MEDWAY CAMPUS LIBRARY

This book is due for return or renewal on the last date stamped below,
but may be recalled earlier if needed by other readers.
Fines will be charged as soon as it becomes overdue.

the
UNIVERSITY
of
GREENWICH

Agribusiness Marketing

Agribusiness Marketing

The Management Perspective

JAMES G. BEIERLEIN
The Pennsylvania State University

MICHAEL W. WOOLVERTON
American Graduate School of International Management

PRENTICE HALL, *Englewood Cliffs, New Jersey 07632*

Library of Congress Cataloging-in-Publication Data
Beierlein, James G.
   Agribusiness marketing : the management perspective / James. G.
Beierlein, Michael W. Woolverton.
      p.   cm.
   Includes index.
   ISBN 0-13-019480-8 (hard cover)
   1. Farm produce—Marketing.   I. Woolverton, Michael W.
II. Title.
HD9000.5.B415   1991
630'.68'8—dc20   90-40552
                                                  CIP

Cover design: Ben Santora
Prepress buyer: Mary McCartney
Manufacturing buyer: Ed O'Dougherty
Page layout: Audrey Kopciak

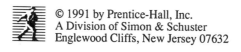

© 1991 by Prentice-Hall, Inc.
A Division of Simon & Schuster
Englewood Cliffs, New Jersey 07632

Printed in the United States of America
10 9 8 7 6 5 4 3 2 1

ISBN 0-13-019480-8

Prentice-Hall International (UK) Limited, *London*
Prentice-Hall of Australia Pty. Limited, *Sydney*
Prentice-Hall Canada Inc., *Toronto*
Prentice-Hall Hispanoamericana, S.A., *Mexico*
Prentice-Hall of India Private Limited, *New Delhi*
Prentice-Hall of Japan, Inc., *Tokyo*
Simon & Schuster Asia Pte. Ltd., *Singapore*
Editora Prentice-Hall do Brasil, Ltda., *Rio de Janeiro*

Contents

9

Production Agriculture   116

10

The Commodity Processing and Food Manufacturing Industries   128

PART FOUR: AGRIBUSINESS MARKETING MANAGEMENT   171

14
Developing the Marketing Plan   173

15
Analyzing the Market   188

Preface

American agriculture has changed. Today's food and fiber system is a vast and complex network of interrelated industries that reaches far beyond the farm gate to include all those involved in bringing food and fiber to the consumer. It includes the people who farm the land, plus those who provide the inputs (feed, seed, fertilizer) and those who process the outputs—the commodity processors, food manufacturers, food wholesalers, and food retailers. In order to capture this expanded view of agriculture, the food and fiber system in this text is referred to as *agribusiness.*

Agribusiness includes *all* the vital activities performed both *on* and *off* the farm that contribute to the food and fiber system's overall success. This three-part system is made up of (1) *the agricultural input sector*, (2) *the production sector*, and (3) *the processing-manufacturing sector.* The use of the systems approach makes it possible to capture the interactions among the various agribusiness industries. It becomes a good deal easier to understand agribusiness when these three sectors are visualized as part of an interrelated food and fiber system in which each sector's performance is heavily dependent on the proper functioning of the other two.

Agribusiness, the food and fiber system, is undergoing profound change. The structure of agribusiness industries in all sectors continues to change in response to a variety of forces. Financial pressures brought on by low commodity and product prices, rapid technological advances, new market entrants and mergers, foreign competition, government intervention, and other factors have combined to change agribusiness irreversibly. As a result, agribusiness firm managers find themselves operating in a new, exciting, and complex decision making environment. Amid all these changes one thing remains clear—success in the future will belong to those agribusiness firms and managers that can profitably market their products in this new, more demanding marketplace.

Students and industry leaders have increasingly recognized the need for stronger instruction in agribusiness marketing in order to be better prepared to meet these new challenges. The result is that agricultural marketing teachers find themselves facing classrooms filled with increasing numbers of students with high expectations and a variety of backgrounds and preparations. As teachers we need a means to meet the needs of students that will (1) carry forth the enthusiasm we feel about the role marketing plays in the successful operation of an agribusiness firm, and (2) give our students the preparation needed to meet the challenges of today *and* tomorrow. We feel *Agribusiness Marketing: The Management Perspective* helps to fill this need, in part because it is written by agribusiness people for agribusiness people.

The Functional-Systems Approach to Marketing. This text takes a functional-systems approach to the subject of agribusiness marketing. It emphasizes that marketing is a series of nine interrelated functions that when performed in a coordinated manner make a successful marketing system. Each firm either creates its own marketing system or adopts one used by similar firms to resolve the differences between the needs of producers and consumers or users. The marketing system is driven by the competition among agribusiness firms who while seeking to maximize their long-run profits must also vie with one another for the consumer's favor. By satisfying consumer needs an agribusiness firm earns the "right" to make a profit.

While the agribusiness marketing system will be examined and evaluated from a general perspective, the primary emphasis will be from a microeconomic, or firm level, point of view. Our primary goal is to develop within the reader the marketing management skills needed to be a successful executive of an agribusiness firm. The perspective will be that of an individual agribusiness firm and how its managers go about earning a profit in the economic and marketing environment that surrounds it.

We feel that the functional-systems approach is the most effective way to teach agribusiness marketing because it gives students a number of advantages over other methods. First, it provides a practical way to address the lifelong learning of marketing. We do this by focusing on *what* has to be done and *why* it has to done for the agribusiness firm to successfully market commodities and products.

In the rapidly changing economic environment that exists today, it makes little educational sense to teach only market organization. What is important and of lasting value is an understanding of the fundamental principles of marketing. These principles are embodied in the concept of consumer sovereignty, where each firm's survival is determined by how efficiently and how profitably it satisfies consumer or user needs.

The fundamental principles of marketing are always present regardless of the market structure or institutional framework. What makes the func-tional-systems approach so appealing is that it provides a way to think about agribusiness marketing that will serve students today and far into the future.

First, the functional-systems approach helps resolve the dilemma facing authors of texts in this area of how to integrate the agricultural input industries into a discussion of food marketing. We do this by making the focus of each firm's marketing effort the satisfaction of *its* customers' or users' needs. Thus, input suppliers become an integral part of the food and fiber system by providing the inputs that producers need to begin the production-marketing of consumer food products.

Second, the functional-systems approach is preferred because it can easily cope with the continuing changes in agribusiness. Structural changes alter the relationships among agribusiness firms. Technological changes alter production possibilities. Consumer tastes and preference changes shorten product life cycles. Each of these factors has contributed to bringing about increases in productivity that have resulted in more than abundant domestic supplies of most commodities and food products. Unfortunately this has come at a time when food production in many other countries has risen to levels that make them less reliant on traditional commodity-exporting coun-tries like the United States.

Because of improvements in communication, transportation, and other marketing services, markets are no longer constrained by national borders. Agribusiness firms operate in a truly international arena. While American agribusiness firms are increasing their involvement in overseas markets, they are also experiencing increased competition from foreign agribusiness firms at home.

In this rapidly changing, highly competitive market environment, a sophisticated approach to marketing and close attention to the needs of consumers is required for agribusiness firms to attain profitability. It is no longer sufficient for food marketers to find ways to quickly and efficiently dispose of what farmers have already produced. Agricultural commodities and food products increasingly compete against one another (and all other goods and services) for the consumers' dollar. This is why agribusiness firms need to devote the same level of effort to marketing management as they have to production management. The functional-systems approach to agribusiness marketing helps firms make better marketing decisions by helping them better decipher the increasingly complex consumer signals in today's competitive marketplace.

We define *marketing* as *all* those business activities that help satisfy consumer needs by coordinating the flow of goods and services from producers to consumers or users. This is an appropriate definition for agribusiness marketers because it includes marketing activities in all three sectors of the food and fiber system. It begins with the input suppliers who manufacture products and offer them along with services to farmers and ranchers. It also includes the farmers and ranchers who use these inputs to produce the grain, livestock, and other commodities that they sell to commodity processors and food manufacturers. This definition of marketing also involves wholesalers and retailers who, in turn, sell food products to the final consumers. The linkages between these parts can easily be seen and understood when students use the functional-systems approach and this definition of marketing.

Audience.   This book is designed to meet the needs of students who are taking the first course in agribusiness marketing. For agribusiness students it will serve as a good foundation for higher level marketing courses. For those trained in other areas of agriculture (food science, agronomy, animal science, engineering, horticulture, and so forth) it will provide a broad and solid understanding of the basics of agribusiness marketing. Much of the material and many of the examples presented in this text come from our experiences as agribusiness marketing managers and our continued involvement with agribusiness firms. This influence should be evident in the practical approach to the subject of marketing and should help agribusiness marketing practitioners relate to and benefit from all that is presented.

Readability.   This text is designed to provide a broad overview of the basic knowledge and skills needed to be an effective marketing manager in agribusiness today. The book is written in a straightforward style that should help students feel comfortable with the material presented. Careful attention is given to definiations: as little jargon as possible is used, and as a further aid, a glossary of some two hundred key terms is included at the end of the text. Each chapter concludes with a summary and a group of review questions.

The material is presented with a one-semester course in mind, but the text can be used with supplemental materials for a two-semester course. A suggested companion text is *Cases in Agribusiness Management* by Beierlein, Woolverton, Hahn, and Niles (Prentice Hall, 1989). It includes a number of case studies that deal with the application of management decision making to marketing.

The text is arranged to tell the reader "the story of agribusiness marketing management." New ideas and concepts are presented in a logical manner. First, a need is established. Second, a procedure is developed to meet that need. Finally, the new material is integrated with what has been previously discussed. This approach helps the student avoids the problem of compartmentalization of knowledge and makes it easier to relate each of the topics to all the other material. As a result, students should gain a strong, comprehensive working knowledge of marketing that will serve them well into their careers.

Organization of This Text.   For agribusiness marketers to be successful they need to acquire skills in three areas. First, they must understand how the food and fiber system operates. Second, they must be able to understand and evaluate marketing's role in society and in the firm. Third, they need to be able to manage the marketing activities within an agribusiness firm. Most textbooks in this area cover only one or two of these topics. *Agribusiness Marketing: The Management Perspective* gives extensive coverage to all three areas.

Part One, "Introduction to Agribusiness Marketing," provides the background against which all the other material will be developed. Chapter 1, "The Agribusiness System," details the size, composition, and complexity of today's food and fiber system. Chapters 2 through 4, on the role of marketing in the economy and in the firm, explain the critical role that marketing plays in the successful operation of an agribusiness firm. Given most students' general lack of understanding of marketing and the role it plays in the successful operation of an agribusiness firm, plus the large number of nonfarm students taking agribusiness courses, we feel that these chapters provide critical preparation for understanding marketing in agribusiness.

Part Two, "Understanding the Marketing Environment," is designed to present the basic elements of economic theory that are necessary to understand and evaluate marketing. While no previous economics background is supposed, our experience is that students with a previous course in microeconomics are generally better able to grasp this material. Chapter 5, "Understanding Agricultural Supply," deals with the biological and technical nature of agricultural production. Chapter 6, "Understanding Consumer Demand," deals with consumer behavior in a free market economy. Chapter 7, "Matching Agricultural Supply and Demand," discusses how the forces of supply and demand interact in the marketplace to allocate scarce resources and satisfy consumer demands.

Part Three, "The Agribusiness Marketing System," is designed to complete the task of describing and evaluating the marketing system. Building on the descriptions from Part One and the economic tools developed in Part Two, this section of the text undertakes a detailed analysis of the six major parts of the agribusiness marketing system. Chapter 8, "The Agricultural Input Industries," deals with the development of that segment of the agribusiness system and shows how it has influenced production agriculture. The impact of technology-induced changes on production practices is examined in Chapter 9, "Production Agriculture," along with the need for increased marketing awareness on the part of producers as a way to achieve greater profitability. The discussion of the post-farm gate part of the agribusiness marketing system begins with a close look at the marketing functions performed in the commodity processing and food manufacturing industries (Chapter 10). Chapter 11, "The Food Wholesaling and Retailing Industries," examines the role that food wholesalers and retailers play in bringing consumers the food and fiber products they desire. Chapter 12, "The Food Service Industry," analyzes the expanding role of the food-away-from-home market and shows the instrumental role that marketing plays in meeting the changing needs of consumers. The section closes with Chapter 13, "Cooperative Agribusiness," a discussion of the development and role of cooperatives in agribusiness.

Management of marketing operations within the agribusiness firm is the subject of the eight chapters that make up Part Four, "Agribusiness Marketing Management." Chapter 14, "Developing the Marketing Plan," explains what a marketing plan is, why it is critical to the success of the agribusiness firm, and how a firm goes about developing such a plan. Chapter 15, "Analyzing the Market," shows the types of market research a firm should undertake in identifying and evaluating the profit potential of the consumer needs identified in the marketing plan. Chapters 16, 17, 18, and 19 each deal with how to manage a different part of the firm's marketing mix of product, price, place, and promotion to realize marketing and financial objectives established in the firm's marketing plan. Chapter 20, "Personal Selling and Merchandising," examines the role that personal selling and merchandising play in successful marketing. The final chapter of this section, "Managing the Market Risk," examines how a firm can manage market price risk through the use of the commodity futures and the options markets. Each offers the agribusiness firm manager a way to minimize exposure to the adverse effects of price fluctuations.

Part Five, "Organizing and Evaluating the Marketing Function," puts all the previously presented material into perspective. Chapter 22, "Organizing and Evaluating the Marketing Function," is designed to help the reader gain some perspective on how to integrate this knowledge into a workable approach to marketing management, and to see how marketing relates to the other areas of agribusiness management. Chapter 23, "The Future of Agribusiness Marketing," describes the role that marketing will play in the future success of agribusiness. Students who can successfully combine the material in these last two chapters with that of the previous chapters will have gained a working knowledge of agribusiness marketing management, and our efforts will have been successful.

Introduction to Agribusiness Marketing

Part One presents the background needed to study agribusiness marketing successfully. The process begins in Chapter 1 with the description of the three-part agribusiness system that includes the agricultural input sector, the production sector, and the processing-manufacturing sector.

The role that marketing plays in the general economic system is discussed in Chapter 2. This chapter establishes the definition of marketing as all those business activities that direct the flow of products from producers to consumers. How society goes about evaluating the performance of its marketing system is the subject of Chapter 3. Chapter 4 takes this broad concept and describes how marketing's role within the firm has changed over time. A firm grasp of these concepts will greatly facilitate understanding of all that follows.

1

The Agribusiness System

When most people hear the word *agriculture* they think of farming and ranching. They conjure up thoughts of someone plowing a field, planting seeds, harvesting a crop, milking cows, or feeding livestock. Until about 1960 this was a fairly accurate picture. But today's agriculture is radically different.

Agriculture has evolved into agribusiness and has become a vast and complex system that reaches far beyond the farm to include all those who are involved in bringing food and fiber to consumers (Figure 1–1). Agribusiness includes not only those that farm the land but also the people and firms that provide the inputs (for example, seed, chemicals, credit), process the outputs (for example, milk, grain, meat), manufacture the food products (for example, ice cream, bread, breakfast cereals), and transport and sell the food products to consumers (for example, restaurants, supermarkets).

Since the 1960s this system has undergone a rapid transformation as new industries have evolved and traditional farming operations have grown larger and more specialized. The transformation did not happen overnight, but came slowly as a response to a variety of forces. Knowing something about how agribusiness came about makes it easier to understand how this system operates today and how it is likely to change in the future.

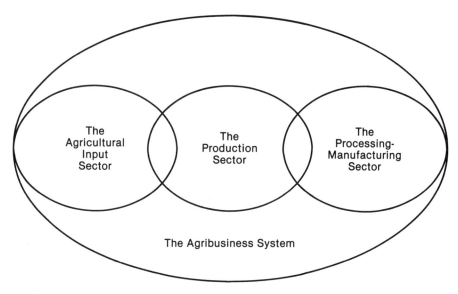

FIGURE 1–1
The Agribusiness System

THE BACKGROUND

When our nation was being settled and for many years thereafter, agriculture was the major industry. It was easy to become a farmer, but productivity was low. As late as 1850 the average American farmer produced enough food to feed just four people. As a consequence most farmers were nearly totally self-sufficient. They produced most of the inputs they needed for production, such as seed, draft horses, feed, and simple farm equipment. Farm families processed the commodities they grew to make their own food and clothing. They consumed or used just about everything they produced. The small amount of output not consumed on the farm was sold for cash. These items were used to feed and clothe the minor portion of the country's population (approximately 10 percent) that lived in villages and cities. A few agricultural products made their way into the export market and were sold to buyers in other countries.

Land was abundant and relatively inexpensive, but labor was scarce. A hired worker would stay only long enough to save enough money to start his own farm. Each time a war occurred farmers saw the prices of farm products rise dramatically. This encouraged them to produce more, but wars also took many young farm workers out of the fields and those that were left became more expensive to hire. In response to this situation farmers were increasingly interested in adopting newly invented labor-saving manufactured inputs.

Farmers found it increasingly profitable to concentrate on production and began to purchase inputs they formerly made themselves. This trend enabled others to build businesses that focused on meeting the need for inputs used in production agriculture such as seed, fencing, machinery, and so on. These firms evolved into the industries that make up the *agricultural input sector*. Input firms are a major part of agribusiness and produce a variety of technologically based products that account for approximately 75 percent of all the inputs used in production agriculture.

At the same time the agricultural input sector was evolving, a similar evolution was taking place as commodity processing and food manufacturing moved off the farm. The form of most commodities (wheat, corn, milk, livestock, and so on) must be changed to make them more useful and convenient for consumers. For example, consumers would rather buy flour than grind the wheat themselves before baking a pie. They are willing to pay extra for the convenience of buying the processed commodity (flour) instead of the raw agricultural commodity (wheat).

During this same period technological advances were being made in food preservation methods. Up until this time the perishable nature of most agricultural commodities meant that they were available only at harvest. For example, cherries for a pie would be available only during the late spring. Many people tried to expand the availability of cherries and other produce through home canning. This was a time-consuming activity even under the best of conditions. Advances in the technology of canning and later freezing led to the formation of food processing firms that could perform these same tasks better and less expensively than most households.

Advances in food processing have enabled consumers to make cherry pies any time of the year for less cost and effort that if they did all the work themselves. In fact, the process has reached the point where many consumers prefer to purchase a ready-to-eat pie at a supermarket or a piece of pie at a restaurant rather than make their own. Today even most farm families use purchased food and fiber products rather than doing the processing themselves. The firms that meet the consumers' demand for greater processing and convenience also constitute a major part of agribusiness and are referred to as the *processing-manufacturing sector*.

It is apparent that the definition of agriculture had to be expanded to include more than production. Farmers and ranchers rely on the input industries to provide the products and services they need to produce agricultural commodities. They also rely on commodity processors, food manufacturers, and ultimately food distributors and retailers to purchase their raw agricultural commodities and to process and deliver them to the consumer for final sale. The result is the food and fiber system.

The food and fiber system is increasingly being referred to as *agribusiness*. The term *agribusiness* was first introduced by Davis and Goldberg in 1957.[*] It will be used in this text to represent this three-part system, made up of (1) the agricultural input sector, (2) the production sector, and (3) the processing-manufacturing sector. To capture the full meaning of the term *agribusiness* it is important to visualize these three sectors as interrelated parts of a system in which the success of each part depends heavily on the proper functioning of the other two.

THE SIZE AND SCOPE OF AGRIBUSINESS

Agribusiness is the largest part of the U. S. economy. Besides providing food and clothing essential to well-being, agribusiness generates approximately 17 percent of the U.S. gross national product and provides employment for approximately 18 percent of all workers. Production agriculture uses nearly half of all the land in the United States, and the total value of farm assets is equal to approximately half of all the assets of the top 500 manufacturing firms in the country. The number of people involved in farming alone is approximately equal to the combined total of all those employed in the steel, transportation, and automobile industries.

The American farmer has become extremely efficient and now produces enough output each year to feed approximately seventy-eight people. Because of the productivity of our farmers, others are freed from the need to produce their own food. This allows them to pursue careers in science, government, education, medicine, computers, and many other fields that contribute to our modern developed economy.

Despite this success, production agriculture represents only a small part of the overall agribusiness system in terms of both the value of output (Figure 1–2) and employment (Figure 1–3). In terms of dollars of sales in 1986, the agricultural input sector sold approximately $93 billion worth of goods and services to farmers and ranchers. Agricultural producers combined these purchased inputs with various other farm-produced inputs to produce com-

---

[*]John H. Davis and Ray A. Goldberg, *A Concept of Agribusiness* (Boston: Graduate School of Business, Harvard University, 1957). See also Michael W. Woolverton, Gail L. Cramer, and Timothy M. Hammonds, "Agribusiness: What Is It All About?" *Agribusiness: An International Journal*, 1 (Spring 1985), 1–3.

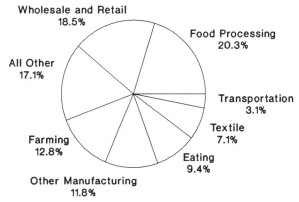

1986 data. Total does not add due
to rounding

FIGURE 1–2
Total Output by Sectors of the Food and Fiber System: Percent
of Dollar Output

Source: USDA, *1988 Agricultural Chartbook*.

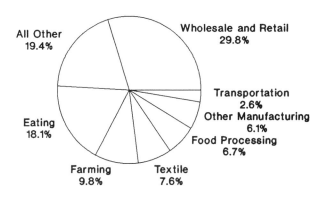

1986 data.
Total does not add due to rounding.

FIGURE 1–3
Food and Fiber System Employment

Source: USDA, *1988 Agricultural Chartbook*.

modities that were sold to the processing-manufacturing sector for $135 billion. The processing-manufacturing firms turned these into food products that they sold to consumers for approximately $350 billion. It is easy to see from these figures that the processing-manufacturing sector represents the largest part of agribusiness.

The importance of agribusiness in the United States is reflected throughout the world, for agribusiness is the single most important contributor to the world's economy. Agribusiness worldwide represents approximately one-fourth of total world economic production and provides employment for nearly half the population on the planet (Table 1–1). Agribusiness also plays an important role in the economic development of most countries. Generally, before economic growth can occur, a country must be able to generate productivity gains in production agriculture. The maturing of the production sector gives rise to the growth of an agricultural input sector and a processing-manufacturing sector, and leads to fewer people being needed for food production. The released workers are available to work in other parts of the developing economy.

THE AGRICULTURAL INPUT SECTOR

The agricultural input sector is a major part of agribusiness. It provides farmers and ranchers with the feed, seed, credit, machinery, fuel, chemicals, etc. that they need to operate. It is generally felt that improvements in the quality of these purchased inputs have been a major source of productivity gains for the entire system. This sector provides three-quarters of the inputs used in production agriculture (Figure 1–4).

Input suppliers provided producers with significant quantities of purchased inputs, including nearly 20 million tons of fertilizer and lime and almost 6 billion gallons of gasoline and diesel fuel (Table 1–2). Farmers are the largest buyers of light trucks in America.

TABLE 1–1 Global Agribusiness: Sales Estimates for Selected Years

	1950	1960	1970	1980
	Billion of Current Dollars			
Farm supplies	44	69	113	375
Farming	125	175	255	750
Processing and distribution	250	380	600	2,000

Source: Ray Goldberg, "A Concept of a Global Food System and Its Use by Private and Public Managers," *Agribusiness: An International Journal*, 1, 1 (1985), 17.

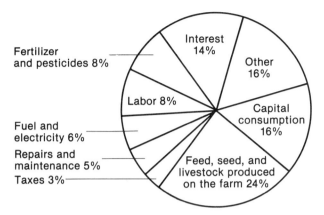

1986 data. Includes operator farm dwellings.

FIGURE 1–4
Components of Farm Production Expenses

Source: USDA, *1988 Agricultural Chartbook.*

The total level of inputs devoted to agriculture has changed little since the end of World War II. However, the makeup of this package has changed drastically. The rising cost of labor relative to the cost of other purchased inputs (especially fertilizer, pesticides, and machinery) has caused a shift away from labor to these other purchased inputs (Figure 1–5).

The replacement of labor on the farm was speeded up by the steady rise in the productivity of these other purchased inputs to the point that farmers can produce more, for less cost, with less labor, than ever before. As a result, the use of farm labor has declined more than 50 percent since 1960 to approximately 3 million people in 1985, with approximately two-thirds of these being family members.

An example of a purchased input whose use has changed drastically is energy. The first change in energy use came with the shift from human to animal power, and then to mechanical power, especially internal combustion engines and electric motors. The second shift occurred in the 1970s as farmers moved to more fuel-efficient equipment in response to rising energy prices. This movement has kept on-farm energy consumption nearly constant over the past decade despite increasing production.

At the distribution level, the agricultural input sector is generally composed of many small, independent, locally owned businesses. However, at the production level, in certain input industries such as chemicals and machinery, a few companies handle most of the business. Some of these

TABLE 1-2   Farm Sector Productivity and Inputs, Selected Years

	1970	1975	1980	1985	1986
			1977 = 100		
Output index:					
Crops	77	93	101	117	108
Livestock	99	95	108	110	111
Total	84	95	104	119	113
Input index	97	96	103	93	N/A
Productivity index	87	99	101	121	N/A
			Millions of Acres		
Principal crops:					
Planted	293.2	332.2	356.7	342.3	328.2
Harvested	283.1	324.0	340.1	349.6	312.6
			Thousands		
Machinery on farms:					
Tractors	4,619	4,469	4,752	4,676	N/A
Motor trucks	2,984	3,032	3,344	3,380	N/A
Grain combines	790	524	652	645	N/A
Corn pickers and					
shellers	635	615	701	684	N/A
Balers	708	667	756	800	N/A
			Millions		
Tractor horsepower	203	222	304	311	N/A
			Horsepower		
Per tractor	56	61	64	67	N/A
			1,000 Tons		
Fertilizer use:					
Nitrogen	7,459	8,608	11,407	11,493	10,439
Phosphate	4,574	4,511	5,432	4,658	4,160
Potash	4,035	4,453	6,245	5,553	5,028
Total	16,968	17,572	23,084	21,703	19,626
Liming materials	25,901	31,128	34,402	N/A	N/A
			Billions of Gallons		
Fuels for farming:					
Gasoline	4.0	4.5	3.0	1.9	1.8
Diesel	1.9	2.4	3.2	2.9	2.9

N/A = not available. Footnotes in original table have been omitted.
Source: USDA, Economic Indicators of the Farm Sector, Farm Sector Review, 1986, ECFS 6–3.

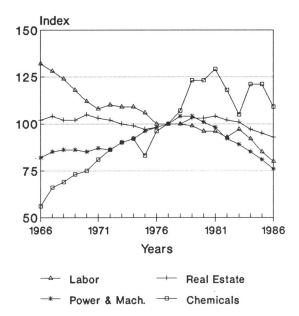

FIGURE 1–5
Farm Input Use, 1966–1986

Source: USDA, *1988 Agricultural Chartbook.*

larger firms whose names might be familiar include John Deere (farm equipment), Purina Mills (animal feed), Pioneer Seed (seed), International Mineral and Chemical (fertilizer), and Monsanto (chemicals).

The trend toward greater use of specialized purchased inputs is expected to continue and should be an ongoing source of productivity gains for production agriculture. However, it is important to remember that this increasing reliance on purchased inputs makes agricultural producers more sensitive to changes in the rest of agribusiness and the general economy.

THE PRODUCTION SECTOR

The middle part of agribusiness is the production sector. It is composed of the approximately 3 million farmers and ranchers who operate approximately 2.2 million farms. These farms and ranches use approximately 1 billion acres of land, nearly half of all the land in the United States. Since the 1930s, the trend in this sector has been toward larger, more specialized farms and ranches. The average farm has continually risen in size and by 1985 had reached 455 acres and had assets worth over $360,000.

However, despite this movement to bigger operations, individuals and partnerships still control almost 90 percent of all farmland. Many farming corporations are owned by families that sought out incorporation to obtain more capital, to limit liabilities, or to solve potential inheritance problems.

By specializing production efforts in one or two crops or types of livestock, producers have been able to increase the efficiency of their operations. This increase in efficiency is seen in Figure 1–6, which shows the total level of inputs remaining nearly constant while output has expanded. Farm productivity (the amount of output generated per unit of input) increased a very respectable 29 percent between 1976 and 1986.

Both gross and net farm income tend to be unstable, while production costs, because of the large portion of purchased inputs, have generally tended to increase each year (Figure 1–7). Gross farm income, which is influenced

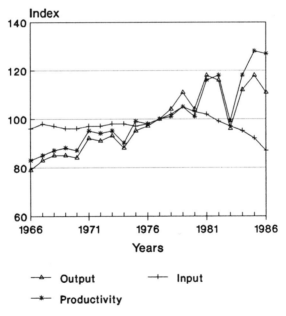

FIGURE 1–6
Farm Productivity, 1966–1986

Source: USDA, 1988 Agricultural Chartbook.

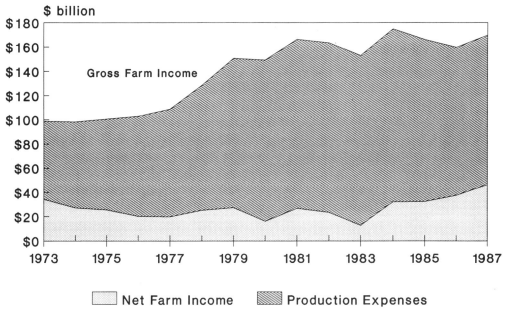

FIGURE 1–7
Net Farm Income

Source: USDA, *1988 Agricultural Chartbook.*

by commodity prices, government payments to farmers, and the level of agricultural commodity exports, tends to vary more. When gross farm income falls significantly as it did in the early 1980s, purchases of inputs generally do not fall proportionately. This puts a tremendous squeeze on net farm income and leaves some farmers in a precarious financial condition.

The trend towards a bimodal distribution of farm sizes has been well documented (Figure 1–8). The first group includes around 300,000 farms with annual sales of $100,000 or more. This group accounts for approximately 75 percent of total farm sales. These farms tend to be large operations that are managed to capture the economies of size that exist in agricultural production. One such economy of size is the reduced cost per unit associated with purchasing large quantities of inputs.

The second group of the bimodal distribution includes the nearly 2 million small farms with annual sales of less than $100,000 that account for 25 percent of total farm sales. While some small farms that specialize in the production of high-value products such as fruit, flowers, purebred animals, and so on are viable commercial operations, the majority of small farm

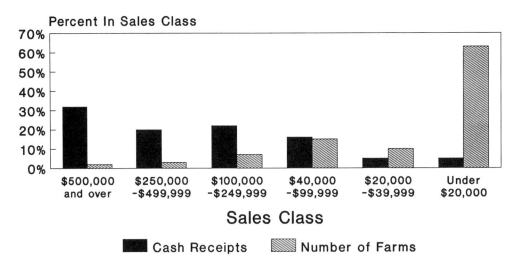

1986 data.
Cash receipts from farm marketings
include net CCC loans.

FIGURE 1–8
Cash Receipts and Farms by Sales Class

Source: USDA, *1988 Agricultural Chartbook.*

owners support themselves with off-farm income. They simply prefer to live in rural communities. While the contribution to total farm output is low, the 2 million small farms represent an important market for sellers of agricultural inputs. However, these smaller farmers often conduct their farming operations differently from those in the first group. These differences are becoming more pronounced as time goes by and are changing the way input markets, commodity processors, and food manufacturers conduct their businesses.

A large part of total farm income comes from the sale of agricultural commodities overseas. Approximately 17 percent of all U.S. agricultural production was exported in 1986 and accounted for approximately 17 percent of total gross receipts from farming (Table 1–3). These exports are not only valuable to farmers but also provide jobs in other parts of the economy. Despite recent downward trends for commodities such as wheat, corn, and soybeans, this country is normally a dominant force in world markets.

The production sector has been at the core of much of the change in agribusiness. Some individual producers have grown larger and more effi-

TABLE 1–3   Share of U.S. Farm Production Entering Foreign Markets, 1980–1986

	Gross Cash Income	Value of U.S. Agricultural Exports	Exported Share of Domestic Production
	Billions of Dollars		Percent
1980	143.3	40.5	28
1981	146.0	43.8	30
1982	150.5	39.1	26
1983	150.4	34.8	23
1984	155.3	38.0	24
1985	156.6	31.2	20
1986	153.0	26.3	17

Source: USDA, Economic Indicators of the Farm Sector, Farm Sector Review, 1986, ECFS 6–3.

cient by specializing in the production of agricultural commodities and letting others supply the inputs and process the outputs. However, for producers to continue to progress, it is important that they recognize the changing nature of agricultural markets and the need to improve their marketing efforts.

THE PROCESSING-MANUFACTURING SECTOR

The processing-manufacturing sector includes all the individuals and firms that process agricultural commodities (for instance, turn wheat into flour), manufacture food products (turn flour, eggs, and other inputs into bread), and distribute and retail food products to the final consumer. It is estimated that this sector employs as many as 14 million people in a variety of establishments ranging from grain elevators to fruit and vegetable processing plants to supermarkets to fast-food restaurants. Some of the nation's largest businesses are agribusinesses. Those agribusinesses listed among the 500 largest industrial and nonindustrial firms in the United States are given in Tables 1–4 and 1–5, respectively.

The businesses in the processing-manufacturing sector acquire raw agricultural commodities from producers, then process them into food products that are sold at times, at places, and in forms that are desired by consumers. The cost of these activities is referred to as the *marketing bill*. In 1985 the marketing bill reached $257 billion and represented approximately 70 percent of the total amount spent by consumers on food (Figure 1–9).

TABLE 1–4 Agribusinesses in *Fortune* Magazine's Directory of America's 500 Largest Industrial Corporations

Rank	Name	Sales ($ million)	Numbers of Employees
	Beverages—8 Companies		
26	Pepsico	13,007	235,000
46	Anheuser-Busch	8,924	41,118
49	Coca-Cola	8,338	18,774
121	Coca-Cola Enterprises	3,874	22,000
191	Seagram (Jos. E.)	2,199	10,200
249	Coors (Adolph)	1,522	10,500
320	Brown-Forman	1,067	5,600
491	Dr Pepper/Seven-Up	510	842
	Total	39,441	344,034
	Median	3,037	14,637
	Food—48 Companies		
14	Occidental Petroleum	19,417	52,500
20	RJR Nabisco	16,956	116,881
36	Sara Lee	10,424	85,700
44	Conagra	9,475	42,993
57	Beatrice	7,505	19,700
59	Borden	7,244	46,300
65	Archer Daniels	6,798	9,006
70	Pillsbury	6,191	101,800
71	Ralston Purina	6,176	56,734
76	General Mills	5,778	74,500
88	Quaker Oats	5,330	31,300
89	Heinz (H.J.)	5,244	39,000
95	Campbell Soup	4,869	48,389
100	CPC International	4,700	32,000
106	Kellogg	4,349	17,461
119	Whitman	3,915	25,396
124	Agway	3,644	16,851
130	United Brands	3,503	42,000
141	Sipco	3,225	5,403
167	Hershey Foods	2,561	12,100
179	Land O'Lakes	2,355	6,724
186	Hormel (Geo. A.)	2,293	7,994
193	Central Soya	2,189	3,360
212	Tyson Foods	1,936	26,000
231	Int'l Multifoods	1,698	9,048
235	Mid-America Dairymen	1,655	4,000
243	Holly Farms	1,583	15,000
247	Dean Foods	1,552	7,100
276	Wilson Foods	1,324	5,100
300	McCormick	1,184	7,626

TABLE 1–4   (cont.)

Rank	Name	Sales ($ million)	Numbers of Employees
	Food (cont.)		
307	Gerber Products	1,166	14,658
325	Amstar	1,057	4,624
328	Gold Kist	1,044	9,100
347	Savannah Foods & Ind.	917	1,665
348	Smithfield Foods	916	4,100
351	AG Processing	910	587
357	Wrigley (Wm. Jr.)	891	5,500
365	IBC Holdings	855	14,700
382	Ocean Spray	767	1,940
392	Flowers Industries	738	9,100
396	Universal Foods	720	4,433
429	Finevest Foods	635	3,050
430	Riceland Foods	633	1,792
452	Thorn Apple Valley	593	2,630
471	Sun-Diamond Growers	554	2,500
474	Amer. Maize-Prod.	548	3,107
490	Prairie Farms Dairy	512	2,000
496	Pilgrim's Pride	506	6,800
	Total	169,033	1,060,252
	Median	1,817	9,048
	Forest Products—33 Companies		
37	Weyerhaeuser	10,004	46,976
42	International Paper	9,533	55,500
43	Georgia-Pacific	9,509	44,000
85	Kimberly-Clark	5,394	38,328
91	Champion International	5,129	30,400
92	James River	5,098	39,000
98	Scott Paper	4,726	27,000
103	Mead	4,464	21,000
112	Boise Cascade	4,095	19,835
122	Stone Container	3,742	20,700
127	Great North. Nekoosa	3,588	19,600
163	Union Camp	2,661	18,508
197	Westvaco	2,134	14,750
200	Temple-Inland	2,099	11,000
217	Louisiana-Pacific	1,903	13,000
219	Fort Howard	1,859	—
229	Willamette Industries	1,716	9,325
240	Sonoco Products	1,600	14,859
244	Avery International	1,582	11,500
262	Bowater	1,410	5,000
267	Esselte Business Sys.	1,401	12,976

TABLE 1–4 (cont.)

Rank	Name	Sales ($ million)	Numbers of Employees
	Forest Products (cont.)		
288	Jefferson Smurfit	1,255	7,600
313	Federal Paper Board	1,117	5,300
317	Potlatch	1,084	7,240
319	Bemis	1,069	7,855
355	Consolidated Papers	897	4,454
394	Dennison Mfg.	722	7,600
399	Chesapeake	711	4,215
412	Gaylord Container	671	3,900
421	Longview Fibre	657	3,450
461	Glatfelter (P.H.)	569	3,439
465	Tambrands	563	4,700
488	Pope & Talbot	515	3,126
	Total	93,478	536,136
	Median	1,716	12,976
	Tobacco—7 Companies		
10	Philip Morris	25,860	155,000
58	American Brands	7,477	48,800
177	Universal	2,414	20,000
263	Lorillard	1,410	4,250
390	Standard Commercial	750	6,500
440	UST	607	3,284
470	Dibrell Brothers	555	24,600
	Total	39,073	262,434
	Median	1,410	20,000

Source: *Fortune,* April 24, 1989. Used by permission of Fortune 500 and Fortune Service 500. © 1989 The Time Inc. Magazine Company. All rights reserved.

The firms in the processing-manufacturing sector have grown to capture the economies available from large-scale operations. While the sector has a small number of large firms, they tend to compete fiercely among themselves and are very responsive to the needs of the market. An example is the increased availability of convenience foods such as microwavable meals, instant potatoes and so on, that came as a response to our changing lifestyles where sitdown dinners may be a thing of the past.[*]

[*]Betsy Morris, "Are Square Meals Headed for Extinction?" *Wall Street Journal*, March 15, 1988, p. 35.

**TABLE 1–5   Agribusinesses in *Fortune* Magazine's Directory of America's
500 Largest Nonindustrial Corporations**

Rank	Name	Sales ($ Million)	No. of Employees
14 Retailers in the Top 50			
4	Kroger	19,053.0	160,000
5	American Stores	18,478.4	165,000
7	Safeway Stores	13,612.4	107,200
10	Great Atlantic & Pacific Tea	9,531.8	83,000
11	Winn-Dixie Stores	9,007.7	83,800
13	Southland	7,950.3	50,724
16	Albertson's	6,773.1	50,000
18	McDonald's	5,566.3	169,000
21	Publix Super Markets	4,803.7	57,791
27	Vons Cos.	3,916.6	34,854
28	Food Lion	3,815.4	35,531
33	Allied Stores	2,977.9	37,300
34	Giant Food	2,721.3	22,700
36	Circle K	2,613.8	24,544
10 Diversified Service Companies in the Top 100			
3	Super Valu Stores	9,371.7	35,595
17	ARA Group	3,917.3	120,000
32	Associated Milk Producers	2,827.2	4,117
34	Castle & Cooke	2,469.2	42,000
35	Harvest States Cooperatives	2,426.3	2,350
54	Super Food Services	1,573.1	2,090
59	Union Equity Co-op Exchange	1,458.4	590
83	Indiana Farm Bureau	1,102.7	858
90	Dairymen	984.7	4,091
98	Pioneer Hi-Bred International	874.9	4,645

This sector of agribusiness is made up of many well-known companies along with some that are not. Some of the lesser known but larger commodity processing firms include: Archer Daniels Midland (grain processing), Anderson Clayton (cotton processing), IBP (meat packing), CPC International (corn processing), Mid-America Dairymen (dairy processing), and Sunkist (citrus processing). Many of these firms are also involved in food manufacturing.

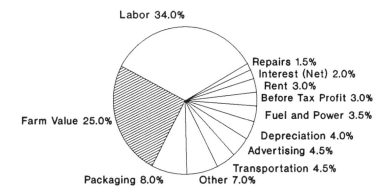

Labor 34.0%

Repairs 1.5%
Interest (Net) 2.0%
Rent 3.0%
Before Tax Profit 3.0%
Fuel and Power 3.5%
Depreciation 4.0%
Advertising 4.5%
Transportation 4.5%

Farm Value 25.0%

Packaging 8.0%   Other 7.0%

1987 preliminary. Other costs include
prop. taxes, insurance, accounting &
prof. services, bad debts, & misc. items

FIGURE 1–9
What a Dollar Spent on Food Paid For in 1987

Source: USDA, 1988 Agricultural Chartbook.

Many of the better known agribusiness firms are found in food manu-facturing. They are better known to the average person because they produce heavily advertised consumer food products and include: Kellogg's, Pillsbury, Coca-Cola, General Mills, Campbell's Soup, Beatrice Foods, Carnation, H.J. Heinz, and Hershey Foods.

While most large agribusiness firms are primarily involved in just one part of the industry, many have subsidiaries in other parts of the system. These diversified firms often do business in a variety of areas. For example, Cargill, Inc. is a privately owned firm with headquarters near Minneapolis, Minne-sota. It is one of the largest grain traders in the world. Yet it is also one of the largest soybean processors, flour millers, wet corn millers, feed manufactur-ers, seed producers, and livestock processors in the United States.

SUMMARY

Since the 1960s, U.S. agriculture has undergone a transformation to a more formalized and specialized system of food and fiber production. The rising cost of labor and changing farmer attitudes toward credit helped to bring about a rapid rise in the use of purchased inputs and the development of a separate agricultural input sector. Changing consumer preferences created opportunities for those firms involved in processing, manufacturing, distributing, and retailing of food and fiber products. The growth of these two sectors on either side of production agriculture requires an expansion of the definition of agriculture to include all three parts: (1) the agricultural input sector, (2) the production sector, and (3) the processing-manufacturing sector of what is now called agribusiness.

The current agribusiness system has resulted in more production and greater efficiency than ever before. However, agribusiness is also more sensitive to changes in other parts of the economy. Agribusiness is in greater contact, and at times in greater conflict, with forces beyond the control of firm managers. Success in the future will go to those agribusiness managers who can operate in this new, more demanding market.

QUESTIONS

1. Does the growth of the three-part agribusiness system mean the end of the family farm? Why or why not?
2. What changes brought about the development of a separate agricultural input sector?
3. Why are some agricultural inputs called durable and others called operating? Explain the difference (if any).
4. Even though the level of energy used in agriculture is unchanged since 1973, some say we use too much energy. Do we?
5. What role should non-farm groups have in determining how agriculture uses land, water, and chemicals?
6. What is the marketing bill for food? Are farmers getting their fair share of the consumers food dollar?
7. Would the removal of all government intervention in agriculture make it a more efficient sector of the economy?
8. Why do agricultural producers now purchase most inputs off-farm and do very little commodity processing on the farm?

2

The Role of Marketing in the Agribusiness System

THE MISUNDERSTOOD MISSION OF MARKETING

Quite often when people in agriculture talk about marketing, they bring up some bad experience they have had such as how someone sold them something they really did not want, or how they fell victim to a deceptive advertisement, or how a shady middleman made a big profit at their expense. This misunderstanding of the role of marketing is unfortunate because marketing has had so much to do with the prosperity that most of us enjoy. This is particularly true in agribusiness where marketing has played a pivotal role in providing consumers with an overwhelming assortment of food and fiber products, at the lowest prices found anywhere.

Marketing's Role in the Economy. Marketing plays a vital role in the success of our economy by bridging the gap between the often conflicting needs of producers and consumers. It does this by helping producers better understand consumer needs. Marketing helps producers decide *what* products to produce and *when* to produce them. Done efficiently, marketing leads to greater satisfaction for consumers and higher profits for producers.

Marketing's Role in Agribusiness. Agribusiness is the nation's largest industry, and marketing is its largest segment. Over 80 percent of

---

The Role of Marketing

- Helps bridge the gap between the needs of the producers and consumers.
- Helps producers better understand the needs of the consumers so they can do a better job of meeting them.
- Helps producers decide what to produce and when to produce.

---

those involved in agribusiness are employed in marketing. Agribusiness marketing activities generate more than 17 percent of America's annual gross national product, and about 70 cents of each consumer's food dollar goes to cover marketing expenses. Agribusiness marketing is clearly a major part of our national economy.

Why It Is Important to Understand Marketing.   Whether or not your future includes a job in marketing, you will find yourself affected by it in just about everything you do. This is why it is important that everyone understand the important role that marketing plays in the proper functioning of our economic system. Regardless of whether you are a producer or a consumer, you will find a knowledge of marketing valuable in helping you succeed in the economic world in which we live.

An understanding of marketing begins with a knowledge of the general economic system and how marketing has evolved from it. The discussion should also include how society goes about measuring how well its marketing system meets the needs of its citizens.

The *macroeconomic* situation is discussed first because it describes the general economic environment in which we operate. It also establishes many of the rules under which businesses in the economy operate. By addressing the general situation first, the reader will be assured of having a thorough understanding of the economic setting that surrounds the typical agribusiness

---

The Role of Marketing in Agribusiness

- 80 percent of all those employed in agribusiness are involved with marketing.
- 70 percent of each consumer's food dollar is spent on marketing.
- 17 percent of the U.S. gross national product comes from agribusiness marketing.

---

firm and the basic rules under which it must operate. This preparation allows us to focus the rest of this text on *microeconomics*, or the activities of the individual agribusiness firm and its managers as they go about trying to earn a profit within our economic system.

THE EVOLUTION OF THE MARKETING SYSTEM

In every part of the world there are unlimited human needs but only limited resources with which to meet them. What is needed is a way to efficiently satisfy as many of these needs as possible. How this dilemma is resolved is what determines a particular society's economic system.

Regardless of how it is organized, every economic system must address these five questions:

1. *What* to produce?
2. *How much* to produce?
3. *When* to produce?
4. *Who* should produce?
5. *For whom* should goods be produced?

In a subsistence economy the answers to these questions are easy. Each person produces everything he or she can. While that may not be all that each person needs, it is what everyone must make do with. There is no trade or exchange of goods. Everyone is both producer and consumer of his or her own products and there is no functioning economic system.

The Advantages of Specialization and Trade

In any economic system beyond the subsistence level, there is an uneven distribution of human talents. Some people will be better at producing certain things than others. This means that people in general can be better off if individuals specialize in the production of the few products that they can make better than anyone else, and then trade that portion of their output over and above personal needs for the other goods they require.

Through specialization and trade everyone in a society can have more of everything (that is, human needs can be better met) since each product is produced by the most efficient producers. This is because a few specialists producing large quantities of a product will result in more total output than if everyone, including the worst producers, tries to produce a little bit more on his own. With specialization, everyone is still a producer and a consumer,

---

The Evolution of Marketing

1. Through specialization of labor, it is possible to achieve greater increases in total output.
2. Trade makes it possible for production specialists to use the goods they produce above personal needs to acquire the other goods they need.
3. The use of money facilitates the trading of goods.
4. The development of central markets makes trading easier.
5. The use of central markets requires that someone be on hand to run them. These people are called middlemen.
6. Middlemen specialize in trading, not production or consumption.

---

but each produces only those few products that he or she can most efficiently produce, and trades for everything else.

The Use of Central Markets.   Trading sounds easy. All that needs to be done is to have all members of the community exchange their surplus production for the surplus production of others. But because of problems of distance, time, and information, prospective buyers and sellers have a hard time finding one another. A better solution might be to have everyone meet at one place and time to form a *central market*.

The use of central markets is helpful because sellers know the buyers will be there, and buyers know they can see all the available surplus production in one place. Buyers and sellers can complete all their exchanges at one time. The greater efficiency of exchange offered by the central market leaves each individual with more time to produce surplus goods for more exchanges, plus more time to consume the goods for which he exchanged. Thus, this system of specialization of labor and free exchange leaves everyone better off.

The Use of Money.   Despite the advantages of this system there are still some problems. Each producer must still barter for each item of exchange (for example, 3 goats for 12 chickens, 1 coat for a wagon wheel). This can leave a trader with too much of some things and too little of others. It can result in long and complicated trails of exchange to get what the trader really does want (for example, 3 goats for 12 chickens for 10 pies for 50 horseshoes for 3 wagon wheels for 1 coat). A better solution is to use a common denominator of trade called *money*, and place the value of all goods in terms of prices in this common unit (dollars, yen, pounds, and so on).

Using money, if 1 goat can be sold for $30, and a coat costs $90, all one has to do is sell three goats and use the money to buy the coat. There is no need to go through goats to chickens to pies to horseshoes to wheels to get to the coat. Thus, the introduction of money hastens the growth of trade and permits economies to become more complex.

The Use of Middlemen.   As the use of central markets becomes more widespread, it becomes necessary for someone to oversee their operation. Someone has to provide the place to conduct the market and keep it presentable. Someone has to build the selling stalls that are used by the producers. Someone has to store the goods between sales. People have to be found to help transport goods to the central market. A few producers may even hire someone else to do their selling so they can concentrate on producing more goods. The people who do all these tasks are called *middlemen.* They specialize in trade, not production. They often finish the production process by getting the producers' goods ready for sale to consumers. They are solely involved in marketing.

The Conflicting Needs of Producers and Consumers

Regardless of how an economic system is organized, it must have a marketing system to bridge the gap between the conflicting needs of producers and consumers. On the one hand, there are producers who seek to maximize their long-run profits by selling large quantities of a small number of products at the highest possible prices. On the other hand, there are consumers who seek to maximize their total satisfaction by consuming small quantities of a large number of products by purchasing these items at the lowest possible prices with their limited incomes.

This conflict of interests requires the development of a marketing system that can mediate the differences between the needs of buyers and sellers. The marketing system helps producers determine what products consumers most desire and which products can provide the greatest profits. The marketing system also makes it possible for consumers to find the variety of products they want at the lowest prices.

The Prerequisites to an Efficient Economic System

When several prerequisites are met in the general economic system, the marketing system can lead not only to an efficient meeting of producer and consumer needs but also to an efficient allocation of society's limited resources.

The Conflicting Needs of Producers and Consumers That Marketing Seeks to Resolve

Producers seek to:	Consumers seek to:
1. Maximize long-run profit	1. Maximize the satisfaction they receive from the products they consume with their limited incomes
2. Sell large quantities of a few products	2. Buy small quantities of many products
3. Seek the highest prices	3. Seek the lowest prices

---

1. A Free Market Economy.   A free market economy must exist where the consumers, with little government intervention, provide the answers to the five questions of what to produce, how much to produce, when to produce, who should produce, and for whom goods should be produced. The level of profits in such a system are a measure of how well producers answer these questions. In a *planned economy*, the government attempts to provide producers with the answers to these five questions, usually with little direct information from consumers. The results are oftentimes less than satisfactory for the consumers.

2. Prices That Reflect the Full Value of Market Resources.   When prices reflect the full value of resources, resources are allocated to their highest and best use. How close an economic system comes to achieving this is a measure of *pricing efficiency*. A high degree of pricing efficiency is desirable because it results in:

- *Producers* using the most efficient technology available and the lowest cost combination of inputs to make their products. This is consistent with their desire to maximize long-run profits. By paying the market price for an input, producers imply that its value to them in the production process is greater than or equal to the price they pay for it in the market. If its value is less than the market price, they should not use it.
- *Consumers* purchasing only those products that lead to the maximization of their total satisfaction. By paying the market price for a product,

they indicate that they are receiving satisfaction greater than or equal to the price of the good in the marketplace. If the added satisfaction consumers receive is less than the price of the good, they should not buy it.

3. A High Degree of Interaction Between Consumers and Producers. When consumers and producers interact, both parties have a good knowledge of the variety and prices of goods available for sale so they can make informed choices.

The satisfaction of these three prerequisites is desirable because it will lead to the development of an efficient economic system where there will be: (1) decision making by the consumers as to the who, what, and where of the economic system; (2) a pricing system that brings about an efficient allocation of resources; (3) the maximization of consumers' satisfaction; and (4) the maximization of producers' long-run profits.

How well these three prerequisites are met largely determines the level of *economic efficiency* present in an economic system. Since the higher the level of economic efficiency, the higher the level of overall consumer satisfaction and producer profits, maintaining a high level of economic efficiency should be a major concern of a society.

The goal of economic efficiency is of sufficient importance in the United States that we have empowered our government to establish laws to protect its existence. These laws insure that everyone plays by the same rules and that all consumers and producers are given the same chance to prosper in the marketplace. The government does this by passing laws that provide for enforcement of contracts, protection of private property rights, fairness in the pricing system, and fair rules of trade. Through the legislative process the people make known what type of economic system and level of economic efficiency they desire.

The Prerequisites to an Efficient Economic System

1. A free market economy
2. Prices that reflect the full value of resources
3. A high degree of interaction between consumers and producers

THE ROLE OF MARKETING IN THE ECONOMY

In any economic system there are always barriers that prevent producers from efficiently satisfying consumer needs. These barriers include separations of: *space*, *time*, *information*, *value*, and *ownership*. The role of the marketing system is to bridge this gap between producers' and consumers' needs and increase the efficiency of the marketing system.

The Nine Functions of Marketing

Regardless of the type of economic system a society employs, its marketing system must perform nine separate functions if the system is to raise the level of economic efficiency in the society. To accomplish this, the marketing system must successfully overcome the separations of space, time, information, value, and ownership.

The most familiar marketing functions to most of us are the *buying function* and the *selling function*. They must be performed in the marketing system if any product exchanges are going to occur. They involve overcoming separations of ownership by transferring legal title of the product from the seller to the buyer. The *storage function* overcomes the separation of time

---

The Nine Marketing Functions and the Barriers to Consumer Satisfaction They Help Overcome

The Exchange Functions
1. Buying—Ownership Separation
2. Selling—Ownership Separation

The Physical Functions
3. Storage—Time Separation
4. Transportation—Space Separation
5. Processing—Value Separation

The Facilitating Functions
6. Grades and Standards—Information Separation
7. Financing—Value Separation
8. Risk Taking—Time Separation
9. Market Information—Information Separation

by maintaining the product in good condition between production and final sale. The *transportation function* overcomes the separation of space by moving the product from where it is produced to where the consumer is willing to purchase it.

The *processing function* involves the transformation of a commodity to a form that has greater value to the consumer. Processing is included as one of the nine functions of marketing since *what* is produced in a free market economy should be determined by the needs of consumers. One of the purposes of the marketing system is to transmit consumer desires to producers so they can provide the products that consumers want. How the products are produced is a technical matter, but what to produce is a function of marketing. Even then, the technology used may depend upon the end use desired by consumers.

The facilitating functions of marketing include those functions that make the system work more efficiently. The *grades and standards function* involves the development of uniform descriptions of commodities and products. It means that buyers do not have to physically inspect each shipment of product before they purchase it. A buyer can be assured that when he orders a certain quantity of a Grade A product over the telephone, he knows exactly the physical specifications of the product he will receive. The *financing function* involves providing the funds necessary to pay for the production and marketing of a product before the money is received from its sale. /

The *risk-taking function* involves assuming the risk of loss between the time of purchase and sale. Various forms of insurance are available to guard against adverse changes in price as well as physical losses arising from such things as fire, flood, theft, and spoilage. The efficiency of the marketing system is also greatly enhanced if there is wide dissemination of information on prices, inventory levels, embargoes, or anything else that could influence the buying and selling of products. The *market information function* involves the development of any means to disseminate this type of information.

These nine marketing functions are normally performed by middlemen in a free market economy. The functions can be performed by buyers or sellers in an attempt to bypass the middlemen, but rarely can they be eliminated if the system is to function efficiently. A middleman may not be able to perform all these functions. Some such as warehousemen perform just one, while others may do three or four. In some cases, such as when they operate their own retail outlets, producers may carry out some of the marketing functions. Even consumers get involved with performing the marketing functions when they buy from a roadside stand or pick their own strawberries in a direct marketing setting.

The Four Utilities of Marketing

Another way to describe marketing is to look at the performance of the marketing functions as a way of adding value to products. Middlemen or marketers continue to exist because they add value to products that consumers want and are willing to pay extra to receive. Middlemen add value by performing the nine marketing functions described above in a production process. The end result of the production process is consumer satisfaction. Economists call this satisfaction *utility.* Consumers receive satisfaction or utility from using the products. Marketers add the following four types of utility to the products they handle:

- Time
- Place
- Form
- Possession

Form utility involves processing the product into a form desired by the consumer. This may be nothing more than collecting and cooking the eggs laid by a flock of chickens for the consumer who is willing to pay for an omelet for breakfast. For those desiring french fries at a fast-food outlet, the farmer may begin the process of providing form utility by converting seed, water, fertilizer, and other inputs into a full-grown potato that is ready for harvest. Those that process the raw potato into frozen french fries are also involved in the process of providing form utility, as are the people who cook it at the fast-food restaurant. Merely handing the consumer the raw potato will probably do very little to provide him with any positive satisfaction when what he really wants is hot, sizzling french fries. Marketing people recognize the profit potential in this desire of consumers for cooked french fries and transform the raw potato to cooked french fries through processing.

Place utility involves transporting the product to a location desired by the consumer. Continuing the french fry example, turning the potato into cooked french fries does only part of the job. If the fries are in Idaho while the consumer is in New Jersey, little is added to consumer satisfaction. Thus, the product needs to be transported to the consumer, since consumption of the fries at a fast-food outlet in New Jersey will give him more utility than if he has to drive all the way to Idaho to get them.

Time utility involves storing the product until the time it is desired by the consumer. Time utility is particularly important in agribusiness where many commodities such as potatoes are harvested just once during the year but consumers want to consume them year-round. Continuing the french fry example, without storage we could enjoy french fries for only a few weeks each year after the potato harvest. Again, marketing people recognize the profit potential in the consumers' year-round desire for french fries and develop ways to store potatoes and french fries successfully to meet this need.

Possession utility involves allowing consumers to gain ownership of the product so they can legally use it. This is why the marketing system must provide a simple way for transferring title of the potatoes and the french fries that does not put the buyer in jeopardy. Possession utility normally completes the utility process as ownership and control pass ultimately to the consumer of the product.

A useful way to think about the utility creation process is to think of the utilities as adding value to the product. Consumers must feel that the process has enhanced the value of a product since they are willing to pay the market price for the addition of time, place, form, and possession utilities to products they purchase.

For example, in 1982 farmers bought $114 billion worth of farm inputs which they transformed into farm commodities which they then sold to middlemen for $144 billion. In that year, farmers added $30 billion to the value of the inputs by transforming them into farm commodities. The middlemen, in turn, transformed the farm commodities into food products that they sold at retail for $358 billion. The consumers must have felt that the middlemen had added $214 billion worth of value to these farm commodities by processing them into food products (Table 2–1).

The function of marketing in our economic system is to make sure that consumers get the products they desire. This means insuring that the right

TABLE 2–1   The Value Added by the Marketing System, Selected Years

Value Added in:	1975	1980	1985
	Billions of Dollars		
Farm sector	43.3	55.1	71.6
Nonfarm sector	282.4	444.8	629.1
Total food and fiber	325.7	499.9	700.8
Total domestic economy	1,598.0	2,732.0	3,998.0
	Percentage		
Farm sector	2.7	2.0	1.8
Nonfarm sector	17.7	16.3	15.7
Total food and fiber	20.4	16.3	17.5
Total domestic economy	100.0	100.0	100.0

Source: USDA, Economic Indicators of the Farm Sector, Farm Sector Review, 1985, ECIFS 5–4, January 1987, Table 7, p. 17.

product (form utility) is available at the right place (place utility), at the right price (possession utility), and at the right time (time utility) to fully satisfy the consumer.

Each of these utilities is added to the product by performing one or more of the nine marketing functions given above. Form utility is accomplished by carrying out the processing function. Place utility is accomplished through the transportation function. Time utility is accomplished through the storage function. Possession utility is accomplished through both the buying and selling functions. Thus, the nine functions of marketing, the four utilities of marketing, and overcoming of the barriers of space, time, information, value, and ownership are all involved in resolving the conflicting needs of producers and consumers in a free market economy. If each part is done well, it contributes to higher consumer satisfaction, higher producer profits, and greater economic efficiency in general. Thus, the proper functioning of the marketing system is a key element in the successful performance of any economy. These relationships are summarized in Figure 2–1.

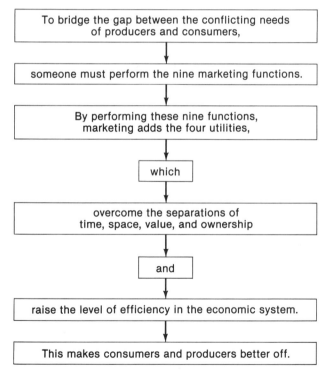

FIGURE 2–1
The Organization of Marketing Principles

THE DEVELOPMENT OF MARKETING IN AGRIBUSINESS

Marketing is a relatively new addition to agribusiness that developed in the years following the Civil War. Before that time farmers were more or less self-sufficient. What buying and selling they did was done locally since transportation and communication systems were minimal and there was little surplus production above family needs to exchange.

The opening of the West around the middle of the nineteenth century brought a tremendous increase in the production of agricultural commodities. It is estimated that the number of acres devoted to agricultural production increased 82 percent from 294 million acres in 1850 to 536 million acres in 1880, while the number of farms rose from 1.5 million to 4 million.

Production grew to feed the rapidly growing population of an expanding nation. The food processing industry was born as entrepreneurs rapidly adopted new technology. Advances in food canning made it possible to preserve food for long periods of time.

It was during this period that the Union Stockyards and the Board of Trade were established in Chicago and the flour milling industry was founded in Minneapolis. This expansion was made possible in part by the development of the transcontinental railroad and telegraph communication systems.

Because of these advances the economic system was under great pressure to absorb the large supply that existed of most agricultural commodities. This led to low farm commodity prices and incomes that deeply depressed the fortunes of the nation's predominantly farm population. The heavy dependence of farmers on the railroads and other basic industries to reach their urban markets made them vulnerable to the formation of monopolies and the use of unfair trade practices. The largely rural population felt threatened by the abuses of big industry and responded by pressuring legislators to pass laws to protect the markets from the unscrupulous actions of a few wealthy individuals. The formation of the Interstate Commerce Commission in 1887 and the passage of the Sherman Act of 1890 are examples of the types of legislation that were designed to preserve the integrity of the marketplace.

The years between World War I and World War II were characterized by low prices and a chronic oversupply of most farm products, despite efforts to ship excess supplies overseas. Domestically, agricultural leadership saw more orderly marketing as the solution to the farm problem. It was during this era that the formation of agricultural cooperatives was legalized. This period ended with the efforts of the New Deal to limit agricultural production as a means to raise farm prices.

In the years immediately after World War II the feeling was that farm prices and incomes would rise if only we had better marketing. The Research and Marketing Act of 1946 renewed this emphasis, and for a while it seemed to work. New technology brought us frozen food, TV dinners, and greater demand for processing and services. The supermarket concept was perfected with the help of many departments of agricultural economics located in colleges of agriculture, and the United States Department of Agriculture (USDA).

Further improvements in the 1960s in transportation (the interstate highway system, air service, and so on) and communications (both television and telephone) plus the advent of computers made it possible for agribusiness firms to operate in regional and even national markets. The resulting gains in productivity led to major declines in the relative cost of food. The period ushered in a growing role for middlemen as well as increased concentration of food processing and manufacturing resources.

Currently, agribusiness is in the midst of another profound change. Central to the system is a group of producers with a productive capacity that greatly exceeds domestic demand. The export markets that were expected to absorb the excess supply have not developed as expected. Competition for foreign markets has intensified as more countries have expanded food production in the name of food security to lessen their needs for imports. In addition, other countries have either begun or expanded their involvement in international commodity and food markets as a way to earn foreign exchange. Many have targeted the United States as the outlet for their food products. As a result, American agribusiness firms face increased competition both at home and abroad for the consumer's food dollar. It is clear that in the future success will belong to

---

The Requirements for Future Success in Agribusiness

1. Greater attention to meeting consumer needs.
2. Assumption by marketing of a more central role in the operation of agribusiness firms in order for them to remain profitable.
3. More sophisicated marketing techniques.
4. The same level of effort devoted to marketing that has been devoted to production.

those agribusiness firms and managers that can profitably market their products in this new, more demanding marketplace.

In this new environment it takes a sophisticated approach to marketing and close attention to the needs of consumers for agribusiness firms to remain profitable. It is no longer sufficient for the food marketing system to find ways to dispose of what farmers have already produced. Agricultural commodities and food products increasingly compete against one another (and all other goods and services) for the consumer's dollar. This is why agribusiness firms need to devote the same level of effort to marketing as they have to production. Marketing can help agribusiness firms compete successfully in today's increasingly competitive marketplace and can help to assure the overall future success of the agribusiness system. This is why in this textbook we define *marketing as all those business activities that help satisfy consumer needs by coordinating the flow of goods and services from producers to consumers and users.*

SUMMARY

Marketing plays an important role in the operation of the economic system as it bridges the gap between the conflicting needs of producers and consumers. Marketing accomplishes this by helping producers better understand consumer needs by assisting them in deciding what to produce, when to produce, and for whom to produce. When this is done efficiently, marketing helps consumers gain greater satisfaction from the products they consume, higher profits for producers, and a more efficient allocation of resources for society.

The marketing system has evolved along with the economic system. As the advantages of specialization of production and the use of trade became more apparent, marketing grew in importance. The use of central markets, the invention of money, and middlemen helped to make the marketing system more efficient. Regardless of the economic system a society employs, its marketing system must perform the nine marketing functions of buying, selling, storing, transporting, processing, uniform grades and standards, financing, risk taking, and marketing information if the system is to raise the level of economic efficiency. Each marketing function helps the society overcome the space, time, information, value, or ownership barriers to greater consumer satisfaction.

The performance of the nine marketing functions also adds time, place, form, or possession utility to products and enhances the level of satisfaction consumers derive from them. Thus, the function of the marketing system is to make sure that consumers get what they desire. This means insuring that the right product is available at the right place, at the right price, and at the right time to fully satisfy the consumer.

Because of the abundant supply of many agricultural products today, marketing must be granted the same level of interest that has typically been devoted to production agriculture. It is no longer sufficient for the food marketing system to find ways to dispose of what farmers and ranchers have already produced. The future profitability of the food system requires a more sophisticated approach to marketing and close attention to the needs of consumers.

QUESTIONS

1. Explain the statement that if marketing did not already exist it would have to be invented.
2. Describe how marketing evolved out of the different needs of producers and consumers.
3. Explain the relationship between the nine functions of marketing, the barriers to consumer satisfaction, and the four utilities of marketing.
4. Why must marketing be given the same level of attention by agribusiness firms as has been devoted to production?

3

Evaluating the Performance of the Marketing System

Regardless of the economic system a society chooses, it must develop a marketing system that can meet the needs of its citizens. How closely that marketing system comes to accomplishing this objective is important because it determines to a great extent the level of consumer satisfaction and producer profits in the general economy. This is why society devotes considerable effort to measuring the performance of its marketing system.

The marketing system is evaluated on two criteria: (1) efficiency—how efficiently goods and services flow from producers to consumers; and (2) fairness—how well the marketing system meets the needs of consumers. Consumers reveal how they feel about the marketing system either directly by "voting" with dollars in the marketplace for the goods they want or indirectly by expressing their opinions through the political system. A good example of indirect voting is the rise of consumerism as a political issue and the subsequent enactment of a number of laws to protect the rights of consumers.

THE STRUCTURE-CONDUCT-PERFORMANCE MODEL

To assist with the evaluation process, economists have developed a method for analyzing the fairness and efficiency of the marketing system. The procedure is the product of the work of a number of economists, but is most closely associated with the efforts of Joe S. Bain. Bain developed an industrial organization model that evaluates the efficiency and fairness of the system by examining the structure, conduct, and performance of individual markets within the economy.

Bain argues that there is a relationship among these three elements that captures the performance of a market (Figure 3–1). The way firms are organized in a market (their structure) tells a great deal about how they make decisions (their conduct), which in turn influences the level of efficiency and fairness present in the market (their performance). Therefore, if society seeks to affect the efficiency and fairness of its markets, it must alter their structure.

There is some evidence that markets with few suppliers operate less efficiently than markets with many suppliers, and that having too few suppliers can result in higher prices for consumers and undue profits for producers. This implies that the best policy for society is to do everything possible to insure that enough suppliers operate in each market to effectively compete against one another.

When a sufficient number of firms are present in a market (structure), individual firms must respond to the market rather than try to control it (conduct). This leads to more reasonable levels of both prices and profits (performance). The result is a more efficient market with higher levels of consumer satisfaction and no undue price enhancement (that is, excess profits) on the part of producers or middlemen.

Who Uses This Model?

The structure-conduct-performance model put forth by Bain has had wide acceptance by government *market evaluators* whose job it is to monitor competition among firms in various markets. The tradeoffs among what is beneficial to consumers, producers, and society in a free market system are not always easy to resolve. For example, consumers may want to consume large amounts of highly salted, fried, fatty foods. Producers may be willing to supply these, but should society warn them that this may lead to serious health problems in the years to come? Should this type of food be banned?

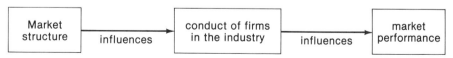

FIGURE 3–1
The Structure-Conduct-Performance Model

Evaluation Criteria for Market Performance

Market Structure
1. Number of Firms in The Market
2. Barriers to Market Entry and Exit
3. Degree of Product and Price Competition

Conduct of Firms in The Market
1. Free Movement of Prices
2. No Price Discrimination
3. No Collusion Between Firms
4. Truthful Product Claims
5. Meaningful Product Differentiation

Market Performance
1. Optimal Output Available at Minimal Price
2. Reasonable Levels of Profits
3. Encouragement of Innovation
4. Reasonable Levels of Investment

These are difficult questions to answer. The issue of how much government involvement there should be in the marketplace and where it should be applied are serious concerns. In our democratic, free market economy these matters are handled through the political process as a response to the needs of the participants in the market.

Now that the general ideas behind the structure-conduct-performance model are in place, it is necessary to examine each component in greater detail.

Details of the Model

Structure. There are certain criteria that a market must meet if its structure is to be conducive to high levels of both economic efficiency and fairness. These criteria include whether:

- There are a sufficient number of firms in an industry given the size of the total market, and firms of the size needed to fully capture the majority of the economies of size (that is, firms large enough to have a low operating cost per unit of output)

- There are no barriers to entry or exit from the market
- Firms are able to differentiate and improve products over time as they compete against one another

It is clear from this that the number of firms in a market plays a critical role in maintaining competition and economic efficiency. This is why market evaluators use *concentration ratios* as a way to measure market structure. The concentration ratio is the proportion of total sales in a market that is accounted for by the sales of the largest firms. The number of firms included in this group depends on the situation, but normally involves the top four to ten firms.

Market evaluators normally get worried when fewer than four of the largest firms account for more than 50 percent of total market sales. When this occurs the firms in these markets tend to behave as oligopolies. This implies that they compete on things other than price, such as advertising, packaging, coupons, and so forth. Efforts to improve and differentiate products may also lag. The result is a loss of economic efficiency and consumer satisfaction. In order to increase competition and raise economic efficiency, the government may step in to limit further market concentration in the form of mergers and acquisitions.

Conduct.   The structure of a market influences conduct or managerial decision making on the part of the firms in it. In a market with many firms, conduct that enhances an individual firm's ability to maximize its long-run profits may be beneficial to the rest of society. However, if there are only a few firms in the market, such conduct pushed to the extreme could lead to monopolistic behavior that would not be acceptable from the standpoint of society.

There are criteria that describe firms' conduct that help to define the level of economic efficiency present in a market. These criteria include whether:

- There are enough firms in the market to create some uncertainty in the minds of firm managers regarding whether price changes both up and down will be followed by competitors
- There is no unjustified price discrimination
- There is no collusion among different firms on pricing or other matters
- Firms are not engaging in unfair trade practices
- Product claims are truthful
- Product differentiation exists and is based on meaningful differences

The satisfaction of these criteria should result in "acceptable conduct" on the part of firms in this market (that is, a high degree of economic efficiency).

Performance. The structure of an industry and the conduct of the firms in it are also reflected in overall industry performance. If the criteria set above for structure and conduct are met, the market should be fair and economically efficient. The level of economic efficiency can also be measured directly by examining several criteria of market performance. These criteria include whether:

- The optimum level of output is being produced at the minimum cost
- Profits are reasonable given the amount of risk, management skill required, and new product development involved
- Innovations are encouraged
- There are reasonable levels of investment, reinvestment of profits, and research and development

Accomplishment of the twin goals of fairness and economic efficiency in a market should bring a balance between the needs of consumers for the highest levels of satisfaction and producers for the highest level of overall profits.

The structure-conduct-performance model provides a way to evaluate the performance of a market. However, much of this evaluation deals with topics normally considered part of marketing. This is why the structure-conduct-performance model is studied here. It is important that marketing managers understand what constitutes economic efficiency and what government regulators will be looking at when they evaluate the performance of a market.

Another reason why marketing managers should understand the structure-conduct-performance model is that these concepts are being used by individual firms to formulate their marketing strategies. The reasons that market evaluators find them valuable for analyzing market structure, conduct, and performance are the very same ones that make them attractive tools for individual firms interested in effective strategic planning. Porter, Quinn, Mintzberg, and others have shown how to use the structure-conduct-performance framework for this purpose.

Under their approach, industry structure is analyzed by the managers of a single firm to determine the basic forces which affect the organization. At the conduct level, firm managers formulate strategy to take advantage of the firm's strength, the weakness of other firms in the industry, and opportunities in terms of unmet consumer needs. Performance, instead of being measured in terms of fairness and economic efficiency, is judged by the profits and market share of the individual firm. This is not quite what government market evaluators normally have in mind for the structure-conduct-performance model, but it has proven to be very effective for individual firms.

GOVERNMENT INTERVENTION IN MARKETS

As we saw earlier, the participants in the economic system establish the rules through the political process and empower government agencies to enforce them. These rules began with the rather basic functions of providing for the common defense, ensuring domestic tranquility, protecting private property rights, and enforcing contracts. Later, Congress expanded its powers to regulate commerce through greater intervention in the marketplace. This includes the enactment of laws against fraudulent trading practices and the establishment of fair weights and measures.

The first major piece of legislation dealing with the operation of the economic system was the Sherman Act of 1890. In the years following the Civil War, because of advances in transportation and communications it became possible to successfully organize and operate large firms. Toward the end of the nineteenth century mergers in steel, railroads, and other basic industries were concentrating the nation's economic power in the hands of a few people. This power was used to control markets. The resulting economic pressure particularly affected the farmers of the day who felt that many of their problems could be traced to the concentrations of market power. Farmers put pressure on their legislators for government intervention in the market to protect farmers and small shopkeepers who lacked market power.

The pressure resulted in Congress's passing the Sherman Act, which states in part that "every contract, combination in the form of a trust or otherwise, or conspiracy, in restraint of trade or commerce among the several states, or with foreign nations, is declared to be illegal." This was the first attempt by the government to affect the structure of the economy so it would perform as its citizens desired. It is the first major antitrust legislation.

In 1914, the Sherman Act was supplemented by the passage of the Clayton Act. This piece of legislation specifically prohibited certain practices that lessened competition or tended to create monopolies. Among them were price discrimination, tie-in contracts and exclusive dealings, and interlocking directorships and stockholdings. The Robinson-Patman Act of 1936 strengthened the Clayton Act's bars against price discrimination.

In addition to these laws, Congress also established a variety of federal agencies to enforce these new rules. Congress created the Interstate Commerce Commission in 1887 to regulate interstate transportation rates, the Food and Drug Administration in 1906 to regulate the quality of food and drug products, and the Federal Trade Commission in 1914 to regulate price competition in interstate commerce.

There were a number of federal laws passed to help insure fair trade in agricultural products. These laws were enacted because farmers and consumers felt they were not being treated fairly by some of the larger agribusiness firms with whom they did business. The first of these was the Meat Inspection Act of 1906, which called for the enforcement of sanitary regulations and federal inspection of meat sold in interstate commerce. The Food Products Act of 1917 established the role of the federal government in food grading and gave the job of carrying out this responsibility to the Agricultural Marketing Service of the USDA.

The Packers and Stockyard Act of 1921 established the rules for fair trade in the livestock markets. It required that all fees be nondiscriminatory, that all weights and measures be accurate, that all transactions be conducted in an open market, and that livestock be sold in a competitive bidding system. The Perishable Commodities Act of 1930 established the same types of regulation for perishable commodities. The Capper-Volstead Act of 1922 exempted farmers as individual businessmen from the antitrust laws and allowed them to come together to organize agricultural cooperatives.

Each of these acts and the others since are directed at assuring that trade remains efficient and fair. Market regulation is designed to insure that competition and innovation are encouraged, and prices reflect true social value. This should lead to greater economic efficiency, fairness in the marketplace, and great consumer satisfaction.

SUMMARY

Once a society selects its economic system it must also develop a marketing system. How well the marketing system performs has a great deal to do with the level of consumer satisfaction and producer profits that are possible in the general economy. Thus, the performance of the marketing system is of great importance to all members of society.

The marketing system is typically measured on two criteria: efficiency and fairness. Efficiency deals with how efficiently goods and services flow from producers to consumers. Fairness deals with how well the needs of consumers are being met. Consumers express their feelings about the performance of the economic system by "voting" either directly (through the goods and services they buy) or indirectly (by expressing their opinions through the political process).

One method used to analyze the efficiency and fairness of the marketing system is the structure-conduct-performance model. Under this approach the way firms are organized in a market (structure) tells a great deal about how they make decisions (conduct), which influences the level of efficiency and fairness present in the market (performance). Therefore, if society seeks to affect the efficiency and fairness of its markets, it must alter their structure. There is evidence that those markets that are the most efficient and fair are those that have a large number of firms competing against one another.

Understanding the structure-conduct-performance model is important to agribusiness marketing managers because: (1) it is one of the measures used by society (through the government) to evaluate the market performance; and, (2) it is used by firms' managers to do market planning.

When citizens have found the marketplace to be unfair and inefficient they have empowered government to intervene in the market to correct these deficiencies. This has brought a number of powerful pieces of legislation from Congress, including the Sherman Act, the Clayton Act, and the Robinson-Patman Act.

QUESTIONS

1. Why is it important to everyone in a society to evaluate the performance of the marketing system?
2. What two criteria are typically used to measure performance and why are they important?
3. Explain the relationship between the three parts of the structure-conduct-performance model and how they help evaluate market performance.
4. What are concentration ratios and how are they used in the market evaluation process?
5. What does the term "excess profits" mean? How are they different from other types of profits?
6. How could a corporate agribusiness manager use the structure-conduct-performance model to help his or her firm achieve greater profits?

4

The Role of Marketing in the Agribusiness Firm

The previous chapters were devoted to explaining the role of the marketing system in a free market economy. In this chapter the general objective is to bring these macroeconomic concepts down to the level of the individual firm so that a workable approach to agribusiness marketing can be developed. The specific objectives are: (1) to describe the role of marketing in the successful operation of an agribusiness firm; and (2) to introduce the basic principles of agribusiness marketing that will be developed in later chapters. By constructing the macroeconomic framework first it is hoped that the reader will be better able to appreciate how marketing helps the firm succeed in the marketplace. With this background in place it should also be easier to understand marketing's role within the firm, and what it takes to successfully manage an agribusiness firm's marketing functions.

This chapter describes how marketing has become more sophisticated in response to the changing economic situation, and then illustrates why this more sophisticated approach to marketing is needed by agribusiness firms if they are to compete successfully in today's more demanding marketplace. The final section of the chapter shows how marketing relates to the overall topic of business management.

THE CHANGING ROLE OF MARKETING WITHIN THE FIRM

The development and growth of the U.S. economic system has caused profound changes in marketing. The combination of a large geographic area with an abundance of untapped natural resources, the ability of products and people to move freely across political boundaries, a relatively high per capita disposable income, a common language, a high level of education, as well as improved transportation and communications, have made it profitable for firms to engage in those activities called marketing. Because of changes in the economic system and the paramount importance of the consumer in the U.S. economy, the attitude of firm managers has had to change. Meeting the needs of consumers is the primary goal of marketing. Reaching this goal profitably requires a high level of marketing management skill.

Five Approaches to the Market

Scholars in the area of marketing have identified a number of approaches that a firm can take to its market. The method used in this text draws heavily on the procedure developed by Philip Kotler. Kotler defines five marketing approaches that he feels represent an evolution of marketing thought. Each succeeding approach represents a higher level of marketing

---

Five Approaches to the Market

1. *The Production Approach*—Produce as much as possible at the lowest possible cost.
2. *The Product Approach*—Make a high-quality product and the world will beat a path to your door.
3. *The Selling Approach*—All any product needs is a strong selling effort to get consumers to buy it.
4. *The Marketing Approach*—Produce a product that fills a consumer need, price it correctly, make it readily available, and promote it properly, and it will sell itself.
5. *The Societal Marketing Approach*—Follow the marketing approach but include only those products that enhance both consumers' and society's well-being.

sophistication as well as a higher level of management skill required to succeed at meeting the needs of the firm, its consumers, and society.[*]

1. The Production Approach. At the earliest stages of market development, when consumer needs are barely being met by emerging technologies, demand normally greatly exceeds supply. In most cases consumers are content just to be able to get a product. As long as it meets some minimum standards of quality, consumers are generally satisfied.

In this economic situation, the proper producer response is to seek production methods that will yield (1) the minimum cost per unit of output and (2) the maximum output per unit of input. This is the correct response to this economic situation because it will lead to the highest profits for the producer. Since demand is seemingly endless relative to supply, and consumers do not appear to be too picky about the product, producers focus their attention on improving production methods rather than on trying to further understand and meet consumer needs. Thus, producers often become insensitive to the needs of consumers, feeling that "they should be glad to get what they do." Under the production approach to the market, marketing deals only with finding ways to lower costs and improve the physical efficiency of moving the product from the producer to the consumer.

2. The Product Approach. Another inward-looking approach to marketing is the product approach. It is the one that most exemplifies the old saying, "Build a better mousetrap and the world will beat a path to your door." The basic premise of the product approach is that it is the duty of the producer to provide a product of good quality and then to improve it over time. Under the product approach it is assumed that discerning consumers will recognize the inherent value of high-quality products and buy them rather than lower-quality products. Consumers are felt to be willing to pay extra to obtain improved versions of the product.

The focus of this approach is still on producers making the products they want to make, and consumers adjusting their needs to what producers want to sell. The result is that rather than being market or consumer-need oriented, producers become product oriented. The result is often a product in search of consumers. A classic example is the buggy-whip manufacturer who concentrates on producing the world's best buggy whip while failing to see the shift away from horses to automobiles. The result is a technically sophisticated buggy whip, but a product with few consumers.

[*]Philip Kotler, *Marketing Management: Analysis, Planning, Implementation, and Control*, 6th ed. (Englewood Cliffs, N.J.: Prentice-Hall, © 1988). Used by permission.

3. The Selling Approach. The selling approach, like the previous two, is primarily producer and product oriented, but it does bring the consumer into the picture. The selling approach is built around the assumption that if left alone consumers will not buy enough of the product that the producer has already decided to make. As a result, it is up to the producer to convince potential consumers that this particular product is really best for them. Thus, the producer must mount an aggressive sales campaign to stimulate sales.

This approach is often used in economic situations where supply exceeds demand and there is growing competition among producers for consumers' favor. The assumption is that with enough sales pressure anything can be sold. However, the selling approach misses the point that management expert Peter Drucker made when he said, "The aim of marketing is to make selling superfluous. You should know your customers so well that products are designed to sell themselves."[*]

Products that need a hard sell probably do not fit consumer needs very well since consumers must be persuaded to accept them. Hard sell is a short-run solution at best. It may get the firm the first sale, but may so alienate consumers that they will not buy from this firm again. This is especially true if consumers are dissatisfied with the product.

4. The Marketing Approach. A major advance in the sophistication of marketing comes with a shift away from a production and selling orientation to one that concentrates on meeting the needs of consumers.

The essence of the marketing approach was explained in a famous article in *Harvard Business Review* by Theodore Levitt called "Marketing Myopia."[†] Levitt explained that firms are myopic or nearsighted in that they often fail to see the true reasons why they are successful. Success does not necessarily come because a firm can produce a technically superior product or can field a force of aggresive salespeople. Rather, success comes to those firms that can best satisfy the needs of consumers.

Thus, the marketing approach proposes that the profitable satisfaction of consumer needs is the driving force that gives direction to all the activities of the firm. Each firm should seek to meet the needs of its customers more effectively, efficiently, and profitably than its competitors. Those that do are rewarded with profits in direct proportion to their level of success in meeting consumer needs.

[*]Peter F. Drucker, *Management Tasks, Responsibilities, Practices* (New York: Harper and Row, 1974).

[†]Theodore Levitt, "Marketing Myopia," *Harvard Business Review*, July–August, 1960.

This approach is also referred to as the *marketing concept*. The marketing concept consists of two parts: first, the determination of the needs of the consumer; second, the organization of the business to profitably fill those needs. However, this approach will be successful only if *all* the functional areas of the firm, such as production, sales, accounting, shipping, and warehousing, accept the idea of *consumer sovereignty* (that is, consumer as king or queen). The profitable satisfaction of consumer needs must be of paramount importance to everyone in the firm if it is to succeed.

The evidence is clear that the marketing approach works. Most of the firms profiled in the popular management book *In Search of Excellence* have adopted this approach.[*] In fact, it was a key element in their success. It is all too easy to cater to the whims of some executive or department within the firm at the expense of the faceless customer who is seldom seen by those at headquarters, but the firm will suffer as a result.

The marketing approach often works best in economic situations where production capacity exceeds demand and there is stiff competition among producers. In this situation how well the firm satisfies consumer needs has a great deal to do with the level of its success.

5. The Societal Marketing Approach.   The fifth market approach offered by Philip Kotler is a refinement of the marketing approach discussed above. It extends the definition of meeting consumer needs to include the phrase "in ways that preserve or enhance the consumer's or society's well-being."

The societal marketing approach recognizes the balance that must exist among the needs of consumers, producers, and society. It also recognizes the need for long-run market solutions to meet the long-run needs of society. For example, the brewing industry has done a magnificent job of meeting the needs of consumers, as the industry's financial success testifies. But has it met the needs of society? There are a lot of societal problems associated with beer consumption such as beer-can litter along the roadways. Society must bear the cost of this unsightly litter since brewers and consumers seem unwilling to do so. Some states have passed container taxes to help society offset these costs. If an industry or firm wants to prosper in the long run, it must consider the long-run needs of society.

Although the societal marketing approach has idealistic appeal, most firms that we would recognize as good marketers remain at the fourth level, the marketing approach. In addition, there are still a great many firms who have not progressed this far. Throughout this text references will be made to

[*]Thomas J. Peters and Robert H. Waterman, *In Search of Excellence* (New York: Harper & Row, 1982).

the marketing approach or the marketing concept, referring to the ideas discussed in the fourth approach. This does not mean that most firms disregard the consumer's or society's well-being, but that they do not put it first in planning market strategies. That next step in the evolutionary process awaits them.

Agribusiness and the Marketing Approach

Just as agriculture evolved into agribusiness, the marketing system that serves it has also evolved. A few years ago, students of agricultural marketing would have studied a very different set of approaches to marketing. Their agricultural marketing course would have taken a functional approach, an institutional approach, a utilities approach, or a commodity approach to the subject.

Under the *functional approach*, one examines each of the nine marketing functions discussed in Chapter 2—the exchange functions of buying and selling; the physical functions including storage, transportation, and processing; and the facilitating functions which include grades and standards, financing, risk taking, and market information. Each of these topics is of great interest to agribusiness firms that deal with perishable commodities (corn, wheat, milk, cattle) whose prices can fluctuate widely.

The *commodity approach* to marketing focuses on a single commodity from the time it leaves the farm until it loses its identity (when the wheat that is processed into flour is used to make bread, for instance). A student would examine the nine marketing functions as they relate to that single commodity. The specialized firms, institutions, laws, and government programs that deal with the commodity would also be studied. This approach is valid for the person who wants to fully understand the market for a single commodity, such as milk.

General categories of marketplace functionaries are studied using the *institutional approach*. For example, one would learn the marketing roles of wholesalers, retailers, brokers, and so on. Specialized institutions which serve agriculture would also be examined. For example, one would learn the risk-shifting mechanism of the commodity futures markets and the facilitating role of the Farm Credit System in providing financing for marketers. To fully understand marketing in agribusiness, one should understand hedging as a risk management tool and the role of a wholesale distributor.

The *utilities approach* was discussed briefly in Chapter 2. Time, place, form, and possession utilities add value to products in the marketing process. These concepts are important to understanding storage, transportation, processing, and market exchange in agriculture.

These traditional approaches to the study of marketing in agriculture give the student who hopes to seek his or her fortune in agribusiness an incomplete view of marketing. Studying the functional, commodity, institutional, and utility approaches gives a person a descriptive understanding of the existing marketing system for agricultural commodities but provides little understanding of how a firm makes marketing decisions or where a new college graduate would fit into a market oriented agribusiness firm.

The traditional approach may give a person a good understanding of the marketing of a single commodity, but an understanding of the dairy marketing system is not transferable to grain marketing or to the marketing of branded food products such as Oreo cookies. An even greater drawback is that for the most part the traditional approaches to marketing ignore the consumers. For a firm in a consumer driven market economy this can be fatal.

The beef industry gives a good example of this point. For a variety of reasons consumers' long-time love affair with beef is apparently over. Per capita consumption of beef has fallen sharply in recent years. Upstart firms such as Iowa Beef Packing, now IBP; Excel, a subsidiary of Cargill, Inc.; and Monfort, now owned by ConAgra, have responded by introducing cost-cutting technologies such as high-speed processing plants and the new marketing concept of boxed beef. They have located plants in areas where they could benefit from lower cost labor. By responding to the shifting realities of the marketplace, these firms have grown to dominate the meat-packing industry. Old-line meat packers who could not or would not respond to their market are out of the meat-packing business. The new companies are now introducing individually wrapped, oxygen-free, branded beef products. They are taking a commodity item (beef) and making it into a branded consumer product (Excel's Country Brand beef) that can be promoted to build a following of loyal consumers. This is the marketing concept in action in agribusiness and an example of why this text uses this approach.

The adoption of the marketing concept by firms in the agribusiness system is one of the keys to success. Those firms that adopt it will survive and prosper. Those that do not will perish. To be a survivor requires that the firm meet the needs of target markets better and more profitably than its competitors.

ADOPTING THE MARKETING APPROACH

Not all firms in agribusiness have adopted the marketing approach. This is partly because its takes more than a memo from the boss's office to make it happen. It calls for a commitment to a whole new way of doing business.

The biggest change is a reorientation of the way the firm views itself. Under the marketing approach, production and processing no longer occupy center stage. In fact, the firm should no longer be viewed as a conglomeration of competing empires each presided over by an anxious manager. Instead, the firm should be viewed as a system that can be organized and reorganized to satisfy changing consumer needs and market situations. Each unit within the firm is there because it plays a pivotal role in the accomplishment of that objective. Marketing's role in all of this is to provide direction or purpose to what the company does—profitably satisfy consumer needs.

Under the marketing approach, marketing does not take over the production department, but it does give it direction. How to produce each product is still left up to the production people. For example, if after extensive market research on consumer food preferences the marketing people find that consumers are looking for a single-serving, hand-held snack food that can be prepared quickly but retails for less than $2.00, they need to pass this information on to the new product development group. It is up to the product development and production personnel to decide how to produce a food product that meets these consumer preferences and sells for a profit when priced at $1.99.

The important difference in this procedure is that marketing identifies what consumers want and transmits this to the rest of the firm. This determines what is produced. The production department now focuses on filling specific consumer needs rather than on on making the products it feels it can make best or at the lowest cost, hoping that the marketing department can sell them.

The dominant role of consumer satisfaction must also be accepted by the staff people in the firm, including the finance department, the personnel department, the legal department, and all the other parts of the firm. It is important that they understand that the level of satisfaction that the firm's products brings to consumers also influences the level of their salaries. The satisfaction of a consumer need is what gives the company its "right" to earn a profit. To do this successfully and profitably requires a coordinated effort on the part of *all* the people in the firm regardless of what they do.

Making this change happen is the job of management. Managers have to implement the marketing concept and see to it that it reaches every corner of the firm, every day. To accomplish this takes a skilled management team.

Marketing and the Four Functions of Management

Being a skilled manager means being proficient at all four of the functions of management—planning, organizing, controlling, and directing.

The Four Functions of Management

1. Planning
2. Organizing
3. Controlling
4. Directing (Implementing)

It also requires that the manager know how to mix just the right combinations of technical know-how and judgment to fit each situation.

Planning is involved in making the decision to adopt the marketing approach in the firm. It also deals with the establishment of the firm's goals and objectives plus any other matters that could affect the future of the company.

Organizing is involved in developing the flow of work through the company so that consumer rather than employee needs are given preference. The organization should be set up so that the goals and objectives established in planning can be accomplished efficiently and effectively. This includes deciding who reports to whom, how the consumer preferences identified by the marketing department will be transmitted to the rest of the firm, how consumer complaints will be handled, and so forth.

Controlling is involved with the development of feedback mechanisms to determine the progress of the company and to measure the effectiveness of its organizational structure in meeting the goals and objectives established during planning.

Directing or implementing is involved with the combining of the plans, the organization, and the controls into something that profitably meets some consumer need. This is the area that consumes about 90 percent of a manager's time. It is also the most critical of the four management functions and is what separates good managers from the rest. Good implementation can overcome even a poor plan with a weak organizational structure and loose controls, and turn disaster into a success. However, poor implementation can result in failure even with the best of plans, organizational structures, and control mechanisms.

The successful management of the marketing function is critical to the success of the firm and should occupy a position within it equal to that of finance, production, and personnel. Each must be performed well for the firm to prosper.

THE FOUR FUNCTIONS OF MANAGEMENT AND MARKETING MANAGEMENT

The management of marketing activities within the firm can be studied within the broad confines of the four management functions—planning, organizing, controlling, and directing or implementing. The only difference is that marketing management focuses on understanding customer needs.

Planning

The first type of planning a firm must do is heavily related to marketing. It must decide which consumer needs it is going to fill and how it will accomplish this *better* than anyone else or *differently*. When this type of planning is done on a companywide basis it is called *strategic planning*. Its primary objective is to look for market opportunities (unmet consumer needs) that can be filled by the company. Once these needs have been identified, management must determine *how* the firm can fill them profitably. This is all explained in the company's *strategic plan*.

This plan includes a clear definition of:

1. *The target market*—the relatively homogeneous group of consumers whose unmet needs the firm hopes to fill efficiently, effectively, and profitably. This market can be small or large. However, it should be as homogeneous as possible. By zeroing in on a homogeneous target or market segment, the firm can gain a competitive edge over other firms by doing a better job of satisfying the needs of this group, and thus increase its sales and long-run profits.

2. *How consumers' needs will be better met by this firm*—the competitive edge that will cause consumers to choose this firm's product over someone else's.

Peter Drucker gets at these two items by asking managers to answer these five tough questions:

- What is our business?
- Who are our customers?
- What is value to our customers?
- What will our business be?
- What should our business be?

These questions should be continually raised and answered to everyone's satisfaction. The answers will indicate whether management has a clear idea of what the firm is trying to accomplish and why. These issues are at the heart of management's planning function and are the cornerstone of marketing.

Organizing

Once the decisions are made about the consumer needs this firm is to fill and how it will be done, a manager's attention should turn to developing an organization to accomplish it.

The chances for success rise if management's efforts are guided by several principles. First, the definition of what the organization is to do should be a market definition and not a product definition. This means the definition should be in terms of the consumer need that is being filled, not in terms of a physical description of a particular product. This is because consumers purchase satisfaction, not specific goods and services. They purchase a particular good because it provides them with satisfaction. Borrowing an example from Levitt's marketing myopia article discussed earlier in the chapter, consumers were not merely buying rides on the railroad but a means to move from one place to another quickly and cheaply. This is why consumers abandoned the railroads when cars and airplanes came along, since they provided greater satisfaction in this area.

Second, the company should be organized so that its primary emphasis is on meeting the needs of consumers. Third, a mechanism should be established for the constant and continued reassessment of consumer needs and the search for better, more efficient ways to meet them.

Thus, the adoption of the marketing approach has a great deal to say about how a business is organized. It can also reveal how the firm views its market and its customers. If a company adopts the marketing approach, marketing activities are given prominence in the organizational structure and the flow of work.

Controlling

With the plans and organizational structure in place, management's next task is to establish a procedure to see that the company is accomplishing what it set out to do. The controlling function depends on developing these feedback mechanisms.

Controls can be both internal and external. Internal controls include reports on production levels, inventory levels, and so on. These reports are not unimportant to people in marketing, but external control reports on sales, prices, market shares, profits, and so on are of greater interest to marketing managers. All these reports help them to evaluate the decisions they made during the planning and organizing functions, and to determine whether there is a need for change.

Controls, regardless of their focus, are valuable only if they give early warning of deviations from what was planned. They should be designed to assist in the measurement of progress, not to impede it by becoming too demanding and time-consuming. Thus, marketing managers have a keen interest in the proper operation of the controlling function of management.

Directing

Marketing managers also have a strong interest in the fourth function of management called directing. It is here that all the previous planning, organizing, and developing of control mechanisms is converted into reality and the consumer need is actually met. This is why directing is often also referred to as implementing.

Directing is the most time-consuming of all the management functions. But if the planning, organizing, and controlling are done well the job of implementing can become a good deal easier. How well this function is done determines to a large extent the overall success of the company. It is here that the manager takes the grand overall strategic plan and develops the *tactical* (short-run) *plans* needed to meet the day-to-day requirements of the market.

THE FOUR Ps OF MARKETING AND THE MARKETING MIX

To assist managers with this function, Jerome McCarthy has identified four controllable variables that make up the firm's *marketing mix.*[*] They must be properly combined to satisfy the needs of the target market.

The marketing mix is composed of four items each of which begins with the letter *P*. For this reason they are referred to as *Four Ps of marketing* and they include:

1. The Product—the firm must develop the right product to give maximum satisfaction to the members of the target market
2. The Price—the right product must carry the right price in light of market conditions
3. The Place—the right product, at the right price, must be in the right place to be purchased by the members of the target market

---

[*]E. Jerome McCarthy and William D. Perreautt Jr., *Basic Marketing: A Managerial Approach*, 9th Ed. (Homewood, Ill.: Richard D. Irwin, 1987).

4. The Promotion—telling the members of the target market in the right way that the right product, at the right price is available at the right location

Developing the proper marketing mix of product, price, place, and promotion in order to satisfy consumer needs is what marketing is all about, and is what marketing managers do to earn their living. Marketing managers use the four Ps of marketing as tactical tools in the satisfaction of consumer needs. By manipulating the marketing mix they are able to implement the company's plans using its organizational structure. The firm's progress toward the accomplishment of these goals is measured by the control mechanisms. *Thus, marketing management is the planning, organizing, controlling, and directing of all the firm's business activities that help satisfy consumer demands and help the firm accomplish its goal of maximizing its long-run profits.*

The objective of all this is to position the firm so that it can maximize its advantage over competitors with respect to changing customer needs and economic conditions. Besides marketing to current customers, marketing managers are always looking for new market opportunities, new consumers, and better ways to meet customer needs.

Successful marketing management is a matter of perspective. It is like the old story of two shoe salesmen who sail away to a distant land. Upon arrival they both note that people in this country do not wear shoes. The first salesman cables home "Send return ticket immediately; no market here." The second one cables home "Send warehouse plans; market appears unlimited." Market opportunities are in the eye of the beholder.

SUMMARY

The marketing concept is the driving force for the entire firm and gives it direction and purpose. The purpose is the satisfaction of discovered consumer needs. Meeting these is what gives the firm its "right" to earn a profit.

The role of marketing has evolved over time as technology and consumer needs have changed. The movement from a product-oriented marketing system to one based on the marketing approach where the needs of consumers interact with those of society and producers has led to higher levels of consumer satisfaction. Agribusinesses must adopt the marketing approach if they are to have continued success.

Marketing management is merely a subset of the general area of business management. As such, it fits well into the four functions of management. Marketing managers use the four Ps of marketing as tactical tools in the satisfaction of consumer needs. Thus, marketing management is the planning, organizing, controlling, and directing of all those business activities that help satisfy consumer needs and help the firm accomplish its goal of maximizing its long-run profits.

QUESTIONS

1. What are the five approaches to the market and how do they differ from each other?
2. What did Levitt mean when he said firms often suffer from "market myopia"; how should firms avoid it?
3. What is consumer sovereignty and what role should it play in how an agribusiness is run?
4. Agribusiness is too important an industry to worry about adopting new approaches to marketing. The old approaches to marketing are just fine. Do you agree or disagree with this statement and why?
5. What steps must an agribusiness take to adopt the marketing approach?
6. What is marketing management and how does it relate to the four functions of management?

PART TWO

Understanding the Marketing Environment

Successful marketing requires that managers understand how markets function. This is important for several reasons. First, the interaction of the market forces influencing supply and demand has a great deal to do with the size of a market and the prices of the products in it, both of which should be of interest to a profit-maximizing agribusiness. Second, the establishment of a successful marketing program requires that marketing managers understand how consumers make their purchasing decisions and how they react to changes in price and other factors.

Third, the maximization of long-run profits requires the producer to have an accurate picture of costs, and how prices of inputs and products purchased for resale are determined. Fourth, success in the marketplace requires managers to be able to correctly determine the market environment their firm faces since it greatly influences marketing decision making.

The social science of economics is largely devoted to examining these issues and can greatly add to a manager's understanding of how markets operate. With this increased knowledge about markets, marketing managers should be able to do a better job of meeting the needs of their consumers and generating higher profits.

This section of the text is divided into three chapters. Chapter 5 explains the profit equation and then examines the demand factors that influence the level of total revenue in the profit equation. Chapter 6 discusses the supply factors that influence the level of production and total cost in the profit equation. Finally, the elements of supply and demand are put together in Chapter 7 in a framework that will permit a careful examination of the profit maximization process. The special features of agricultural markets are examined as part of this process.

5

Understanding Consumer Demand

This chapter will develop the first part of the profit equation and then will examine the factors that influence the total revenue side of the profit equation. First, let's define the profit equation and see why it is important to marketing managers.

INTRODUCTION: THE PROFIT EQUATION

Under the marketing approach adopted in this text, the primary goal of a firm is the maximization of its long-run profits through satisfaction of consumer needs. The two ideas of maximizing long-run profits and satisfying consumer needs are closely related.

As was seen in Chapter 4, price is one of the four P's of the marketing mix (product, price, place, and promotion). The setting of an acceptable price has a great deal to do with consumer satisfaction. The lower the price, the more of a product consumers are likely to buy and consume. The level of prices of inputs is also of great interest to producers. The lower the prices paid for inputs and the higher the prices received for outputs, the larger the firm's profits.

Let's begin the discussion of what economics can reveal about the behavior of markets and consumers by examining the profit equation. Profit (π) is the difference between total revenue (TR) and total cost (TC). The *profit equation* is:

$$\pi = TR - TC$$

The objective for the firm is to maximize the difference between TR and TC by either raising TR, lowering TC, or doing both.

TOTAL REVENUE

A critical part of any firm's profit equation is total revenue. It is calculated by multiplying price per unit (P_y) times quantity sold (Y), or

$$TR = Py \cdot Y$$

It is important for firm managers to remember that the objective of the firm is to maximize long-run profits, not just quantity sold. All too often, using a production, product, or selling approach to the market, the corporate goal becomes sales maximization. With these approaches, profits are assumed to take care of themselves. Unfortunately, they rarely do.

A good part of the success in trying to maximize profits comes from understanding the interrelationships between the size of total revenue and the various levels of price and quantity. High levels of total revenue can be obtained from selling just one unit if the price is high enough and someone is willing to pay it. For example, a TR goal of $1,000,000 can be reached if just 1 unit is sold provided the selling price per unit is $1,000,000.

This same total revenue goal can be accomplished by selling a large volume of the product at a more reasonable price. For example, TR can still be $1,000,000 if the price is lowered to $1 per unit and the firm is able to sell 1,000,000 units.

In fact, there are a whole host of intermediate prices and quantities that can yield the same total revenue. However, given cost factors and the characteristics of consumers in the market, the solution is generally found somewhere between these two extremes. Table 5–1 gives some examples of this.

More realistically a manager might look at a chart of prices and quantities like those in Table 5–2.

TABLE 5–1

Total Revenue	=	Price	×	Quantity
$1,000,000		$ 1		1,000,000
$1,000,000		2		500,000
$1,000,000		5		200,000
$1,000,000		100		10,000
$1,000,000		1,000		1,000
$1,000,000		10,000		100
$1,000,000		100,000		10
$1,000,000		1,000,000		1

TABLE 5–2

Price	×	Quantity	=	Total Revenue	Elasticity
1.00		90		$ 90	
1.50		80		120	-0.22
2.00		70		140	-0.38
2.50		60		150	-0.57
2.75		55		151.25	-0.83
3.00		50		150	-1.00
3.50		40		140	-1.20
4.00		30		120	-1.75
4.50		20		90	-2.67
5.00		10		50	-4.50

A closer look at the Table 5–2 shows that as price and quantity move in opposite directions the level of total revenue does not remain the same. This means that the price the firm charges has a great deal to do with the level of its total revenue. Tables such as 5–2 are extremely useful to marketers and economists. Economists call such tables which show how much consumers are willing and able to buy of a product at various prices a *demand schedule*.

Putting these prices and quantities on a graph (Figure 5–1) would show a line sloping down and to the right. This indicates that there is an inverse relationship between price and quantity sold. The higher the price, the smaller the quantity sold. The lower the price, the larger the quantity sold. This illustrates the *law of demand*, which states that consumers buy less of a good as the price rises and more as the price declines.

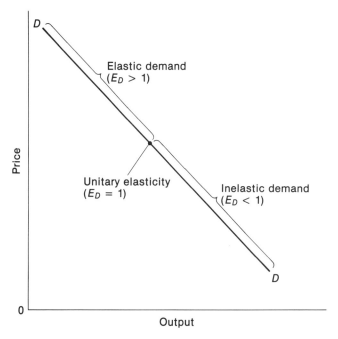

FIGURE 5–1
A Typical Demand Schedule

Total Revenue, Price Changes, and Elasticity

One of the major concerns of marketers is the effect on total revenue of product price changes. Using the data from the demand schedule in Table 5–2 it is possible to calculate the change in total revenue and quantity sold at different prices.

As price declines, quantity demanded increases, showing that the law of demand works. Total revenue increases as we would expect, but eventually it reaches a maximum at a price of $2.75 and a quantity of 55 units, and then declines. Aren't higher sales at lower prices better?

The answer rests in the size of the relative changes in quantity sold and price. When price rose from $1.00 to $1.50 (a 50 percent increase), quantity sold decreased from 50 to 45 (a 10 percent decrease). The fairly large percentage rise in price (50 percent) brought about a much smaller percentage decrease in quantity sold (10 percent) and total revenue rose.

However, when prices rose from $4.50 to $5.00 (an 11.1 percent increase), quantity sold declined from 15 to 10 (a 33.3 percent decrease), and total revenue decreased.

From Table 5–2 it is possible to develop some conclusions about what happens to total revenue *when price increases.*

The conclusions are:

1. When the percentage change in quantity demanded is *greater than* the percentage change in price, total revenue *declines.*
2. When the percentage change in quantity demanded is *equal to* the percentage change in price, total revenue *stays the same.*
3. When the percentage change in quantity demanded is *less than* the percentage change in price, total revenue *increases.*

When the percentage change in quantity is greater than the percentage change in price, and total revenue increases, demand is called *elastic.* When the percentage changes are equal and there is no change in total revenue, demand is called *unitary.* When the percentage change in quantity is less than the percentage change in price, demand is called *inelastic.*

Doing this same thing for price declines reveals just the opposite outcomes for total revenue. A decline in price from $5.00 to $4.50 (a 10 percent decline) brings an increase in quantity demanded from 10 to 15 (a 50 percent increase), and total revenue increases.

Thus for *price decreases* the following conclusions apply:

1. If the percentage change in quantity demanded is *greater than* the percentage change in price, total revenue increases and demand is *elastic.*
2. If the percentage change in quantity demanded is *equal to* the percentage change in price, total revenue *stays the same* and demand is *unitary.*
3. If the percentage change in quantity demanded is *less than* the percentage change in price, total revenue decreases, and demand is *inelastic.*
   To summarize, when:

$$\frac{\text{Percent change in quantity}}{\text{Percent change in price}} \quad \begin{array}{l} > \ 1, \text{demand is elastic} \\ = \ 1, \text{demand is unitary} \\ < \ 1, \text{demand is inelastic} \end{array}$$

Looking back at the graph of the demand schedule in Figure 5–1 it is possible to show the elasticities of different sections of the demand schedule. In the upper half of the schedule, demand is elastic (>1). In the middle of the schedule, demand is unitary (=1). In the lower half of the schedule, demand is inelastic (<1).

Why Knowing Elasticity Is Important.   In order to establish a price that will permit the firm to achieve its goal of maximizing long-run profits, a marketing manager must first know whether the demand for the product is elastic or inelastic. For example, if a manager knew that within a certain price range demand for a product is inelastic, he could be fairly confident that raising its price would raise the firm's total revenue. But if demand for the product is actually elastic, raising its price would be the wrong thing to do since this would reduce the firm's total revenue. On the other hand, if product demand is elastic, higher total revenue can be achieved by lowering the price of the product. It is important for managers to know the elasticity of demand of the products they handle so they will know what type of pricing policy to pursue to reach the goal of long-run profit maximization.

Looking at Table 5–2, it is apparent that a firm would want to sell products with an inelastic demand since each price rise would bring greater total revenue. Unfortunately for firm managers, there are only a few items with inelastic demand over a broad range of prices. They are usually necessities like salt or gasoline where there are few substitutes. Most items fall into the general area of elastic demand, where price increases normally lead to declines in total revenue. Quantity demanded decreases because customers can readily find substitutes for the higher priced item. For example, if the price of butter rises, many consumers substitute lower-priced margarine for higher-priced butter. If the price of butter is lowered, both quantity sold and total revenue for the dairy industry would rise as consumers turn back to butter and decrease consumption of margarine.

The general category of food has an inelastic demand (that is, the demand curve is nearly vertical). However, within the general food category there are a large number of substitute goods, and demand becomes more elastic (that is, the demand curve is more horizontal).

Let's look at an illustration (Figure 5–2). Assume demand schedule A represents all food items. It is the most inelastic. The next line, line B, could represent the demand for all dairy products. Line C could be the demand for all ice cream, while line D may be for all vanilla-flavored ice cream. The last line, E, and the one that is the most elastic, could be for Haagen-Dazs vanilla ice cream. As a food product is more narrowly defined the demand becomes more elastic as the list of substitutes grows longer.

For example, you may have a craving for vanilla ice cream. Nothing else will do. But on your way to Haagen-Dazs you notice a sign that says that Baskin-Robbins is having a half-price promotional sale on vanilla ice cream. The lower price on the Baskin-Robbins vanilla ice cream causes you to substitute it for the Haagen-Dazs.

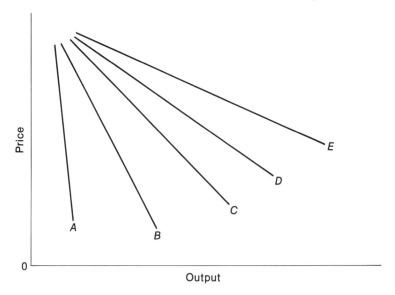

FIGURE 5–2
Shape of Demand Schedules

In this example there are few substitutes for food. For dessert dairy products there are many substitutes such as candy, baked goods, and fresh fruit. By the time the demand is refined all the way down to Haagen-Dazs vanilla ice cream the number of substitute items is large. This is why increases in the general level of food prices are easily passed along to the consumer, while the producer of a single food item like Haagen-Dazs vanilla ice cream has a harder time raising prices.

Consumer Demand

In a free market economy where the doctrine of consumer sovereignty is accepted, consumers direct what is produced by what they purchase. Economists have studied this behavior and have developed some general principles that explain it.

The first principle is that consumers always seek the highest level of total satisfaction (utility) from the collection of goods they consume. When choosing each additional good to consume they always pick the one that gives the greatest addition to their overall total level of satisfaction. By consistently following this principle individual consumers select the bundle of goods that gives them the greatest total satisfaction.

The second principle of consumer demand is that the amount of satisfaction obtained from consuming each additional unit of a product diminishes as more of it is consumed. For example, if you are really hungry the first hamburger you eat will probably taste great and give you a tremendous amount of satisfaction. But after you have eaten several burgers, the additional satisfaction you get from eating another one will probably be much lower. In fact, you can experience negative satisfaction from consuming too many hamburgers.

Hence, the additional satisfaction or *marginal utility* obtained from the consumption of each additional unit diminishes. This illustrates the principle of *diminishing marginal utility* where the additional satisfaction provided by the consumption of each added unit of a good declines. If utility did not decline with additional consumption, people would consume nothing but enormous quantities of the single product that gave them the highest utility. Since utility does decline, the consumer eventually reaches the point where given a choice of another burger or green beans she will choose the green beans. Diminishing marginal utility is what leads consumers to demand a variety of products in order to maximize their total utility.

The Role of Price

If the world had unlimited resources, this discussion of consumer demand would be at an end. However, limits of time, money, land, labor, and so forth prevent the consumption of everything that consumers want. Because of this we have to live within budgets, and are forced to make choices. We look for those items that will give us the most satisfaction for the amount of money we can afford to spend. This helps us receive the largest total amount of satisfaction possible from our limited resources. The combination of the consumers' desire to maximize satisfaction on a limited budget and the producers' desire to maximize profits by meeting consumer needs with the lowest cost production methods is what drives the economic system. Price is a key piece of information that helps both consumers and producers allocate scarce resources to the best use.

Consumers, by being willing to pay a certain price for an item, indicate that they are receiving at least as much additional satisfaction from consumption of that good as they could from the consumption of any other good they could purchase at the same price. If the price is lowered, more consumers will feel this way and quantity demanded will increase. For example, by paying $1.79 for a Super Burger at a fast-food restaurant, as many as 25 million customers will indicate that they derive at least $1.79 worth of satisfaction from eating one. At a price of $1.00, this number may increase to 50 million consumers.

Producers operate much the same way. They assemble scarce resources to produce items demanded by consumers. By paying a particular price for an input, producers indicate that it is worth at least that much to them in the production process. How much the producer is willing to pay for the input is dependent on how much he thinks consumers are willing to pay for his product. Thus producer demand for resources is dependent on the consumer demand for the firm's product. This illustrates the principle of *derived demand*, where the demand for an input is largely determined by the demand for the end product.

In agribusiness the demand for barns, feed, processing plants, frozen food display cases, dairy cows, and so on is derived in part from consumer demand for retail food items. For example, the demand by farmers for fertilizer is derived partially from the consumer demand for turkey. If consumers demand more turkey, the price of turkey rises. This encourages producers to enlarge their flocks. Increased flock size leads to greater demand for turkey feed, which leads to increased demand for corn, and finally for the fertilizer to grow it. Thus, the turkey grower, the corn farmer, the turkey processor, and the fertilizer producer are all linked together in the agribusiness system. The demand schedule faced by each firm is at least partially derived from the consumer's demand for turkey. This is why they all need to be aware of consumer demand for turkey and other food products, and why agribusiness must be viewed as a system. At each step along the way it is price that helps each of the firms to allocate its scarce resources, and price that communicates any need to realign resource allocations.

The Factors That Influence Demand

Because of its importance to firms at all levels, a great deal of effort has been expended to understand and predict consumer behavior. The definition of demand that was offered earlier stated that "demand is a schedule of how much consumers are willing and able to buy at various prices." The words *willing and able* mean that the concern of the firm is with those consumers who are able, not just willing, to buy. Therefore, the concern of marketers is with *effective demand*, with those who desire the product and who have the ability to actually make a purchase. In the rest of our discussions when we speak of demand we will be referring to effective demand.

In general there are seven factors that influence the level of consumer demand. They include:

The Seven Factors That Influence Demand

1. Price of the good
2. Price of substitute goods
3. Price of complement goods
4. Income
5. Population
6. Tastes and Preferences
7. Seasonality

---

1. *Own Price.*   The price of the item whose demand is being examined is called "own price." Under normal conditions, the law of demand will hold true so there is an inverse relationship between price and quantity demanded.

2. *Price of Substitute.*   The price of a good that consumers could substitute for the item being examined is the second factor influencing demand. A rise in the price of the substitute good will stimulate the consumption of the good in question because consumers will buy the now relatively lower-priced good rather than the higher-priced substitute good. For example, if the good being examined is coffee, a rise in the price of tea should lead to an increase in coffee consumption even though the price of coffee has not changed, and vice versa.

3. *Price of Complement.*   A complementary good is one whose consumption normally goes hand in hand with that of the item being examined. A rise in the price of the complementary good should discourage the consumption of the good in question. Continuing the coffee example, a significant rise in the price of sugar could lower coffee demand to some degree if some consumers simply could not drink their coffee unsweetened.

4. *Income.*   The level of consumer income also affects the level of consumer demand. For most goods there is a direct relationship between changes in income and demand. For example, one would anticipate that people would purchase more coffee as their incomes rose. However, the demand for some goods such as bagged flour, dry beans, and raw potatoes falls as consumer incomes rise and people trade up to "better" foods.

5. *Population.* Changes in population can also affect the level of product demand. The more people there are in a market the greater will be the demand for the product at every price. A marketer would want to know whether increased sales of his product are coming from a larger population or increased interest. The difference is important in market planning.

6. *Tastes and Preferences.* Consumer demand rarely remains constant. Consumer tastes and preferences are continually changing. If in the long run consumption of a product is decreasing because it no longer fits the needs of consumers, a marketer needs to know this in order to make adjustments in the marketing mix.

7. *Seasonality.* Consumer demand is also influenced by the time of year. For example, freshly cut evergreen trees certainly sell better between Thanksgiving and Christmas than at any other time of the year. A marketer must know the seasonal patterns of consumption for a product to schedule the production and plan marketing activities.

Demand Shifters

An important concept in the area of consumer demand is the difference between a change in the quantity demanded by consumers and a shift in consumer demand. If a change in the own price of an item brings a change in the number of units of a product sold, this implies that a change in demand has occurred. On the other hand, if price remains the same but the quantity sold changes, this implies that demand has shifted.

For example, let's look at Table 5–3, which modifies the demand schedule used earlier.

TABLE 5–3

Price	Quantity 1	Quantity 2
$1.00	80	90
1.50	70	80
2.00	60	70
2.50	50	60
2.75	45	55
3.00	40	50
3.50	30	40
4.00	20	30
4.50	10	20

If at an own price of $2.00, 60 units are sold, and now at a price of $3.00, 40 units are sold, one can say that the change in sales merely reflects the law of demand. The rise in the price brought about the decline in the quantity sold. But if instead of selling 60 units at a price of $2.00 the quantity sold increases to 70 units, there must have been a shift in demand from $Q1$ to $Q2$ (Figure 5–3).

The factors that cause this movement of the demand schedule are called the *demand shifters*. They include changes in:

1. Price of substitute goods
2. Price of complement goods
3. Income
4. Population
5. Taste and preferences
6. Seasonality

Changes in any of these can lead consumers to demand more or less of a product even though own price does not change. Producers must pay careful attention to changes and anticipated changes in these factors so they do not get caught off guard by major shifts in any of them. Such movements can have a powerful impact on the long-run level of producer sales and profits. It is also important to see what this list does not include: own price and

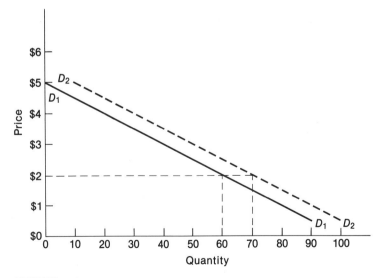

FIGURE 5–3
A Shift in Demand

quantity. They are normally associated only with changes in quantity demanded.

SUMMARY

This chapter is devoted to explaining the revenue side of the profit equation and examining the factors that influence it. A major part of the discussion focuses on the role of price in determining total revenue. Price is one of the four Ps of the marketing mix and the only one that deals with revenues. Thus, the establishment of an acceptable price has a great deal to do with both consumer satisfaction and producer profits. This is why this subject should be of interest to marketing managers.

The role that price plays in the profit equation and how it affects the level of sales and total revenue are examined through the concept of elasticity. An important element in an firm's pricing decisions is knowing whether its products face elastic or inelastic demand.

It is also important for agribusiness firms to understand the factors that influence consumers' demand for their products. The concept of diminishing marginal utility explains why people consume a large variety of goods. Price plays a role in consumer choice and helps the economic system allocate its scare resources to their best use. These concepts are applied to the discussion of derived demand and effective demand. One should know the seven factors that can lead to a change in the demand for a product; but it is also important to be able to tell the difference between a change in demand and a shift in demand.

Each of these concepts is important to agribusiness firms that are attempting to fully understand the factors that influence their customers' demand for the good and services they sell. Each influences total revenue by impacting on either the price or the quantity sold and thereby leads to changes in the firm's profits. In today's world where consumer demand can change rapidly and unexpectedly, a solid understanding of and attention to consumer demand is important to the long profitability of the agribusinesses.

QUESTIONS

1. Why does raising prices not always lead to higher total revenue?
2. Since the demand for food is inelastic why don't food firms just raise their prices to make more money?
3. How is the demand for fertilizer tied in to consumer demand for turkey?

4. What seven factors influence the demand for goods?
5. What is the difference between a change in demand and a shift in demand? What factors cause a shift in demand but do not cause a change in demand?

6

Understanding Agricultural Supply

This chapter continues the discussion of the profit equation (total revenue – total cost = profit) by examining the factors that influence total cost. Again economics will be used to help understand how costs behave. Since most costs have their origins in the production process, the discussion will begin there.

THE PRODUCTION PROCESS

Agribusinesses use materials, equipment, buildings, trucks, people, and a variety of other things to produce the goods and services they sell to others. Managers are charged with the responsibility of combining these items in a profitable manner in the production process.

The traditional idea of production in agribusiness is to turn seed, water, and soil into wheat or some other farm commodity. But production can also take many other forms. It can involve the conversion of milk to cheese or ice cream. It can mean converting hogs to pork chops and bacon. It may involve processing soybeans into oil for use in home cooking. It can also involve the production of a promotional campaign for a food product that turns consumer needs into sales. Regardless of what is done there are similarities among all these activities that allow a definition of production to emerge. *Production is the use of input(s) to create an output that has economic value.*

Inputs to the production process include items such as grain, animals, chemicals, labor, money, and anything else that an agribusiness uses to create an output. *Output* from the production process can be a *commodity* such as feed, fertilizer, milk, or grain. It can also be a *food product* such as hamburgers, breakfast cereal, ice cream, or corn chips. Services such as financial planning, insurance, market price news, and so on are also considered outputs. Regardless of what is done *the production process is how an agribusiness combines the various inputs to create an output.*

The Production Decisions

When agribusinesses decide to undertake the production of an output they face four major production decisions:

1. *What to produce?* What products and services can this business profitably offer?
2. *How to produce?* What is the most efficient technical combination of inputs to use in producing the output?
3. *How much to produce?* What is the correct amount of output to produce that will maximize the firm's long-run profits?
4. *When to produce?* What is the correct time to produce the output?

The answers to these four production questions rest heavily on the level of demand for the output at various prices. But the answers are also heavily influenced by cost factors such as the availability and prices of inputs. For example, a firm may sell a candy bar in a retail market where there is a high level of price competition among the sellers but find that its most important input, chocolate, is hard to get and rapidly rising in price. In this case the firm may find that its long-run profits may be affected as much by production efficiency and cost controls as good marketing.

So being a successful manager requires having a production process that is both technically and economically efficient. A process is *technically efficient* when the maximum physical output per unit of input is obtained at all levels of input use. This must be done first. Once maximum technical efficiency is achieved, the manager can turn to reaching economic efficiency. A process is *economically efficient* when the level of output maximizes profits. Given that the manager's primary objective is to maximize the long-run profits of the firm, he or she should be keenly interested in how to accomplish both.

The Production Function

At the heart of the production process is the production function. The *production function* summarizes the output possible from various levels of input use. A production function might describe the amount of grain output possible from various levels of fertilizer use. For a beef processing plant it might show the number of pounds of boxed beef that can be produced using various amounts of labor.

A representative production function for a milk processing plant is shown in Figure 6–1. The ice cream output possible using various amounts of labor input is shown by the line labeled total product (*TP*). The more technically efficient the plant is, the higher the *TP* line is at each level of labor use. The less technically efficient the plant is, the lower the *TP* line is at each level of labor use. Because this book is concerned with marketing, *it will be assumed from here on that the production processes presented represent*

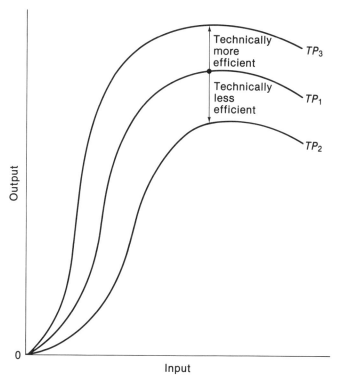

FIGURE 6–1
Production Functions for a Hypothetical Milk Processing Plant

maximum technical efficiency so the discussion can focus solely on achieving economic efficiency.

The shape of the *TP* curve in Figure 6–2 shows the level of output (ice cream) possible as more and more inputs (workers) are added to the production process. Notice that output increases rapidly with the addition of the first few units of labor. Beyond point *A*, output continues to increase but at a decreasing rate until output reaches a maximum at point *B*, and then declines. The decline comes because beyond a certain point adding more workers causes a decline in efficiency as the extra workers simply get in each other's way.

Diminishing Marginal Returns

The shape of the total product curve shown in Figure 6–2 also illustrates the *principle of diminishing marginal returns.* This principle states that as more and more units of a variable input are added to the production process,

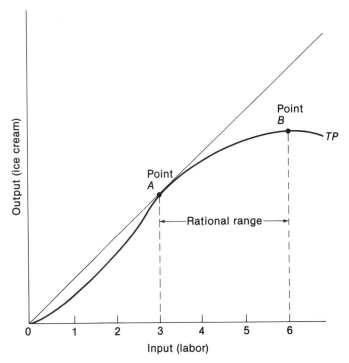

FIGURE 6–2
Determining the Rational Range for Production

TABLE 6–1

Amount of Variable Input	Amount of Output
0	0
1	30
2	100
3	168
4	220
5	240
6	252
7	245

where at least one other input is being held constant, total output will increase at an increasing rate, then increase at a decreasing rate, reach a maximum, and then decline.

Table 6–1 shows a hypothetical production function for milk processing that illustrates this principle. In this case the size of the processing plant is held constant while more and more labor is used. The exhibit shows that 2 workers achieve more than 3 times the output of 1 worker, and that 3 workers can generate more output than 2. From 1 worker to 3, the percentage change in output (30 to 168 tons—460 percent) is greater than the percentage change in workers (200 percent), and total product increases at an increasing rate.

The use of 4 to 6 workers brings additions to total output, but the contribution of each additional worker to output (that is, the change in output that comes from the use of each new worker or marginal product) becomes smaller and smaller, and total product increases at a decreasing rate. The use of 7 or more workers results in a decline of total product. The workers must simply get in each other's way and cannot work very efficiently.

The rational range of production can be defined using this information (Figure 6–2). The lower end of the range is where yield or the efficiency of input use (that is, amount of output divided by amount of input used to produce it, or average product) reaches its maximum (Point A), and total product begins increasing at a decreasing rate. This occurs after the third worker is employed. The upper end of this range comes with the use of the sixth worker since total product declines with the use of any more workers (Point B). Thus, the rational range of production comes between the third and sixth worker. However, for this information to be useful in determining economic efficiency, it must be converted to dollars and cents.

DETERMINING ECONOMIC EFFICIENCY

The determination of economic efficiency (that is, the point of maximum profits) requires the use of economic theory. Economic theory shows that profits will be maximized when output is expanded to where the increase in revenues is just equal to the increase in costs necessary to produce that last unit of output.

In simple terms, what this concept says is that if the production of the last unit of output costs $9, but can be sold for $10, expand output. If the last unit costs $12 to produce but can be sold for only $10, reduce output. And finally, if the last unit costs $10 and sells for $10, economic efficiency has been met. Economists call the cost of producing the last unit of output *marginal cost* and the revenue received from selling the last unit of output *marginal revenue*. Thus, economic efficiency is achieved when marginal cost equals marginal revenue.

Continuing the milk processing plant production example and combining it with what has been presented here, it is possible to determine the level of output within the rational range of production that will achieve economic efficiency (that is, maximum profits). Suppose the ice cream yields a net revenue of $10 per unit which covers all costs except labor. Labor costs $200 per worker and all other costs are fixed. Table 6–2 summarizes all the technical and economic data needed to determine economic efficiency.

A look at the profit column on the far right shows the greatest profit $1,400 coming with the employment of 4 to 5 workers. Each of the first 4 workers adds more to net revenue than to costs (change in revenue is greater than the $200 change in costs). The sixth worker adds $120 to total revenue, which is less than the cost of the worker, and profits fall. The addition of the

TABLE 6–2

Output	Revenue @ $10/unit	Marginal Revenue	Labor #	Labor Cost @ $200	Marginal Cost	Profit
0	$ 0	$—	0	$ 0	$ 0	$ 0
30	300	300	1	200	200	100
100	1000	700	2	400	200	600
168	1680	680	3	600	200	1080
220	2200	520	4	800	200	1400
240	2400	200	5	1000	200	1400
252	2520	120	6	1200	200	1320
245	2450	−70	7	1400	200	1050

fifth worker adds $200 to total revenue (marginal revenue of $200) and also adds $200 to total cost (marginal cost of $200). This is also where profits are maximized. Thus, profits are maximized where marginal revenue is equal to marginal cost.

SUMMARY

This chapter covers the elements of production and costs that influence the total cost part of the profit equation (profit = total revenue - total cost). The production process is the combination of various inputs to create an output. The chapter looks at what constitutes costs and how they are measured. It also examines the effect of the cost items on the level of production.

The chapter combines the cost and revenue concepts to begin a discussion of what constitutes economic efficiency and how it differs from technical efficiency. Technical efficiency is a prerequisite to economic efficiency and is always assumed to have been achieved prior to seeking economic efficiency.

The role of the principle of diminishing marginal return is introduced and used to show why production doesn't always increase as more inputs are used in production. Economic efficiency (that is, profit maximization) occurs where the change in the cost (marginal cost) is equal to the change in total revenue (marginal revenue).

QUESTIONS

1. What is the difference between technical efficiency and economic efficiency? Why is technical efficiency a prerequisite to economic efficiency?
2. Describe the three stages of production. Identify and explain which one is the most relevant for production.
3. Why aren't profits normally maximized at the points of maximum yield (maximum of average product) or maximum output?
4. What kind of costs comes from the passage of time? What kind of costs comes from the undertaking of production? Can they be combined, and if so, what is the result?

7

Matching Supply and Demand in Agricultural Markets

This chapter completes the discussion of markets by drawing upon the basic elements of consumer demand developed in Chapter 5 and the production and cost concepts presented in Chapter 6. The process of how a price is determined in a market, and how it keeps markets separated by time, space, and form in equilibrium will be discussed. The four major types of market environments are then examined from a marketing perspective with an eye toward developing the proper marketing mixes. The chapter closes with a discussion of some of the unique features of agricultural markets and the special challenges that they present to agribusiness marketing managers.

PRICE DETERMINATION AND PRICE DISCOVERY

Throughout the discussion of maximizing profits, the role of price recurs. As was seen earlier, price plays an important role in allocating and reallocating scarce resources in a free market economy. Before proceeding it is important to make a distinction between the terms *price determination* and *price discovery.*

Until now supply and demand were assumed to have been known and the market price has been found at the intersection of the two schedules.

Whenever supply and demand schedules were shifted, the full impact of changes in the prices of substitutes, technology, inputs, and so forth was known or was assumed to be known before the shift was made. Because of this information the shifts that were made closely matched the actual changes in the schedules that occurred in the market. This type of price analysis is typically carried out by economists who are trying to understand the forces that affect market prices. This process is referred to as *price determination*.

The price determination process is important to an agribusiness marketing manager because the level of market prices arising from the intersection of supply and demand determines profitability to a great extent. Therefore, an agribusiness manager who seeks to maximize his profits over the long run needs to understand the forces that influence current market prices and that are likely to affect future prices of his products, his inputs, and his competitors' products.

A situation which more closely reflects the real-life dealings of an agribusiness manager is how buyers and sellers agree on a mutually acceptable price during an actual sale when they do not have complete information about the market. This process is called *price discovery*.

Price discovery takes place through the interaction of buyers and sellers of a product at a particular point in time (a day, an hour, or minute) when neither party in the negotiation has perfect knowledge about the true levels of supply and demand, or exact measures of the impact of changes in technology, the price of substitute goods, the price of inputs, and so forth. The process of price discovery is not an exact science. Unlike price determination where one waits until all the relevant information is gathered before calculating the proper price, most people in agribusinesses find themselves involved in price discovery situations where they must make pricing decisions long before all the data they would need to do a thorough economic analysis is available.

Whether the agreed-upon price is above or below the general price level for similar transactions depends on: (1) the amount, quality, and timeliness of information available to both parties; and (2) the relative bargaining ability of each participant. Thus, information plays a vital role in an individual's success in the price discovery process. For example, a grain buyer who is the first to learn about a major purchase by a large foreign buyer might be able to buy up large quantities of grain at the prevailing price and later reap a great profit when price rises as exporters buy grain to fill the purchase contracts. The price discovery process generally works very well, meaning that when there is a free flow of accurate, timely information among all market participants there are few transactions at prices very much above or below the prevailing market price.

The role of information in maintaining a high level of market efficiency is of such importance that it led to the passage of federal legislation (for example, the Packers and Stockyards Act and the Perishable Food Act) and the establishment of specific federal agencies (for example, USDA's Market News Service and the Crop Reporting Service) to prepare and widely disseminate information important in agricultural markets.

Marketers need to understand the difference between price determination and price discovery. Both are important since price to a large extent determines both the size of a market and its profit potential. Price determination helps managers see the long run impacts of changes in the marketplace, while price discovery helps to establish prices in day-to-day operations.

THE LAW OF ONE PRICE

When markets are operating efficiently there should be only one price for each product in a market after adjusting for the costs of adding time, place, and form utility. This phenomenon is called the *law of one price*.

If prices differ by more than the cost of the added utility, prices are "out of line." When this happens there is an economic incentive to shift the allocation of resources from the current use to the production of a product whose price is "too high" in order to gain additional profits. However, as others see this opportunity they too will shift their resources to the product with the higher profits. The result should be larger supplies of the "higher profit" good and an eventual decline in its price to "normal levels" so that prices are back "in line." The process of capturing extra profits in situations where prices are "out of line" is called *arbitrage*.

Finding Equilibrium in Current and Future Markets Separated by Time, Place, and Form

- *Time*—The cost of adding time utility (the cost of storage) should be just equal to the difference between the current price and future price.
- *Place*—The cost of adding place utility (the cost of transportation) should be just equal to the difference in price between the two locations.
- *Form*—The cost of adding form utility (the cost of processing) should be just equal to the difference between prices paid for inputs and the price received for the output.

Arbitrage is what helps to keep markets that are separated by time, place, and form in equilibrium. Any time prices deviate beyond what is justified by the costs of adding time, place, and form utility, someone will try to take these profits away. Doing so keeps the markets in equilibrium.

Time.   In markets separated by time, for example the fall harvest-time market for apples versus the springtime market, the difference between the current price and the expected market price some time in the future must be equal to the cost of storage for that period of time. If the difference between the current price and the price in the future exceeds the cost of storage, people will be encouraged to store more for the future and not enough of the product will be available today. On the other hand, if the price difference is less than the cost of storage, people will try to sell their products now and not enough will be stored for the future. *For the current and future markets to be in equilibrium, the cost of adding time utility (the cost of storage) should be just equal to the difference between the current price and the future price.*

Place.   In markets separated by distance, the difference in price between the two locations must be equal to the cost of transporting the product between the two points. If the price difference is greater than the cost of transportation, too much will be shipped from the lower-priced location to the higher-priced location. If the price difference is less than the cost of transportation, nothing will be shipped between the two locations. This can lead to unmet needs in each market and lower overall profits for market participants. *For two distance-separated markets to be in equilibrium, the cost of adding place utility (the cost of transportation) should be just equal to the difference in price between the two locations.*

Form.   In markets separated by differences in product form, the difference between the prices paid for inputs and the price received for the output must be equal to the cost of processing. If the difference in price is greater than the cost of processing, output will be expanded. If the difference is less than the cost of processing, no output will be produced. *For markets separated by different product forms to be in equilibrium, the cost of adding form utility (the cost of processing) should be just equal to the difference between the prices paid for inputs and the price received for the output.*

Thus, the law of one price is what keeps markets that are separated by space (place utility), time (time utility), and processing (form utility) in equilibrium. If the returns from adding these utilities are not equal to their costs, markets get "out of line." Arbitrage activities help insure that markets gravitate toward the equilibrium that underlies the law of one price. If markets are functioning efficiently, whatever deviations there are should be small and short lived so that resources are always being allocated efficiently and prices differ only by the cost of the added utility.

MARKET ENVIRONMENTS

It is imperative for marketing managers to correctly identify and understand the different market environments a firm is likely to face. Each type of environment calls for different behavior on the part of the firm with respect to pricing, terms of trade, product innovation, and so on. If marketing managers incorrectly identify the market environment, they may adopt a marketing mix that will lead to lower sales and profits.

Economists have identified four basic types of market environments: (1) perfect competition, (2) monopoly, (3) monopolistic competition, and (4) oligopoly. Each of these market environments will be examined using the structure-conduct-performance analysis procedure developed in Chapter 2. Under that procedure the competitive structure of the firm in a market determines the decision-making options that are available. This helps to define the firm's conduct, which is reflected in overall economic performance. The discussion here will focus on how each type of environment affects marketing decisions made by the firm.

Perfect Competition

When economists began studying markets one of their first tasks was to develop an idea of what makes the best or perfect environment for competition. Under this ideal situation markets would be efficient, scarce resources would be correctly allocated, prices would reflect full social value, producers would have maximum profits, and consumers would have maximum satisfaction from all that they consume. This ideal situation is called *perfect competition*. It serves as the standard against which all other market environments are measured.

The accomplishment of this ideal requires that a number of prerequisites be met. First, there must be a large number of small firms in the market so that the actions of any single firm cannot influence prices. This implies that prices are determined solely by the interaction of market supply and market demand. The individual firms must take the resulting market price as their selling price and have no power to set their own price.

Second, the product must be homogeneous. This implies that the product produced by each producer is exactly like that produced by all other producers. Agricultural commodities are good examples of homogeneous products. For example, number 2 yellow corn from a farm in Illinois is the same as that from a farm in Arizona.

Third, it should be easy to enter and leave the production process. This implies that if selling prices get high enough it should be relatively easy to get into the business. It also implies that if prices get low enough it should be just as easy to get out of the business.

Based on these three prerequisites it should be easy to see why many people feel that farming is the best example of a perfectly competitive market environment. In production agriculture there are still a large number of relatively small farms that produce homogeneous commodities and that generally can fairly easily enter and exit the production process.

Using the knowledge of supply and demand developed earlier, it is possible to outline how a perfectly competitive market operates. For the firm that buys and sells in such markets, the prices it pays and receives are determined at the market level by the interaction of market supply and market demand. Since the firm in this type of market environment is a *price taker* and cannot affect the level of prices, it can buy and sell all it wants only at the prevailing market price.

From the perspective of the four Ps of the marketing mix, perfect competition is the worst possible situation. The firm has no control over price since it is determined at the market level and must be accepted. At the market *price* the firm can sell all it produces, so there is no incentive to cut price. At prices above the market price, no one will buy the firm's product since the *product* is homogeneous. Every producer's product is exactly the same, so arbitragers will see that prices at different locations are in line and that the product reaches all the right *places*, so it does not need *promotion*. In such cases there is little marketing to do, and what is done focuses on improving the physical efficiency of the activity.

While there are few situations of true perfect competition, this discussion helps illustrate the absence of pricing and production decisions for a marketing manager in this type of market environment. It explains why commodity-based agribusinesses had little interest in marketing until recently. It also explains why consumers prefer this type of market environment, while firms seek ways to avoid operating in a perfectly competitive market environment.

Monopoly

From the perspective of the producer, *monopoly* offers the best of all worlds. In this market environment a single large producer provides all of the product that the market needs. In fact, the monopoly firm is the industry. It can maximize its profits by setting either market price or market output because of its total control over supply. It can also exercise total control over each of the four Ps of the marketing mix since it is the only supplier of the product. Because of its dominant position the demand schedule facing the monopolist firm is also the same as the industry's downward sloping demand schedule.

To see why producers prefer monopoly to a perfectly competitive market environment one only has to look at the quantity produced and the price of the product. Under monopoly the market price is higher and the quantity produced is less than would be found under perfect competition. In addition, the monopolist earns an economic profit that is not possible under perfect competition. This added profit is what is so attractive to producers seeking to become monopolists.

It should also be clear that while producers prefer this market environment, consumers and society do not. The presence of a monopoly means less output is available and at higher prices than would be the case in a perfectly competitive market environment. This is the reason why society seeks to prevent monopolies. This discussion gives some insight into the incentives as well as the pricing and production options facing a monopolist that are not present in perfect competition. These will prove useful in the discussion of monopolistic and oligopolistic competition.

Monopolistic Competition

Between the extremes of perfect competition and monopoly lies *monopolistic competition*. Industries characterized by monopolistic competition have a structure that is very similar to that found in a perfectly competitive market environment. There are a large number of small buyers and sellers, and the possibility exists of reasonably easy entrance and exit from the market. What is missing is a homogeneous product. This means that producers have found ways to differentiate or make their product appear different to the consumer.

When differentiation is accomplished producers gain some control over the price of their product. They are no longer price takers and they do not face the horizontal demand schedule found in perfect competition. The demand schedule for the firm's product has some slope to it and there is a marginal revenue curve below price at every level of output. In monopolistic competition there are economic profits available to the producer compared to the zero economic profits possible to the firm in perfect competition. Thus, there is great incentive for a firm to differentiate its product in order to gain these additional profits.

A firm's ability to break away from a perfectly competitive market environment depends on its ability to: (1) differentiate its product from all other similar products, and (2) get buyers to pay extra for the differentiation. These two points are closely related. The greater the perceived difference, the more a buyer should be willing to pay to get this particular product. This is the reason why some agricultural marketers are willing to go to great lengths to differentiate their commodities. Examples of this include: Sunkist oranges, Diamond walnuts, Vermont turkeys, Long Island ducks, Washington apples, Pennsylvania mushrooms, and so on. Whether these are truly superior to other nonbranded commodities (oranges, walnuts, turkeys, ducks, apples, and mushrooms) is not important. What is important is whether consumers feel they are and whether they are willing to pay for the difference.

By differentiating the product a marketer gains some control over its price plus a chance to enhance profits. The amount of this enhancement is determined by the elasticity of the demand curve. The more inelastic (vertical) the demand curve, the greater the profit potential.

The marketing mix employed by a marketing manager in a monopolistic market environment will involve: (1) the development of a product promotion program that will strongly emphasize why this product is different, (2) the establishment of a price as high above the price of the undifferentiated commodity as the competition will allow, and (3) the placement of the product in locations where its differences can be best promoted to unique target markets. A good example of such a marketing mix is that used by various brands of exotic coffees and teas that are sold only in specialty shops at prices above those found in supermarkets.

Thus, there are great economic incentives for marketers to develop a differentiated product. Such a move may also benefit consumers and society if the product truly fills a "special need" not being filled by the undifferentiated homogeneous product. Overall consumer satisfaction may increase. If the differentiated product is to capture the "extra profits" over the long run, the product must have characteristics that other producers cannot easily duplicate. If it does not, competitors will quickly copy the product and the extra profits will soon be taken away. Given the advantages of monopolistic competition and the legal restrictions against monopolies, monopolistic competition is the preferred market environment for a firm.

Oligopolistic Competition

The last market environment examined is *oligopolistic competition.* In oligopolistic competition, not only is the idea of a homogeneous product lost

Prerequisites for the Four Basic Types of Market Environments

Prerequisites for Perfect Competition
1. There must be a large number of small firms in the market.
2. The product must be homogeneous.
3. It must be easy to enter and leave the production process.

Prerequisites for a Monopoly
1. A single large producer provides all the product the market needs.
2. The producer exercises total control over the 4 Ps of the marketing mix.

Prerequisites for Monopolistic Competition
1. There are a large number of small buyers and sellers.
2. There is reasonably easy entrance and exit from the market.
3. There are ways to differentiate the product.

Prerequisites for Oligopolistic Competition
1. There are only a few large firms.
2. A firm's actions can influence the level of production and prices within the market.
3. The chief means of competition is through product differentiation.
4. Firms in the industry try to avoid competition based on price.

but also any recognition of the existence of many small buyers and sellers that cannot influence the level of market price.

The key features of oligopoly are: (1) there only a few large firms; (2) a firm's actions can influence the level of production and prices within the market; (3) the chief means of competition is through product differentiation which is heavily promoted to prospective buyers; and (4) firms in the industry try to avoid competition based on price.

Producers in an oligopolistic market environment face an unusual demand situation. If one firm raises its price above the current market price, consumers will substitute a competitor's lower-priced product (unless the product is truly unique and has a strong consumer demand), and demand will fall off. So for prices above the market price the demand schedule is more elastic (horizontal), and a rise in price is likely to lead to a relatively larger decline in quantity and a drop in total revenue. If one firm lowers its price, so will every other producer in the market to prevent a large decline in its sales. So for prices below the market price the demand curve is more inelastic (vertical), and a decline in price is likely to lead to only a relatively small increase in quantity and a drop in total revenue. Thus, there is little incentive to compete on price since movements in either direction by one firm alone are likely to lead to lower total revenue and profits for the firm.

This structure leads to conduct where competition is focused on non-price activities. Oligopolistic firms spend heavily on advertising and on ways to enhance product differentiation. The goal of these efforts is to make the portion of the demand schedule above the market price more inelastic so that a price rise will not cause a loss of customers, but rather an increase in total revenue.

The proper marketing mix in this environment is to avoid price competition and focus on greater product differentiation, better distribution, and stronger promotional efforts. In the agribusiness system the processing-manufacturing sector contains the best examples of firms that operate this way. The competition between the leading cola soft-drink producers is a classic example of oligopolistic competition.

Throughout the agribusiness system there are examples of each of the four types of market environments. The degree of control the firm can exert over the elements of its marketing mix is determined largely by its market environment. The correct identification of the market environment is a critical first step in developing a successful marketing mix.

Workable Competition

While none of these four market environments exists in its pure form, and perfect competition is not readily attainable, economists have developed a concept called workable competition to allow them to evaluate markets and firm behavior. *Workable competition* exists when there is sufficient effective competition to give both consumers and society most of the benefits that arise from perfect competition.

The criteria for workable competition are as follows: (1) there should be a reasonable number of buyers and sellers so that none has undue control over market prices; (2) there should be no collusion between or among the buyers and sellers; (3) all buyers and sellers should be independent; (4) there should be essentially free exit and entry to the market; and (5) buyers and sellers should have free and unobstructed access to one another. These criteria recognize the reality of the economic world where consumer needs are varied, products are differentiated, and competition can take on a variety of forms. Workable competition provides a general yardstick with which to measure market efficiency.

UNDERSTANDING AGRICULTURAL MARKETS

The markets for agricultural commodities and food products are often very different than those for other products. To be a successful agribusiness marketer requires an understanding of the unique physical features of the products and the special requirements they place on the marketing system. By understanding the factors that affect total revenue and total cost it is possible to draw some inferences about how to profitably market agricultural commodities and food products.

Physical Characteristics

The first step is to focus on the physical characteristics. Most agricultural commodities: (1) are bulky, (2) have a low value per unit of weight, (3) are perishable, (4) are normally produced in areas located far from consumers, and (5) because of the biological nature of the production process, are in fixed supply in the short run. This means that those who handle the commodities must seek the most efficient means to quickly process and move the resulting products to distant consumers.

Characteristics of Agricultural Supply

The biological origins of the production process give producers little control over the level of output once the process is underway. Output levels and yields during the crop or marketing year are largely determined by uncontrollable variables such as weather and disease.

For commodities such as grains, the supply is relatively fixed between harvests regardless of price. The result is a nearly total inelastic (vertical) supply. If the time horizon is expanded to two years or longer, there is greater room for adjustment and supply can become more elastic (Figure 7–1).

In the short run of the hypothetical situation shown in Figure 7–1, producers are unable to respond with greater output even if the price were to rise to $5 from $4. In the intermediate and long run producers are able to adjust input usage to raise output to 90 and then 100 units. This greater responsiveness of output to higher prices over time is seen in the increase of the *supply elasticity* coefficient (E_s) from 0 to 1.00.

For most agricultural commodities supply elasticity is less than 1 (inelastic). This implies that small percentage changes in quantity are associated with large percentage changes in price. This is why small variations in yearly crop production levels bring such large swings in farm level commodity prices and farm incomes.

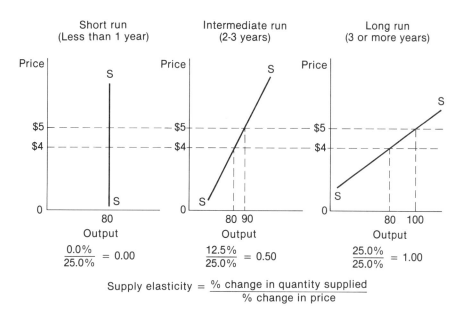

FIGURE 7–1
Agricultural Supply in the Short Run, Intermediate Run, and Long Run

This can be seen using the price and output relationships shown in Figure 7–1. In the short run, the fall in price from $5 to $4 (20 percent) lowers total revenue by $80 ($400 – $320) or 20 percent. In the intermediate case, the fall from $5 to $4 (20 percent) lowers total revenue by $130 ($450 – $320) or nearly 29 percent. In the long run, the fall from $5 to $4 (20 percent) lowers total revenue by $180 ($500 – $320) or 36 percent. In each instance the percentage decline in total revenue was equal to or greater than the percentage decline in price.

Fortunately for producers the reverse is also true; that is, small price increases bring greater percentage gains in total revenue. This greater variability in total revenue for small changes in price is due to the biological nature of most agricultural production processes which limits the short-run adjustments a producer can make in output. This results in most agricultural commodity supply functions being inelastic.

Characteristics of Agricultural Demand

Unlike agricultural supply, the domestic demand for agricultural commodities is generally stable from year to year. There may be some variation

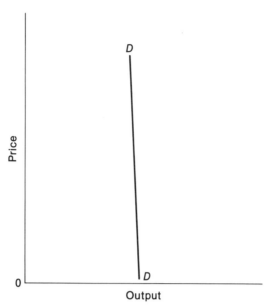

FIGURE 7–2
General Demand for Agricultural Products

for particular products from period to period, but the general situation remains fairly stationary over time. This is because people's demand for food is largely a function of habit. This results in the overall demand for food being basically inelastic (vertical) (Figure 7–2).

A closer look at food demand causes several interesting facts to emerge. First, the demand for specific food products tends to be elastic (horizontal) at the retail level since there are usually a variety of substitute goods available. For example, if the consumer is looking for sausage there may be several brands to choose from such as Jimmy Dean, Bob Evans, Swift's Brown n'Serve, plus two or three local or store brands. In addition, the consumer has the choice of link, patty, or loose forms of sausage.

Second, demand is more inelastic the closer one gets to the farm level since there are fewer substitutes for farm-produced commodities. The hog buyers for the various pork processors are all probably looking for the same types of high-quality hogs to keep their plants operating at peak efficiency throughout the year. To them there are no substitutes for a good-quality hog, and the demand for hogs is more inelastic than the demand for a particular brand of sausage at the retail level. Thus, the demand for most raw agricultural commodities is inelastic, while the demand for specific food products tends to be elastic.

The Intersection of Supply and Demand in Agricultural Markets

The combination of a highly inelastic but unstable supply and a highly inelastic but stable demand leads to short-run situations at the farm level where prices and incomes are more volatile than at the retail food level. The inelastic nature of these supply and demand functions brings about situations where even small changes in quantity supplied bring large changes in farm level prices and incomes.

For example, in the short run where the supply of a feed grain is fixed until the next harvest, supply is totally inelastic (Figure 7–3). If demand increases due to an unexpected surge in export sales, the market price for the grain should rise from $4 per bushel to $8 per bushel. Both price and total revenue increase 100 percent with no change in output.

Let's pursue this same situation from the supply side and look at what happens when supply shifts out and to the right by 20 percent due to a good growing year for grain, while demand remains constant (Figure 7–4). The increase in output to 12 bushels from 10 (a 20 percent gain) results in the market price declining to $4 from $8 per bushel (a 50 percent loss) and total

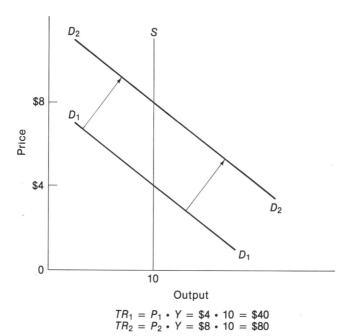

$$TR_1 = P_1 \cdot Y = \$4 \cdot 10 = \$40$$
$$TR_2 = P_2 \cdot Y = \$8 \cdot 10 = \$80$$

FIGURE 7–3
Intersection of General Agricultural Supply and Demand

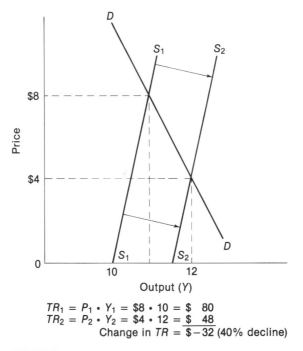

$$TR_1 = P_1 \cdot Y_1 = \$8 \cdot 10 = \$\ \ 80$$
$$TR_2 = P_2 \cdot Y_2 = \$4 \cdot 12 = \underline{\$\ \ 48}$$
$$\text{Change in } TR = \$-32 \text{ (40\% decline)}$$

FIGURE 7–4
Intersection of General Agricultural Supply and
Demand When Supply Increases

revenue falling by 40 percent. This is why even a good crop may leave farmers worse off.

The large shifts in price for even small changes in supply and demand are a source of great income instability for farmers. Add to this the fact that most farm input prices rarely decline or may even increase in periods of low farm prices and one can see the making of a farm cost-price crunch. Marketing managers need to understand the nature of these relationships and their impacts since most agribusiness firms either sell to farmers or buy commodities from them.

Agricultural Price Patterns

Many agricultural commodities exhibit recurring price patterns over time. These patterns reflect the biological nature of food production and consumption. Those patterns that recur within one year are called *seasonal price patterns*. Those patterns that repeat in periods longer than a year are called *price cycles*. Understanding these patterns can go a long way toward helping a marketing manager achieve the objective of maximizing long-run profits by providing a basis for forecasting prices.

Seasonal price patterns are primarily caused by the seasonality of production and consumer demand. For grains, fruits, and vegetables there is generally only a single crop per year, while demand is fairly constant throughout the year. This inconsistency between supply and demand is reflected in the pattern of prices throughout the year.

A graph of these monthly prices would show the price lowest at harvest time, followed by a slow rise each month thereafter throughout the year, followed by another slow decline as the next harvest approaches (Figure 7–5). The increase in price each month immediately after harvest is the market's method of encouraging someone to store part of the annual crop in order to meet year-round demand.

This same type of supply-caused price pattern can also be seen for livestock. Producers have a tendency to reduce holdings during the winter months when production costs are the highest. Seasonality of market prices can also occur on the demand side. Certainly the prices for Christmas trees are the highest during November and December. Understanding seasonal price patterns can help an agribusiness obtain higher profits by timing purchases and sales to receive more favorable prices.

Similar price patterns can be found that extend beyond one year and are referred to as *price cycles*. They have their origins in biological and producer

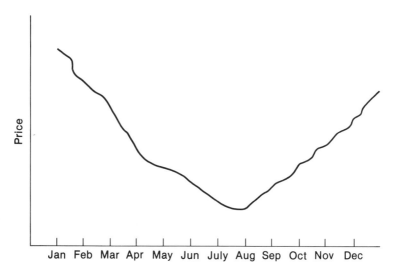

FIGURE 7–5
Illustration of Seasonal Price Patterns for a Typical Agricultural Commodity

behavior just as do the seasonal patterns. In these cases the underlying biology does not permit as rapid an adjustment of supply. Good examples of commodities with longer supply-adjustment processes are cattle and hogs. A full cycle of expansion and contraction for hogs may take 3 1/2 to 4 years, while for cattle it may take as long as 11 to 12 years.

Knowing where you are in the price cycle is critical for planning. Producers certainly do not wish to expand output at the peak of the price cycle since it may be years before it repeats. But it might be profitable to consider expansion at the bottom or on an upward leg of the price cycle. Having knowledge about this process can improve profit levels for producers and all those who serve them.

SUMMARY

This chapter completes the discussion of markets. At this point the reader should have a full knowledge of the factors that influence consumer demand, supply, costs, and production. This knowledge was applied to a discussion of how these factors come together to produce a price in the market. This process was examined under the four market environments of perfect competition, monopoly, monopolistic competition, and oligopoly. The best type of marketing mix under each environment was then reviewed. The last part of the chapter dealt with how agricultural markets operate and the special marketing challenges they offer agribusiness marketing managers.

The concepts of price determination and price discovery were introduced. Price determination was shown to be generally done after the sale as a way to explain prior price changes. Price discovery explains how the participants arrived at an agreeable price in a particular situation when they did not know the full impact of all the factors that could influence their decisions. It was shown that price discovery is likely to be the situation faced by agribusiness managers but that it can be close to the best price in markets where there is a large free flow of accurate, timely information.

The law of one price was used to explain how markets separated by time, place, and form utility remain connected to one another. The prices in these markets should differ only by the cost of overcoming each separation.

Of the four markets examined, monopolistic competition was shown to offer both producers and consumers the best solution. It affords consumers greater choice and producers the possibility for greater profits.

The last section of the chapter explained how understanding the unique characteristics of agricultural supply and demand can help an agribusiness manager achieve greater efficiency and profits.

QUESTIONS

1. What is the difference between price determination and price discovery and why are both important to an agribusiness marketing manager?
2. Define the law of one price and explain the role of arbitrage in enforcing it.
3. Briefly define the four types of market environments that an agribusiness firm can face. Determine which is the best for consumers, which is best for producers, and which offers the best middle ground between the needs of producers and consumers.
4. Explain why small changes in quantity demanded or supplied lead to larger changes in farm level prices than in retail food prices.
5. Explain the differences between seasonal price patterns and price cycles.

The Agricultural Marketing System

Part Three is designed to complete the task of describing the agribusiness marketing system. It does this by examining six industries that constitute the major portion of the system. The section begins in Chapter 8 with a discussion of the input industries and how they have influenced production agriculture. The history of agricultural technology is traced through the development of several key industries.

The next four chapters are devoted to describing the processing, manufacturing, wholesaling and retailing, and food service industries that take the raw agricultural commodities produced on the farm and turn them into food products that are desired by consumers. The final chapter in this section describes the role that cooperative agribusinesses play in the agribusiness system.

8

The Agricultural Input Industries

Agribusiness, like the rest of the economy, is constantly changing, reflecting the dynamic nature of the world in which we live. Members of the agribusiness system continually attempt to stay abreast of changes in technology and consumer needs since these changes profoundly affect their competitive edge in the market and their profits.

The ability to apply new technology has certainly been the hallmark of the industries that make up the agricultural input sector. One can easily trace the development of these industries and much of their success to their ability to supply the agricultural production process with the latest technologies in the form of highly productive, cost-reducing inputs. These efforts spawned the development of a whole new set of firms exclusively devoted to supplying inputs to the production sector. In the process they brought about a major change in production practices as farmers began to buy inputs that they had previously made or grown themselves. By purchasing rather than making many inputs, producers are now able to concentrate more on production, and this has led to unprecedented productivity gains.

The agricultural input industries include those firms that supply feed, seed, equipment, credit, insurance, chemicals, and a whole host of other inputs that farmers use to produce crops and livestock. This sector provides approximately 75 percent of the total inputs used by farmers and ranchers. The remaining 25 percent includes items such as hay, livestock, grains, and so on that are produced on the farm for use as an input to other production activities.

While the total level of input use has changed very little since the end of World War II, there has been a dramatic shift in the mixture of inputs used. Machinery and chemicals have largely replaced labor on the farm. This shift has reached the point where it is not uncommon for one or two people to handle 1,000 or more acres of crops or several hundred head of livestock. Farmers are now able to produce more output, for less cost, with less labor than ever before.

This chapter focuses on the development of this important sector of agribusiness and illustrates how many of the productivity gains in agribusiness have come from the rising quality of purchased agricultural inputs. The discussion will trace the development of individual inputs from a marketing perspective. Each will be shown to have been successful because of its ability to profitably meet farmers' needs. The history of agricultural technology will be traced in the following agricultural input industries: (1) farm equipment, (2) seed and fertilizer, and (3) agricultural chemicals.

THE FARM EQUIPMENT INDUSTRY

Until about 1850 agriculture changed very little from generation to generation. Most tasks, including sowing, tilling, and reaping, were performed using human muscle power. Farming practices where handed down from father to son. As late as the year 1800 approximately 90 percent of all the people in the United States lived on farms. Most farmers were nearly totally self-sufficient. They produced nearly everything they needed including clothing, tools, feed, and farm equipment. They were forced to do so because the typical farmer had to struggle each year just to produce enough food to feed his own family. There was little surplus production left to exchange.

The nineteenth century brought the beginnings of change. The century began with the Louisiana Purchase in 1807 and the opening of the farmland west of the Allegheny Mountains. Between 1850 and 1880 the amount of land devoted to farms increased 82 percent to 536 million acres from 294 million acres, while the number of farms rose 167 percent to 4 million. The rise of the industrial age near the middle of the century brought about shortages of farm laborers as workers flocked to northern industrial cities.

The Civil War brought increased interest in the development of labor-saving tillage and harvesting tools by simultaneously raising farm commodity prices and reducing the supply of farm laborers. It was during this period that John Deere developed the steel plow that gave newly settled prairie farmers the ability to plow the tough sod that covered most of the country's midsection. Cyrus McCormick developed the mechanical grain reaper that took much of the backbreaking labor out of harvesting and greatly increased harvesting productivity. These and other developments led to a great expansion of agricultural output. The increased supply of food was used to feed the growing number of people who now worked off the farm.

By the close of the century only 50 percent of Americans lived on farms and the transition from manpower to horsepower was nearly complete. Farmers were still largely self-sufficient, but they had raised their productivity to a level where they could afford to purchase some horse-drawn farm equipment and a few other inputs produced off the farm.

The onset of World War I marked another turning point in the development of agriculture. Spurred by higher incomes from feeding war-ravaged Europe, U.S. farmers began the process of replacing their horse-drawn equipment with gasoline-powered tractors and the larger tillage implements they could pull. This brought still further increases in productivity.

The higher commodity prices soon withered away with the resumption of European agricultural production, and the next twenty years were characterized by chronically low farm prices and incomes. These events slowed the conversion to mechanized farm equipment, but the pattern of continually adopting new technology in order to enhance profitability was firmly established in production agriculture. This process was not completed until after the end of World War II.

The conversion to mechanical power from horsepower lessened the demand for animal feed. It is estimated that if horses were still the major source of power on the farm they would consume the output of approximately 25 percent of grain acreage. This would be a major drain on food production capabilities. The conversion to mechanical power not only increased farmers' productivity but also increased the amount of production available for human consumption by lessening the amount of output needed by animals.

The Depression years of the 1930s were characterized by a number of government programs designed to aid farmers and rural America. One of the major advances was the development of the Rural Electric Administration (REA). It brought electricity to farms and ranches for the very first time long after it had been commonplace in most urban areas. It enabled rural areas to catch up with their urban neighbors. The adoption of electric lights and the use of electric motors to do much of the backbreaking farm labor soon followed. This greatly reduced the labor burden on the farm, led to still further productivity gains by farmers, and helped reduce the harshness of farm life.

The changes from manpower to horsepower to mechanical power each came in response to felt economic needs on the part of farmers. Each advancement was accepted by farmers because it helped them enhance their productivity, and, more importantly, their profits. By helping farmers get what they wanted (higher output and profits), farm equipment manufacturers got what they wanted (higher sales and profits). In fact, Peter Drucker credits Cyrus McCormick with pioneering the development of marketing, particularly market research, pricing policies, parts and servicing departments, and the idea of installment credit purchases. The purchasing patterns established for farm equipment soon spread to other agricultural inputs, especially in the years following World War II.

THE SEED AND FERTILIZER INDUSTRIES

The typical family farm at the beginning of the twentieth century produced a variety of outputs and was a nearly self-sufficient business. Grains, fruits, and vegetables were raised for human consumption and to feed animals. Horses ate the feed and provided the power needed to grow crops. Their manure was used for fertilizer. No pesticides were used. Children provided the unpaid supplemental labor needed to run the farm. Nearly all the food and most of the clothing needed by the family was produced on the farm.

Under this system corn yields were less than 25 percent of what they are today. The adversity faced by farmers of that day is illustrated by the common practice of corn growers of planting three seeds of corn together in a hill. The first seed, according to tradition, was for the rootworm to eat. The second was for the blackbird to eat. The third one was for the farmer. Imagine a planting system where two-thirds of the seeds are never expected to produce anything!

Things began to change during the 1930s when hybrid seeds were first developed. Hybrid seed grown under specially controlled pollination soon replaced open-field-pollinated seeds. This shift occurred because the hybrid seed resulted in plants that nearly doubled corn yields to approximately 60 bushels per acre with minimal increase in cost. However, since these plants were not able to generate their own seed for the next year's crop, farmers had to buy new seed each year from firms that specialized in seed production. Farmers were able to use acreage for current production that they had previously devoted to growing seed corn for the next season, and output was enhanced even further. In this manner farmers took one more step in the direction of being specialized producers and letting others meet their input needs.

These same types of changes were also occurring with respect to fertilizer. World War II brought a tremendous increase in the demand for nitrogen for explosives. The U. S. production capacity for nitrogen was greatly increased to meet this need. After the war the nitrogen plants were sold to private firms who converted them to the production of nitrogen fertilizers. This provided farmers with access to low-cost chemical fertilizers. The declining use of horses on the farm added further to their need for purchased fertilizer to replenish soil nutrients. Again in the name of greater productivity and profits, farmers increased their use of another purchased input.

Each of the major components of fertilizer—nitrogen (N), phosphorus (P), and potassium (K)—is produced by a different production process. Nitrogen is normally used as a form of ammonia which has the chemical configuration NH_3—one molecule of nitrogen to three molecules of hydrogen. It is produced by a natural gas–driven compressor that extracts nitrogen from the air and combines it with hydrogen from natural gas. This explains why the price of nitrogenous fertilizers is so closely tied to the price of natural gas. Phosphorus is found in several places in the world. In the United States there are large deposits in Florida as well as North and South Carolina. North Africa and Chile also have major phosphorus deposits. Potassium was once produced by collecting the ash from burning wood in iron pits and thereby acquired the common name potash (even though ashes are no longer used). Potassium is found naturally in the form of the salt potassium chloride (KCl). Some of the largest deposits of potassium chloride in the world are found in Canada.

The effects on productivity from increased fertilization are well documented and have helped to boost crop yields still further. Abundant supplies of fertilizer have kept prices relatively low and have made it profitable for farmers to use large amounts of them. Suppliers have met the need of farmers for plant nutrients by providing fertilizer at the time, in the place, in the form, and in a way that made possession easy and convenient. In short, they did a good job of marketing their product.

THE AGRICULTURAL CHEMICAL INDUSTRY

World War II also brought dramatic developments in the ability of chemicals to control weeds, insects, and other pests. During the war a chemist working for the Geigy Chemical Company discovered the insecticidal properties of DDT. Its ability to kill a large variety of insects helped to improve the health and sanitation of those involved in the war. After the war these same properties made DDT a popular insecticide for farmers since it drastically reduced the amount of crops lost to insects.

The war years also saw the development of the herbicide 2,4D. Originally developed as a potential crop-destroying chemical, it was found to be very effective in killing broadleaf weeds while it did not control grasses. It too soon found wide use in production agriculture as a way to cut crop losses to broadleaf weeds.

Both DDT and 2,4D were widely used throughout the 1950s and 1960s. Toward the end of this period scientists began to question the use of DDT because of unwanted side effects from use. Chemical producers continued their research to find safer and more effective products to control weeds and insects. The late 1960s saw the development of atrazine and other pesticides that raised crop yields still further.

The decades of the 1970s and 1980s saw renewed concern for the environment and the need to keep our air and water unpolluted. Agricultural chemical producers continued their search for selective yet effective herbicides and pesticides that would minimize environmental damage.

AGRICULTURE AND TECHNOLOGY

The evolution of agribusiness has gone hand-in-hand with the growth of technology. The Industrial Revolution brought a new demand for factory workers and reduced the supply of farm laborers. This shortage increased farmers' interest in labor-saving methods and devices. The resulting rise in productivity made possible by the application of new technology has permitted both sectors to prosper.

This process has been so successful in production agriculture that currently less than 3 percent of our labor force is directly involved in food production. Many people who otherwise would have been involved in agricultural production are now involved in the production and marketing of agricultural inputs. To achieve higher productivity, producers now purchase rather than make about 75 percent of all the inputs needed in the production process. On the other side, food processing has also moved off the farm. The shift to off-farm processing has been so complete that farm families, like nearly everyone else, depend almost entirely on the firms in the commodity processing and food sector for their daily food needs.

Technology and the Future

The decade of the 1980s gave us just a glimpse of what technology holds for us in the future. Technological developments in the agricultural input industries appear to be affecting production agriculture in two ways. First, there is the need to better manage the technology that already exists. This means input suppliers need to help farmers to understand the full potential of new, improved inputs and to coordinate these inputs (equipment, chemicals, seeds, etc.) as part of their business, financial, and marketing decision making.

Today's full-time commercial farmers cannot be content to be just tillers of the soil. They must be technically efficient in each production activity they undertake in order to get the maximum output from each unit of input. They must be able to combine the various crops and livestock systems into an efficient farming system. And they must be able to accomplish this in the most profitable way possible. This requires that farmers be managers, not just producers. They need to be as proficient at financial planning and marketing as they are at crop and livestock production. The management challenges in production agriculture are as great as those found in any industry in the economy.

The second effect of technology on agricultural production pertains to changes in the way production is done. Biotechnology holds great promise in bringing about gains in productivity. Until the 1980s scientists exploited the genetic potential that already existed in crops and animals by careful crossbreeding. The next step is to adjust the genetic potential by rearranging the genetic material inside reproductive cells.

Genetic engineering, including gene splicing and other recombinant DNA techniques, offers the potential to develop improved plants and animals with unheard-of production capabilities. Embryo implants give the potential for multiple births from beef and dairy animals. Changes in bioregulation can speed up or even eliminate the ripening process of crops and make harvesting more efficient and less costly.

The tremendous effects of technology on agricultural production call for greater reliance on computers to help farmers better manage the people, machinery, and money in their operations. Each crop, livestock, and financial system will generate enormous amounts of information that only a computer will be capable of analyzing in the time needed to make a decision. Computers also hold the potential to automate many routine farm activities such as turning on irrigation systems, monitoring seed placement during planting, and measuring temperatures in milk storage tanks. This will release the farmer to spend time on other more important matters.

The growing sophistication of full-time production agriculture makes it a high-tech industry. This means that producers have to become more sophisticated managers. They will buy even larger amounts of increasingly technologically complex production inputs. This means that input suppliers will need to maintain strong networks of support personnel in the field to see to it that their products work effectively and efficiently for their farmer customers.

Where Does New Technology Come From?

A recurring question in these types of discussions is, Where does this new technology originate? The answer is that it comes from a variety of sources and that we all pay for it in one way or another.

Farmers are good sources of many ideas for improved technology. Those closest to the problem are often the ones with the best ideas for a solution. Many refinements and improvements in the production process have come from farmers. For example, the idea of using a front weight on a tractor (made from a tank filled with water to keep the front wheels on the ground when using heavy implements) came from a farmer. He refined the idea and later sold it to a major implement maker so they could manufacture the item on a large scale. But new basic technology is not likely to come from farmers. They simply do not have the time, money, or capability to perform the research necessary to add to our knowledge of basic technology.

Government (state and federal) has been a good source of funding for new technology research. The federal government in particular has been a major supporter of new technology research. Much of this research has come from work that has been administered by the USDA and done either in its own laboratories or at land grant universities throughout the country.

Agribusiness firms have also added significantly to our base of technology. These firms have been involved in developing new and better feeds, seeds, fertilizers, tractors, and so on to better meet the needs of their farmer customers. The motivation to develop technologically improved inputs comes in part from the desire of the input supplier to have a differentiated product that can provide it with a competitive edge and a means to higher profits. Commodity processors and food manufacturers also engage in similar types of research.

Regardless of the source, the cost of new technology is included in the price of the inputs and food items we purchase, and in the taxes we pay. Analysis shows that expenditures on new technology continue to be a good investment since each $1.00 spent on agribusiness research is calculated to yield $10.00 in benefits. In a world with a rising population we can ill afford to lessen our search for new technology in agribusiness.

SECTOR STRUCTURE

The structure of the agricultural input sector varies by industry. Each of the industries has evolved in a slightly different manner in response to different forces. Because of this the discussion will focus on the following three input industries: (1) pesticides, (2) farm implements, and (3) seeds.

Pesticides

The pesticides industry includes all those firms that produce chemicals used for the control of organisms that are considered to be pests. Pesticide products include insecticides, herbicides, fungicides, miticides, and so forth. They are used to control the most destructive of the 10,000 species of insects, 600 species of weeds, and over 1,500 different types of plant diseases that destroy $15 to $20 billion worth of crops, livestock, and forest and food products each year in the United States. Sales of pesticides in the United States amount to over $4 billion a year.

The industry is made up of three major components. First, there are the basic manufacturers. This group includes a small number of large chemical, petroleum, and drug companies such has Ciba-Geigy, Monsanto, Dow, and Elanco. They are the firms that do much of the research and development work on new pesticide products.

Finding new products is an increasingly difficult task. Once a promising product has been discovered it can take up to seven to ten years and $14 to $20 million of testing to receive government clearance for use. This leaves only seventeen years of patent protection for the firm to recover its costs and earn a profit before other firms are allowed to produce the product. The basic manufacturers normally maintain sales representatives in the field who sell directly to wholesale distributors, work with retailers on various promotional campaigns, and provide technical service to retailers and farmers.

The second major component is the wholesale distributors. This small group of firms takes an ownership risk position in pesticides, warehouses the products, distributes them to the retailers, and provides the dealers with the training and technical assistance they need. The third component of the industry is the retailers who are sometimes called resellers. They sell the products to the farmers. They normally do some warehousing and product distribution, provide some technical expertise, extend credit, and offer custom application. There are a large number of retailers of agricultural chemicals, and they can be found in just about every farming community. They tend to be local agribusiness firms and include farmer owned cooperatives as well as independently owned retail outlets.

The Farm Implement Industry

There are around 1,200 firms involved in producing farm machinery in the United States. However, there are only five or six that offer a full line of equipment (that is, tractors to planters to manure spreaders, plus combines, hay balers, and so on). Most smaller firms offer only a few specialized pieces of equipment that are designed for use on specific crops (for instance, pea planters and cranberry harvesters).

Most equipment manufacturers sell through independently owned dealerships. These retail outlets are often given an exclusive selling territory by the full-line manufacturers. The key to much of a dealer's success is his ability to meet customers' needs for service, repairs and parts. The speed and quality of service provided is vital since the breakdown of a piece of equipment during planting or harvesting can be very costly to the farmer. To maintain a high level of service, retailers usually employ a number of service technicians plus sales representatives who call on farmers to see how well their needs are being met.

The Seed Industry

There are a large number of firms involved in seed production. However, there are only a handful that operate on a wide geographic scale. The industry grew because of the higher-yield potential of hybrid seeds and because of the ability to produce seed to meet specific local growing conditions such as short growing seasons, resistance to certain insects, or low rainfall.

The first hybrids were developed in the 1930s by the U.S. government in its laboratories or by state agricultural experiment stations at land grant universities. Many farmers attempted to enter the business by selling seed to their neighbors that they had grown, cleaned, treated, and bagged. In some states the quality of the product was certified by state agricultural officials. So many people entered the business that it soon became saturated. Finally, during the 1940s several national companies emerged that sold branded seed.

At first the seed companies attempted to sell their product through local farm supply stores and elevators, but they had limited success. Dekalb found a profitable solution by using farmer-dealer representatives to sell to other farmers in a local area. This established the basic marketing channel for seed that exists today. The major seed companies generally sell through a district sales office to the farmer-dealers who in turn sell to other farmers. Farmers become dealers because of the chance to earn extra income and to obtain their own seed at a discount.

SUMMARY

The agricultural input industries have developed for the most part since the end of World War II. The main reason for the existence of these industries is that the inputs they sell are cheaper and more productive than the ones the farmer could provide for himself. The development of these industries has permitted farmers to concentrate more on production and has made the input firms a major force in agribusiness today. The firms in the agricultural input industries have made a major investment of time and money in the development of highly technical and sophisticated inputs. Thus, they have a great interest in the efficient and effective marketing of these products to agricultural producers to help insure the continued health and profitability of the food and fiber system.

QUESTIONS

1. What were the major forces that led to the development of the agricultural input industries?
2. Why must a farmer or rancher be more than just a producer to be successful today?
3. Why do many people see agricultural production as a high-tech industry in the near future?
4. In what two general directions does technology seem to be taking agribusiness, and what are the implications of these changes?
5. Should the government or private industry pay for the research needed to support new technology?

9

Production Agriculture

Central to the food and fiber system are the farmers and ranchers that use the inputs provided by the agricultural input industries to produce raw agricultural commodities. These commodities are sold to commodity processors and food manufacturers in the processing-manufacturing sector of agribusiness. Farmers and ranchers are at the heart of the food and fiber system and are definitely part of agribusiness. This chapter explains how and why they are rapidly becoming more businesslike in how they run their individual operations.

In recent years the markets for nearly all agribusiness products including inputs, commodities, and food products have been characterized by excess supply, intense competition, and low market prices. Agricultural producers, even though they are often referred to by economists as part of the last bastion of pure competition, have felt competitive pressures. Farmers face tough competition not only for major inputs such as land but also in output markets. For example, if a farmer wants to grow popcorn, seed corn, or even sweet corn to increase his returns over commercial field corn, he often finds that his neighbors have already contracted for all of this year's crop from the buyers of these specialty crops, and he is closed out of these markets.

A sadder case is the farmer that does not consider anything but traditional crops. He raises corn and soybeans in rotation because that is what he has done for the past twenty years, and then grumbles about the low price of these commodities at the local elevator on the day he hauls his crop in. To be successful in today's evolving agribusiness system, producers need to think about the price they are likely to receive for their crops long before they take them to market. This is a direct application of the marketing approach discussed in previous chapters.

The objective of this chapter is to show how agricultural producers can increase their chances for economic prosperity by adopting the marketing approach. As was discussed earlier, the successful functioning of the total agribusiness system requires that all parts of this system operate efficiently. Thus, farmers and ranchers in the production sector must understand the marketing approach.

THE BACKGROUND

As a people, Americans have always been concerned with food production, commodity and food prices, and farm income. On the one hand, as consumers we want an adequate supply of wholesome food at reasonable prices. On the other hand, we want farmers to receive fair prices for the commodities they sell so they can achieve incomes that are comparable to their nonfarm neighbors. Unfortunately, these two goals are often at odds with one another.

The concern for farm commodity prices and incomes originated when the majority of people in this country made their living as farmers. More recently we have become more concerned that low commodity prices and farm incomes would cause many of the remaining farmers to go out of business. This could reduce the supply of food, forcing prices to the consumer to rise dramatically. This is why even though most of us are not involved in food production, there is widespread popular support for government programs that protect agricultural commodity prices and farm incomes and assure us of an adequate supply of reasonably priced food.

Beginning in 1933 with the Agricultural Adjustment Act, Congress enacted a series of farm programs that were designed to solve "the farm problem" of low farm incomes and prices. There have been government farm programs ever since, and "the farm problem" still exists.

"The farm problem" is really a series of problems, many of which are related to the marketing of farm commodities. The first problem has to do with the revenue farmers receive from marketing their crops and livestock. Simply put, most of the time there is not enough revenue to cover expenses and leave the farmer with a fair profit. Revenue fluctuates, and most farmers would say it always fluctuates downward. But farm income can increase as it did in the mid-1970s, when the world supply of commodities was low and the prices farmers received increased dramatically. Farm income also increased sharply in the mid-1980s due to massive government payments to farmers that offset extremely low commodity prices.

A related problem is the relationship between farm income and comparable nonfarm income. At one time government economists would compare average farm family income to the income of an average nonfarm family using a concept called parity. Usually the farm family fared badly in the comparison. Not much has been said about this in recent years because it is so difficult to equate farm income to nonfarm income. The farm family has a considerable investment in their farming operation, the whole family is usually involved in the farm business, and they supply nearly all of their own labor. None of this equates to the typical suburban family where the husband and wife may work for different companies with no ownership interest.

Central to the discussion of farm problems is the problem of unstable farm commodities prices. (Livestock prices and the prices of livestock products such as milk, eggs and wool are also included here.) The factor which usually has the most impact on prices is weather. It can be too dry, too wet, too cold, or too hot. Hurricanes, droughts, tornadoes, hail, floods, frozen rivers, and so on, all can cause commodity prices to fluctuate. Besides the weather, the biological nature of agricultural production can cause yields and prices to fluctuate. For example, the southern corn blight caused a significant reduction in corn yields in the early 1970s. The resulting rise in the price of corn was a boon to the corn farmers whose crops escaped the blight. However, the higher price did not help those who had infested fields. Their incomes moved sharply downward.

Other factors can cause prices to be unstable. In the past, demand for farm products has been relatively stable, at least compared to the wide fluctuations in supply. Domestic demand is still relatively stable. However, export demand has proven to be very unstable. Countries such as Russia, China, and India buy large amounts of farm products one year, but the next year they may buy nothing. It all depends on how their weather influenced the level of crop production that year and their current purchasing policies. With such a large proportion of U.S. crops destined for the export markets, the fluctuation in export demand causes correspondingly large fluctuations in market prices.

THE DIFFERENCE BETWEEN SELLING AND MARKETING

Historically, farmers have taken the commodities not used on the farm to town and have sold them for whatever a local buyer would pay for them. If the price seemed too low to the farmer, he could try to bargain for a higher price. But the buyer could usually buy all he wanted at the posted price. Unable to bargain for higher prices, the farmer could take his wheat, hogs, eggs, or cream back to the farm. Usually, he did not. He took the price offered.

This is not marketing. It is selling. When individual farmers were small and the amount of excess commodities they wanted to sell was also small, the difference between selling and marketing didn't matter very much. The farmer involved would feel shortchanged and go away muttering, but there was always next year and the hope of higher prices.

Today, we have larger farm units which specialize in the production of one or a few commodities. The quantities of commodities produced and sold are very large. The margin between revenues and expenses is small at best. A difference in price of a few cents per bushel or hundredweight can mean the difference between prosperity and bankruptcy.

Too often when the crop is harvested or is ready for market the farmer hauls it to the local market and takes whatever price is offered. Sometimes the price offered is good and the farmer does well. More often than not the farmer receives a poor price because many other farmers are doing the same thing and there is a relative glut on the market at harvest time. The farmer who sells a crop in this way is merely selling, not marketing, commodities. He has very little if any influence on the price received because of his poor bargaining position. If he threatens to withhold his product from the buyer, the buyer will probably yawn with indifference. The buyer can purchase the same commodity from a number of other farmers at the price offered. Even farmer bargaining groups have not been very successful in withholding commodities from the market to force buyers to pay higher prices.

Becoming Involved in Marketing Functions

Many farmers now market their commodities instead of just selling them. Marketing starts with analyzing the market to see what is needed before beginning production. It may be a different variety of wheat; hogs with longer, leaner body types; earlier maturing apples; or perhaps new or exotic crops such as jojoba. By being willing to shift production to a different crop or livestock animal the farmer may be able to substantially increase revenues and profits.

For example, many vegetable producers plant a crop only when they have a sales contract in hand. This takes the marketing uncertainty out of the picture for farmers who would rather not speculate on price but do want to make a reasonable profit by being capable, efficient producers. The vegetable buyers are assured of a supply of product at a known price so that uncertainty is eliminated for them too. Marketing contracts are becoming more common in production agriculture, particularly where quality of product is important or where buyers must have a specific raw material to use in a food manufacturing process. Examples include tomatoes for sauce and catsup, malt barley for beer, white corn for tortillas, chickens for brand-name products, and so on.

Some farmers perform many of the middleman's marketing functions by selling products through roadside stands or pick-your-own operations. For a farmer located close to a population center, this form of marketing can be profitable. The farmer captures a large part of the middleman's profit margin and passes some of it on to customers in the form of lower prices. In return for increased profits the farmer must take on some of the marketing functions ordinarily performed by middlemen such as the risk of continued ownership, processing, storage, transportation, and financing.

The consumer performs some marketing functions too. By driving to the farmer's location the consumer provides some of the transportation that would ordinarily be provided by the middleman. By purchasing large quantities the consumer performs some storage and financing. When consumers pick their own fruits and vegetables they are actually performing some of the farmer's production functions as well!

There is an old maxim of marketing, "You can eliminate the middlemen, but you can't eliminate the marketing functions they perform." Middlemen become very proficient at performing marketing functions. It is unlikely that a farmer or a consumer can perform the same functions as efficiently. Most farmers and ranchers are not willing to make the investment in time and money necessary to perform middleman marketing functions. As consumers, we are looking for ways to conserve our precious time. As the rapidly growing market for convenience items suggests, we are more willing to give up money than time. We want middlemen to provide more marketing functions, not fewer. However, in some specialized markets, farmers who are willing to assume even a few of the middleman's marketing functions can significantly improve revenues.

Strategies to Increase Revenues

Farmers are assuming marketing functions on the input side as well through their role as purchasing agents. Farmers buy large amounts of input such as seed, fertilizer, equipment, and petroleum products. These raw materials are transformed into commodities and food products which the farmer markets to recover expenses and, if there is any money left over, make a profit.

A farmer's profit picture can be improved by purchasing the inputs at the lowest possible prices. Because of specialization in production and the resulting large-scale buying, some farmers have become very proficient at buying input products. In a large business organization a person performing this marketing function would be called a purchasing agent. The purchasing agent must have a high level of technical knowledge and be skillful in handling purchase negotiations. Often, substantial savings can be gained by assuming some of the middleman's marketing functions such as storage, transportation, or financing. Farmers are taking on some of the middleman's functions primarily to reduce the cost of purchased inputs. A few farmers are also assuming the reselling function.

In one case a farmer became so effective as a purchasing agent that his neighbors asked him to purchase inputs for them. Eventually this farmer's input purchasing and reselling business became more lucrative than his farming operation. He rented his land to a neighbor and moved to town. His input business expanded to include fertilizer, agricultural chemicals, feed, seed, and an implement dealership. This "farmer" recently added a small grain elevator to his agribusiness holdings. His operation is now a one-stop service center for farmers in that community.

Farmers who are limited to the production of traditional crops or livestock can usually increase revenues through better timing of sales. Four years out of five, grain farmers can receive a higher price by storing grain at harvest time and selling later in the year. As the harvest glut is used up, prices tend to rise. Near the end of the marketing year, prices may rise dramatically if *pipeline supplies* become short. The pipeline supply is the amount of a commodity needed to allow the marketing channel to function smoothly without disruption.

Another marketing action by farmers that can add to revenue is to offer their commodities for sale where they are most needed. A grain farmer may

---

Strategies for Farmers to Improve Their Profit Picture

- Analyze the market to see what products are needed.
- Purchase inputs at the lowest possible prices.
- Assume some of the middlemen's functions such as storage, transportation, and financing.
- Carefully time sales to receive the best price.
- Offer commodities where they are most needed.

find the price to be significantly higher at a terminal or a grain processor's plant than at the local country elevator. Many farmers now call around to find the highest offering price and haul their grain to that buyer. They can hire truckers or they can haul the grain themselves. It is not uncommon for farmers to own their over-the-road rigs. The higher price for their grain more than pays for their hauling costs and they can utilize their own slack time.

Farmers don't have to be sellers. They can become marketers and have some control over the prices they receive. But they have to be willing to adjust to the marketplace and become active participants in the marketing process. By altering production plans, timing sales better, and moving commodities to buyers willing to pay higher prices, farmers can usually increase their revenues.

DEVELOPING THE PRODUCER'S MARKETING PLAN

Many producers have a wide range of marketing alternatives available to them. The number of alternatives depends upon crops or livestock products involved. There are three steps to developing a producer's marketing plan:

1. Identify the marketing alternatives
2. Evaluate the seller's financial position and attitude toward risk
3. Choose the appropriate marketing alternative(s)

To illustrate how a marketing plan is developed let's look at the marketing decision process for a grain producer and the marketing alternatives worth considering. A cash grain producer who has adopted a marketing approach should develop a marketing plan long before the crop is planted. It may be possible to have the grain already sold for a known price before pulling the planter into the field. By separating the marketing of grain from physical production, the farmer gains marketing flexibility. By developing a marketing plan, he or she knows before beginning production that the crop to be planted is needed in the marketplace, and where, when, and how he or she is going to market it to realize the best possible profit.

Identifying the Marketing Alternatives

There are many different ways to market grain. The following represent some of the marketing alternatives available to grain producers:

1. Sell in the Cash Market at Harvest Time. This usually means hauling the grain to the nearest local elevator as it comes off of the combine. The farmer, perhaps after a lengthy wait in line to dump the grain, receives the price posted on the elevator's price board for that day.

This marketing alternative has some advantages for the farmer in that no special grain-handling equipment such as grain dryers or storage bins is required and immediate cash payment is made. Unfortunately, because of the harvest glut the farmer may receive the lowest price in the grain marketing year by choosing this marketing alternative. It may also be the riskiest approach, since the farmer will not know what a whole season's work will bring until pulling onto the scale to weigh the grain and looking at the elevator's price board.

2. Store at Harvest, Sell Later. Aided by government programs which encouraged storage of grain on the farms where it was grown, farmers have built on-farm grain storage systems. In fact, there is now more grain storage capacity on-farm than off-farm in the United States. Commercial grain handlers, except for the large terminal grain elevators whose business it is to store grain, generally do not want to store any more grain than is necessary to efficiently run their businesses.

In most years a farmer can get a higher price for grain by storing at harvest time and selling later in the marketing year. At harvest time grain prices are usually lower than at any other time of the marketing year. (The marketing year is the twelve-month period between harvests.) After harvest, grain is slowly but continuously consumed. In most years price rises more than the cost of storage to reflect the growing relative shortage of the grain in the commercial pipeline. In years when the shortage of a particular grain becomes acute near the end of the marketing year, the price of that grain can rise dramatically. Under those conditions astute farmers can substantially improve the selling price of their grain by holding it until near the end of the marketing year.

There are years, however, when grain prices do not rise following harvest or at least do not rise enough to justify the cost of storage. Large supplies of surplus grain in government storage, a bountiful harvest in the Southern hemisphere, or a large anticipated acreage expansion in the United States can keep grain prices depressed throughout the marketing year.

On-farm storage is not without risk. Grain is a living organism and must be managed carefully while in storage to avoid a loss in quality. Grain that becomes moldy or insect infested may be severely discounted when taken out of storage and sold. Unless a farmer is willing to spend the time and money necessary to maintain the grain quality, it is much better to sell at harvest time.

3. Cash Forward Contract Before Harvest.   Farmers routinely sell grain before it is harvested. In fact, some farmers sell their grain before it is planted. They do this by contracting with a willing buyer, usually a livestock feeder or local elevator, at a time when they find the market price is acceptable. The determination of what makes an acceptable price is done beforehand as part of the producer's marketing plan.

Once the contract is signed, such farmers know exactly what price they will receive for their grain. They can lock in a profit and avoid the risk of loss caused by a downward movement of price. Of course, if the current price of grain does not provide a profit, they would not contract immediately but would wait for the price to improve before signing. Contracting allows grain producers to time the sale to capture the highest price they think possible. Of course, if they are wrong and prices rise after the contract is signed they cannot take advantage of those price increases. And they are contractually obligated to deliver the amount of grain specified in the contract. If the crop yield is reduced by a drought, hail, or other natural cause, they must still fulfill the contract even if it means buying grain from someone else.

4. Forward Contract in the Futures Market.   Using the futures markets it is possible for a farmer to lock in a price through a technique called hedging. When John Jones, a grain farmer, sees an acceptable selling price in the futures market any time before harvest, he sells futures contracts equal to the amount of grain whose price he wishes to protect. (For a full discussion of the workings of the futures market, see Chapter 20.) At harvest time he hauls his grain to the local country elevator and sells it at the going market price on the day of delivery. Immediately after the cash sale he must buy the same number of futures contracts that he previously sold to lift his hedge and be released from his futures market obligations.

Jones's profit or loss from the futures market transaction should be just about equal to the profit or loss he would have experienced in the cash market price from the day he entered the futures market. Since the profit in one market just about offsets the loss in the other market, his original target cash price for the grain is preserved. The process is called hedging because Jones takes equal but opposite positions in the cash and futures markets (that is, buying in one market while selling in the other).

The major advantage of hedging compared to cash forward contracting is that the farmer can take advantage of favorable price movements. If the price of grain starts to increase, the farmer lifts his hedge early to take advantage of the rising price in the market. If price starts to falter, he can place a new hedge to lock in the higher price.

5. Market Grain as Livestock Feed.   For many grain farmers, feeding livestock is a good alternative for marketing their grain. In actuality they sell the grain to themselves. In practice the grain is transferred from the grain enterprise to the livestock enterprise. The transfer price should be the prevailing market price.

By feeding grain on-farm rather than selling it, farmers are adding value by processing the grain into a higher value product (livestock). When animals or livestock products are sold, farmers capture the profit on the grain as well as on the livestock enterprise. When grain prices are extremely low, feeding livestock may be one of the few profitable grain marketing alternatives available.

There are some drawbacks to marketing grain through livestock. It takes additional investment capital and management skill to feed livestock. And there is no guarantee of profit. What appears to be a profitable livestock enterprise when the commitment is made may turn out to be unprofitable if many other farmers make the same decision.

Some livestock producers sidestep this risk by placing a hedge to lock in a profit. In fact, the entire operation may be hedged. The grain crop is hedged while it is growing and in storage awaiting conversion to feed. The hedge is lifted in increments as the grain is fed to the livestock, which are also hedged. This is called a complete hedge. It eliminates most of the risk of adverse price fluctuations and allows the farmer to concentrate on making a profit by running efficient grain and livestock enterprises.

6. Sell to the Government.   The government's farm program was not designed as a marketing mechanism. It was designed to stabilize erratic markets while providing price and income protection for farmers. In other words, it was meant to solve some of the farm problems discussed earlier in this chapter. Regardless of the intent, farmers have sold billions of bushels of grain to the U.S. government over the years through the nonrecourse loan program.

When an eligible farmer harvests and places grain in approved storage he or she can obtain a loan from the U.S. government using the grain as collateral. For example, if the loan rate is $3.00 per bushel, the producer can receive a loan equal to the number of bushels of qualified grain in approved storage times $3.00. The farmer can use this loan money received from the government to pay off debts at the bank or to provide operating capital for the next crop or for any other purpose.

To get the grain out of storage all the farmer must do is to pay back the loan at the loan rate ($3.00 per bushel) plus storage costs. He or she will do that when the market price rises above the $3.00-per-bushel loan rate. When this occurs the farmer enters into a transaction to sell the grain and uses part of the proceeds to pay back the government loan. The farmer pockets the difference. The program allows the farmer to store grain at harvest for later sale while providing the money needed to conduct a farm business until the grain is sold.

In times of large surpluses, the market price may not rise above the loan rate. The loan rate sets the price floor and the weight of the surplus grain on the market keeps it there. If the farmer never redeems the grain for sale on the open market he or she in effect reneges on the loan. Because it is a nonrecourse loan, the government cannot force repayment. It simply takes title to the grain. The result is that the farmer sells the grain to the U.S. government at the loan rate price per bushel.

Each of the five marketing alternatives offers the producer a different way to turn a crop into cash. The producer who has adopted the marketing approach and established a marketing plan will know the marketing alternatives before entering into production.

Evaluating the Financial Position and Attitude Toward Risk

Once the marketing alternatives have been identified it is up to the producer to weigh them in light of his or her financial position and attitude toward risk. If the farmer is the type who likes to avoid risk at all cost or is in a difficult financial position, then a less risky marketing alternative such as selling grain under loan to the government may be most appropriate. Planning should be done with that option in mind. Depending upon finances and ability to handle risk, the farmer might consider either cash forward contracting or the use of the futures markets. Remember, these situations are usually not all or nothing. In other words, it may be possible to forward cash contract or use futures markets for just a portion of the crop, while selling the rest in the cash market at harvest time.

Selection of the Best Alternative

The selection of the best marketing alternative depends on the individual, the situation, and the marketing alternatives that are available. It is important to achieve a good match. What might be right for one farmer may not be acceptable to other farmers who have completely different financial situations, or who have a different approach to risk. If the thought of a particular marketing alternative leaves a farmer tossing and turning at night, then it is not an acceptable marketing option. Oftentimes just sitting down and reviewing the various marketing options that are available will give a farmer ideas about how to improve an operation and achieve a higher income. What is important is that this type of decision making be done long before harvest, not on the day the crop is ready to be hauled to market.

SUMMARY

This chapter has reviewed some of the problems that surround production agriculture and offered some ways for producers to raise their incomes through better marketing. These suggestions are all based on the idea that producers, like others in the agribusiness system, must be responsive to the needs of the marketplace if they hope to be more profitable. By adopting a market oriented approach, producers can take an active role in solving farm income and price problems.

QUESTIONS

1. What is the Farm Problem and how has the government attempted to solve it?
2. What is the difference between selling and marketing farm commodities?
3. Why are producers able to get a higher price for their commodities when they sell them at a roadside stand?
4. Describe the three steps in developing a marketing plan, and explain when the plan should be made.
5. Why is it that a single marketing alternative cannot be used by all producers of the same commodity?

10

The Commodity Processing and Food Manufacturing Industries

The commodity processing and food manufacturing industries owe their existence to advancements in technology. Until the Civil War most food processing and manufacturing was done on the farm. Around this time advances in the technology of food preservation such as safe canning procedures, and later more reliable refrigeration, made it easier and in many cases safer to buy processed food products than to process food at home. The new technologies also permitted better utilization of existing food supplies by extending the useful life of perishable food items. Many of the advances in technology came as a result of efforts to develop low-cost, high-volume commodity processing and food manufacturing procedures. The result was the development of a separate processing-manufacturing sector in agribusiness.

This chapter is devoted to discussing the commodity processing–manufacturing sector of the agribusiness system that stretches from the farm gate to the final consumer. The specific topics to be covered include: (1) a review of the development of the sector, (2) a discussion of the differences between commodity marketing and product marketing, (3) a discussion of the marketing functions performed by the firms in the sector and how economic factors help determine their location and the size of their marketing areas, and (4) a presentation of the dominant core–competitive fringe model to explain the conduct and performance of firms in the commodity processing and food manufacturing industries.

The firms that make up the commodity processing and food manufacturing industries are a critical link between producers and consumers. They normally add the greatest amounts of value to food products. Thus, commodity processors and food manufacturers have a strong interest in efficient and effective marketing.

THE SIZE AND STRUCTURE OF THE SECTOR

There are approximately 22,000 firms in the commodity processing and food manufacturing sector. In 1986 they added over $215 billion of value to the items they handled. About half of the sector's output comes from the 100 largest firms. They include such well-known companies as General Foods, General Mills, Kelloggs, Pillsbury, Sunkist Growers, Land O'Lakes, and a host of others.

The size of these firms and their limited numbers are a cause of concern to some economists. The top 100 firms have continued to increase the proportion of total sector assets and sales under their control. The concern is that such an increase in the concentration of resources by a few firms might lead to declines in market efficiency. Opponents of this point of view point out that these firms compete fiercely among themselves and must compete against foreign competitors in order to maintain their share of U.S. and world markets.

THE MARKETING CHANNELS

The structure of the sector has also influenced the development of food marketing channels. *Marketing channels* define the path that a food product follows from the farm gate to the consumer. The length of this path depends on the product. For example, for wheat used for bread, the marketing channel could be as long as this:

> *farmer→local elevator→terminal elevator→flour miller→baker→wholesaler→food retailer→consumer*

For fresh tomatoes sold at a farmer's roadside stand the channel could be as short as this:

farmer→consumer

The market channel for most food products is as follows:

producer→assembler/procurer→processor/manufacturer→
wholesaler/food broker→food retailer/food service→consumer

The marketing functions that each firm performs are largely determined by their position in the marketing system and by the marketing strategy employed by the firm. The market channel includes the participants discussed below.

Assemblers/Procurers

Assemblers/procurers do just what their name implies. They assemble many smaller-sized lots of commodities produced by individual producers into larger-sized lots needed by processors. This permits the processors to capture more of the economies of size possible in shipping and plant operation. For grain this function is performed by assemblers such as the local elevators. For livestock this function is performed by a procurer such as a commission buyer who for a fee buys animals from individual producers on behalf of a processor.

In recent years, as the raw product requirements of commodity processors have become more definitive, there has been an increase in purchasing livestock and crops by specification. A growing practice is for the processor to contract with individual growers to produce a specific type of crop, planted at a specific time, harvested in a specific way at a specific time. This practice is becoming more and more common in the livestock industries. It insures the processor of the uniform quality and quantity of input that is available on a known schedule so that the processing plant can be operated at peak efficiency. Thus, the role of the assembler/procurer is to increase the efficiency of the marketing system by getting the right quality of products, at the right time, at the right price, at the right place, and in the right quantity to meet the needs of the processor.

Processors

The processor is normally the first one in the marketing system to alter the form of a raw agricultural commodity. Good examples are the flour millers who process the raw commodity wheat into flour that is sent to bakers to make bread, or the meat packers who take 1200-pound live steers and process them into 600 pound carcasses or primal cuts that are shipped to food retailers for further processing into steaks, roasts, and hamburgers. In each case the form of the product is greatly changed, yet flour and meat still retain some of the characteristics of the initial raw commodities since they are still largely undifferentiated products.

Some of the larger and better-known processors include Cargill (grain and meat), IBP (meat), Central Soya (oilseeds), AMPI (dairy), and Monfort (beef).

Food Manufacturers

Food manufacturers continue the job started by the processor by adding more form utility to crops and livestock by increasing the level of preservation, convenience, and quality. Food manufacturing includes firms that bake bread, cookies, and crackers; firms that manufacture prepared breakfast cereals; firms that manufacture ice cream; and so on. In each case the firm takes a raw agricultural commodity (wheat, corn, milk) that has had its initial form altered by a processor (turned into flour, processed corn, pasteurized milk) and further changes its form into a manufactured food product (bread, corn flakes, ice cream) that is desired by consumers.

In this process the undifferentiated raw agricultural commodities (wheat, corn, milk) completely lose their identity and emerge from the food manufacturing process as part of a food product (such as Hostess Twinkies, Kellogg's Corn Flakes, Haagen Dazs ice cream). The undifferentiated commodities no longer exist but are now part of the ingredients found in a food product such as Twinkies—a highly differentiated, branded, manufactured food product. This transformation from undifferentiated commodity to food product is a major breaking point in the agribusiness marketing system. As will be seen in Chapter 15, marketing a branded food product is very different from marketing agricultural commodities.

Some of the largest and best-known food manufacturers are Pillsbury, General Mills, Coca-Cola, and H.J. Heinz.

Food Wholesalers

There are a number of firms that buy products from commodity processors and food manufacturers for sale to food retailers and food service firms. Food wholesalers buy railroad car or truckload quantities of food products for delivery to their warehouses where they break these larger-sized lots into smaller units of pallet or case size for shipment to individual food retailers and food service establishments.

Food wholesalers exist in the agribusiness marketing system because they provide a range of services to food retailers including giving them a wide assortment of products and in some cases providing short-term credit. By purchasing large quantities of single products, wholesalers obtain price savings in the form of volume discounts that retailers would be unable to obtain for themselves. Wholesalers maintain a variety of products and inventory levels that the retailer could not sustain. All of these services are valuable to food retailers and food service operators. They are willing to pay a middleman's margin to the wholesaler rather than try to perform these functions themselves.

The presence of the food wholesaler makes it possible for the retailer to place an order on Tuesday afternoon for: five cases of Post Raisin Bran cereal, five cases of Hershey's chocolate bars with almonds, eight cases of Charmin toilet tissue, sixty cases of Green Giant canned corn, forty-five cases of Del Monte peaches, and five pallets of Tide laundry detergent, all from the same source, for delivery on Wednesday.

Wholesalers normally take title to their products and resell them to their customers. They not only store the product but usually deliver it to individual stores. In addition, they often finance the shipment for a limited time through the use of credit sales. Thus, food wholesalers provide valuable services to the industry by performing the storage, transportation, and financing marketing functions.

For many years the larger food retail chains have performed their own wholesaling rather than rely on independent wholesalers. They have been able to perform pre-retailing activities with enough efficiency that they could pass some of the cost savings on to customers. This gave the retail chains a competitive advantage in the marketplace. In order to counter this advantage, independent retailers have banded together to provide their own wholesaling or have contracted with a wholesaler. Such arrangements where wholesalers and retailers are linked by ownership or contractual arrangement is called *integration*, more specifically *integrated food wholesaling/retailing*.

Food Brokers

For some products food brokers are used as the link between the manufacturer/processor and retailers. A food broker serves as the sales representative of the food manufacturer. Brokers are paid a commission for their work but normally do not take title to the products they sell, even though they may perform many wholesaling functions.

Food brokers normally work in a specific geographic area and represent a number of manufacturers. When orders are written, the food broker passes them on to the manufacturer who ships directly to the retailer or food service company. Sometimes brokers perform other services for clients such as assisting in promotional campaigns, introducing new products, and collecting or exchanging out-of-date or damaged merchandise.

Food Retailers and Food Service Operators

The next major step in the food marketing system is made up of food retailers and food service companies. This group includes the grocery stores as well as the HRI (hotels, restaurants, and institutions) trade. Both of these industries are of such size and complexity that they are the subjects of the next two chapters.

LOCATING PROCESSING AND MANUFACTURING FACILITIES

Technology and economics determine to a large degree where commodity processors and food manufacturers locate. When looking for the best place to build new processing facilities, managers look for a site that allows them to minimize the sum of: (1) the cost of transporting inputs to the processing facility, (2) the cost of processing, and (3) the cost of transporting the finished product to retailers.

If the inputs are of low value and bulky compared to the output, and the cost of processing is the same regardless of where it is located, processors locate close to the source of the inputs. This lowers the cost of transportation for the lower-valued inputs and focuses most of the transportation expense on moving the higher-valued product to market. Where significant weight is lost in processing, significant reductions in transportation costs can be realized.

This is the case for dairy products and meat. Milk is bulky, has a relatively low value per unit, and is highly perishable. Cheese, on the other hand, is not nearly as bulky since it takes about eight pounds of milk to make one pound of cheese. It has a higher value per unit than milk, and is less perishable. This is why cheese processing plants are located close to milk production areas rather than near consumption areas.

The location of meat processing has also changed because of changes in technology and economics. Before there was reliable refrigeration, live cattle were shipped to population centers for slaughtering even though processed beef was less costly to ship, since about half of carcass weight is lost in processing. Because of the availability of refrigeration, livestock processing is done near production areas in the West and the processed meat is shipped to consumers. Livestock producers also face a location decision with respect to the economics of shipping feed grains. For many of the same reasons, large-volume feeding facilities are located adjacent to grain production areas. The result is that livestock feeding and meat processing facilities both tend to be located in the major grain-producing regions of the country, and feed grain is shipped to the consumer in the form of processed meat.

These economic forces have led to a general movement of processing facilities away from large population centers to locations closer to production areas. This has generally meant a movement of livestock processing and meat product manufacturing to the South and West, away from the northern and eastern sections of the country. This movement of livestock producers to areas of lower costs and higher yields, the clustering of processors nearby, plus the availability of low-cost transportation have resulted in greater efficiency for the meat marketing system and lower prices for consumers.

Determining the Size of the Marketing Area

The size of the geographic area in which a firm can profitably market its product is largely determined by the cost of transportation. This explains why some products such as milk are sold only locally or regionally, while other products such as canned vegetables are sold nationwide. The *law of market areas* was developed to explain this situation. It may be illustrated best by using an example.

Let's assume there are two processing plants, Plant #1 and Plant #2, owned by the same firm. They are located 1,000 miles from each other (Figure 10–1). The president of the firm needs to decide which plant can most efficiently serve each segment of the firm's total market. Plant #1's cost of processing is $5 per case, and Plant #2's cost of processing is $7 per case for the same product. It costs $1.00 for transportation to move 1 case 100 miles from either plant.

As can be seen in Figure 10–1, Plant #1's marketing area will extend 600 miles from the plant. At this point the cost per case of processing and transportation is $11 ($5/case + $6/case). This is just equal to the cost of processing plus transportation for servicing this location from Plant #2 ($7/case + $4/case). Beyond 600 miles from Plant #1 it is cheaper to service a location from Plant #2. At distances less than 600 miles from Plant #1 it is cheaper for Plant #1 to service the location. The size of a plant's marketing area is determined by the sum of its processing costs plus transportation costs per unit relative to that of other plants.

The law of market areas says that the location with the lowest total cost (processing + transportation) should service an area, and that boundaries

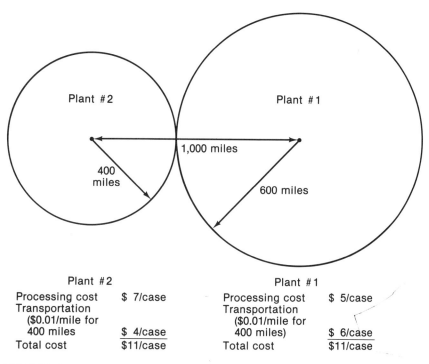

Plant #2			Plant #1		
Processing cost	$ 7/case		Processing cost	$ 5/case	
Transportation ($0.01/mile for 400 miles	$ 4/case		Transportation ($0.01/mile for 400 miles)	$ 6/case	
Total cost	$11/case		Total cost	$11/case	

FIGURE 10–1
The Law of Market Areas

between marketing areas are determined where costs are equal. In this example the boundary between plants falls 600 miles from Plant #1 and 400 miles from Plant #2 where the costs of servicing ($11/case) are equal. Thus, by applying the law of market areas it is possible for a multiplant processor to determine how large a geographic market area will be served from each location.

THE DOMINANT CORE–COMPETITIVE FRINGE MODEL

Economists have developed a number of models to explain the actions of markets. In Chapter 3 the structure-conduct-performance model was used to explain these interrelationships and how they influence market behavior. A refinement of this approach is offered by the dominant core–competitive fringe model. It is particularly useful in explaining the actions of firms in the commodity processing and food manufacturing industries.

The dominant core–competitive fringe model does this by separating the firms in each industry into two categories by size. The first group is the dominant core. The dominant core is made up of a few firms that produce well-known, brand-name food items. The sales of these dominant firms represent a significant portion of total sales in each industry. The second group of firms is the competitive fringe. It is made up of many small firms that produce products that are less well known nationally or known only in limited geographical areas. This group includes firms that can products such as upper Michigan cherries and blueberries or bake specialty products like Pennsylvania Whoopie Pies.

Conduct Comparisons

The firms in each group conduct themselves very differently in the areas of product innovation, quality, and advertising. In the realm of product innovation, firms in the dominant core spend large sums of money on product development and are continually introducing new products. Firms in the competitive fringe group specialize in private label goods and sell their products under a variety of wholesaler and retailer brand names with few product changes from year to year.

In terms of product quality, firms in the dominant core strive to consistently put out a high quality product. Oreo cookies are the same each and every time you buy them. Firms on the competitive fringe, on the other hand, produce products that are of standard quality. These products may not measure up to the quality of products from the firms in the dominant core, but lower manufacturing costs allow them to be sold at prices below those of products from the dominant core firms. These products are attractive to many customers because they offer value at the lower price.

As for product advertising, firms in the dominant core make extensive use of national advertising to gain brand recognition for their products. Dominant core food manufacturers are among the heaviest users of every form of advertising and spend large amounts of money every year for this purpose. Those firms on the competitive fringe spend very little on advertising since their products are usually sold under another firm's name.

Structure of the Marketing Channels

Differences are also found in the structure of the marketing channels between the food processors/manufacturers and food wholesalers/retailers. The dominant core is composed of the large food processors/manufacturers who often operate their own salesforces. Their approach to the market works well with independent food wholesalers who sell to independent retailers and small grocery chains.

These retailers can be thought of as the competitive fringe of grocery retailers. This is not to imply that they are weak. Many have large market shares in local markets but may not be large enough in terms of number of outlets to justify having their own private label products. They rely on the big name manufacturers to provide them with a wide variety of high-quality products, to do the national brand advertising, and to provide them with new products. The smaller retailers use the consumer interest in the nationally advertised, branded, high-quality products to create demand in their local market. This enables them to be competitive with the regional and national chain stores.

Independent grocery retailers can be strong in local markets by finding a niche. These stores maintain their niche in the market by offering special (and high-profit) services to their customers such as live lobsters, fresh flowers, in-store restaurants, and so on. They can concentrate on servicing this upscale segment of the retail grocery market by going along with the national marketing programs offered by the processors/manufacturers in the dominant core. The marketing strategy of the grocers in the competitive fringe is to serve those customers who are attracted by the marketing efforts of the dominant core of manufacturers who have pre-sold consumers with nationally advertised branded products.

In the competitive fringe group there are more than 20,000 small to medium-sized food processors. Some are even owned by food retailers as part of integrated wholesaling/retailing businesses. They tend to specialize in a single processing activity such as cookie making, vegetable canning, or popcorn making. These firms normally have little or no marketing capability and produce products that do not have national recognition. As long as they can achieve their profit margin goals they are happy to sell their product to anyone under a private label. Their success and survival rests with their ability to be very efficient in the physical aspects of food processing and manufacturing.

Integrated wholesalers/retailers and national grocery chains (which can be thought of as dominant core food retailers) like to buy products from these smaller independent processors because they can obtain large volumes of low-priced, private label products which enable them to perform their wholesaling functions more efficiently and profitably. For example, they may be able to reduce the operating costs per unit of their physical distribution systems by handling higher volumes of standardized products. The chains pass some of these cost savings on to the customer in the form of lower prices or special sales to draw people into their stores, hoping to gain increased overall sales and customer loyalty. Thus, the limited marketing capability of the competitive fringe processors fits together nicely with the marketing needs of the dominant core national chain stores. Some large, integrated retailers carry this concept a step further by purchasing or developing their own processing and manufacturing facilities to take advantage of their in-house brand name products (such as Anne Page products at A&P).

The convenience of fit between fringe processors and dominant core retailers can break down when dominant core processors attempt to sell products to the dominant core retailers. For example, when the Campbell's sales representative calls on the A&P buyer to sell canned pork and beans there can be a conflict. A&P has its own in-house brand of canned pork and beans (A&P) that sells for less but probably yields a nice profit margin. Campbell's offers a nationally known brand name and high quality but perhaps a lower profit margin to A&P. The buyer for A&P may be reluctant to stock both products but may have to since some A&P customers expect to find Campbell's brands on the shelves. This type of competition is called the *battle of the brands*, where private label products battle nationally advertised, well-recognized brands for supermarket shelf space.

Channel Leadership

In almost every marketing channel there is a *channel leader*. The channel leader is the firm in the market channel that is recognized as the leader or the innovator whom everyone else follows. Channel leaders initiate new marketing methods such as selling milk in supermarkets in paper or plastic containers instead of in glass bottles delivered to the door. They initiate new business organizations such as franchised fast-food outlets. They often set the pricing standards upon which all other firms in the marketing channel base their pricing decisions.

A market channel leader's power is not absolute. In other words, a leader firm cannot raise its prices to a higher level than competitors without facing a certain loss of market share. But a market channel leader may be the first to raise price following a general increase in operating expenses. All other firms who have experienced a similar increase in expenses will see the wisdom of increasing prices to protect profit margins. If all firms raise prices by approximately the same amount, overall sales may fall slightly but individual firms' market shares should remain roughly the same.

Channel leadership sometimes arises from market power gained through group action. In agribusiness, group action often takes the form of cooperation. There are grower groups such as Sunkist in fresh oranges, Ocean Spray in cranberries, and Diamond Walnuts in walnuts that have been able to achieve this type of leadership. Few assemblers/procurers have been able to amass this type of market power without integrating vertically forward into food processing or backward into agricultural production.

At the food manufacturing level the structure of the industries has evolved to include channel leaders such as Campbell's Soup, Pillsbury, Kraft, Heinz, Mars Candy, Coca-Cola, Anheuser-Busch, and so on. At the retailer level the channel leaders include A&P, Safeway, and Kroger. In food service, the channel leaders include McDonalds, Kentucky Fried Chicken, Pizza Hut, etc.

Channel leadership comes not only from size and financial strength but also from having a well-known product that is highly regarded by consumers. The potential for large sales and profits is what gives market channel power to the owners of a good product or service. For example, a chance to operate a franchise under the name of a popular fast-food chain is considered by many as almost a license to print money, and they will do just about anything to become franchisees. Because of this, these parent firms have market channel power.

The secret to obtaining a high level of power in a market channel is to build overwhelming consumer demand for a product by developing the proper marketing mix. It starts with having a good product with a high level of consumer demand that competitors cannot easily copy. The product needs to be made available in all the right places. It needs to be priced so the firm can maximize its long-run profits without encouraging competitors to enter the market with a similar but lower-priced product. An effective promotional program will help pre-sell the product and encourage market channel participants to cooperate.

In most cases effective promotion means developing a *brand name*. A brand name is a word or group of letters or words that can be recognized and pronounced, that customers will readily associate with the product.

How to Build Channel Leadership

- Start with a good product with a high level of consumer demand that cannot easily be copied.
- Make the product available in all the right places.
- Price the product so the firm can maximize its long-run profits.
- Use an effective promotional campaign to pre-sell the product and encourage market channel participants to cooperate.

McDonald's is a good example of this with its Chicken McNuggets, Egg McMuffins, Big Macs, and so forth. The right promotion may also include use of *trademarks*. A trademark is a symbol that need not be pronounceable but that customers can recognize and associate with a particular firm's products. McDonald's golden arches are a good example of this.

The use of brand names and trademarks is a good way to earn the *consumer's franchise*—the consumer's tacit agreement to continue to buy this firm's product over everyone else's provided the manufacturer lives up its end of the bargain by providing a consistently high level of quality and quantity at a reasonable price. Firms that can achieve this over time have market channel power.

SUMMARY

This chapter discussed the workings of the commodity processing and food manufacturing industries, a major part of the agribusiness marketing system. It explained how processing moved off the farm and how it was one of the first agribusiness industries to capitalize on technological change. The role of each of the participants in these industries was described. The economic factors that influence the geographic size of the marketing area and the location of processing facilities were also discussed. The conduct of these industries was examined using the dominant core–competitive fringe model and the concept of market channel leadership.

QUESTIONS

1. What factors led to the development of the processing-manufacturing sector?
2. What are the differences between marketing agricultural commodities and marketing food products?
3. What determines which firms in the agribusiness marketing system perform the marketing functions?
4. What is the dominant core–competitive fringe model and why is it valuable to those who study the agribusiness marketing system?
5. Define the term *marketing channel* and determine who the typical members are in agribusiness.

11

The Food Wholesaling
and Retailing Industries

Change is a thread that runs throughout all of agribusiness. It is certainly present in the food wholesaling and retailing industries where the final marketing functions for many food products are performed. The activities of food wholesalers and retailers are so closely related that it is difficult to discuss one industry without talking about the other.

This chapter deals with growth and change in these two industries. It begins with a discussion of food retailing and the development of chain stores, supermarkets, and convenience stores. It then moves to the food wholesaling industry and the marketing channels that have developed with food retailing. The chapter also discusses the role that merchandising plays in the success of supermarkets.

THE FOOD RETAILING INDUSTRIES

The history of food retailing in this country is marked by two major developments. Each has had a profound and long-lasting effect on the way Americans buy food. The first was the development of the retail food chain store. The second was the development of the supermarket concept.

The Development of Retail Food Chain Stores

Retail food chain stores developed in response to a number of market forces present during the latter part of the nineteenth century. First, technological advances in the commodity processing and food manufacturing industries made large quantities of a wide variety of food products available for the first time. This meant that these firms had to find reliable markets to absorb the rapidly expanding output from their plants. Second, improvements in transportation and communications made it possible for food retailers to successfully operate large numbers of stores located across wide geographic areas.

A number of food retailers recognized the opportunities these events offered. First, the operation of a large number of retail stores by a single firm would insure that they had a place to market the large volumes of food these suppliers could provide. Second, the purchase of large quantities of food from these suppliers should enable them to buy at lower prices. This combination of large volume and low prices gave these stores a competitive advantage in the market, and the retail food chain store was born.

The retail food chain stores passed some of the cost savings on to their customers in the form of lower food prices. Customers loved it and flocked to this new type of food store. During the 1920s the chain stores' share of the market increased from practically nothing to more than 25 percent of total retail food sales.

At the top end of the scale are such national retail food chains as Safeway, Kroger, A&P, and others, with the largest chains operating as many as 5,000 stores. In addition to these giants there are many other chains that operate fewer stores on a local or regional basis. (A chain store is defined as the operation of eleven or more stores under a single owner.)

The chain stores revolutionized the way food was sold at retail. Their lower prices and wider selection led to a decline in the family-run, single-outlet food stores which are sometimes called ma and pa stores. The age of the chain store meant consumers could now buy an appealing assortment of food for less cost than ever before. People came to rely more and more on purchased food and less on food they produced and processed themselves.

The Growth of Supermarkets and Convenience Stores

In the years following World War II food retailing underwent a second change with the advent of the supermarket. Supermarkets offered the customer a full line of 10,000 to 15,000 items, plus many nonfood items such as household cleaners, health and beauty aids, and so on. A supermarket is set up to be strictly self-service and operates on a cash-and-carry basis. This new arrangement put even more competitive pressure on the ma and pa grocery stores. These family-run operations did not offer much selection with a limited line of only 4,000 to 5,000 items, but they did offer considerably more service, such as phone-in ordering, home deliveries, credit with monthly billing, and often a convenient neighborhood location. What happened to change all this was a major shift in American lifestyles after World War II.

The war years brought a huge upheaval in the way people lived and looked at the world. Americans emerged from this period looking for new ways to do just about everything. In the years after the war consumers were richer, more mobile, and had a wider variety of tastes than ever before. They were also willing to forgo some customer service if it meant lower prices. Supermarkets filled the bill perfectly, and consumers flocked to the new stores with their wide aisles and thousands of items.

Interestingly, it was not the chain food stores that first adopted the supermarket concept. Supermarkets were started by several independent ma and pa stores as a way to compete with the national chains. They were so successful that it became hard for the chains to ignore them. The national chains finally accepted the concept and by the mid-1950s the supermarket method of food retailing was firmly established. As consumers, the way we purchased food was again dramatically changed.

The demise of the ma and pa retail grocery stores left a void in the marketplace. People still needed a local, convenient food store in which to buy a newspaper, get a quart of milk, or grab a pack of cigarettes, sometimes during hours when supermarkets are closed. The convenience store evolved to fill this market niche.

The typical convenience store stocks a limited line of 2,000 to 3,000 high-turnover items often at prices above those found in supermarkets. In return for slightly higher prices the stores offer the convenience of being open almost around the clock, being close by, being fast, and being easy to get into and out of. While there are usually a number of stores where people can buy these convenience items for less, if someone needs a bottle of aspirin or a quart of milk at 11 P.M. on a Sunday, convenience stores are open while other stores are not. Few people buy all their weekly groceries at convenience stores, but just about everyone stops at them occasionally for one or two items. Many convenience stores are part of a chain. The largest chain is the Southland Corporation, which operates 7-Eleven stores.

Retail food stores are classified according to the dollar value of their annual sales. To be classified as a supermarket a store must have annual sales in excess of $1,000,000. To be classified as a superette market a store must have annual sales of between $500,000 and $1,000,000. A small grocery store has yearly sales of less than $500,000. By comparison, convenience stores normally have annual sales of about $300,000 per year. Of the 170,000 retail food outlets in the United States, 20 percent are supermarkets, 60 percent are superettes and small grocery stores, and 20 percent are convenience stores.

MARKETING CHANNELS AND THE FOOD WHOLESALING INDUSTRY

The rise of chain stores coupled with the adoption of the supermarket concept dramatically changed the traditional food marketing channels between wholesalers and retailers. With the rapid growth of chain stores, retailers could exert market channel leadership over the wholesalers because of their financial strength, purchasing volume, and, perhaps more importantly, their control of shelf space in their stores.

One way chains exerted their power was to *integrate* vertically backward in the marketing system by doing their own wholesaling. Some retailers even became processors and food manufacturers. This forced other retail chains to begin operating their own dairy processing plants, meat processing plants, bakeries, and so forth. Some even resorted to contractual integration to reduce costs, bypassing the established wholesalers entirely. By contracting for private label goods, retailers bought directly from processors and food manufacturers and had them ship directly to individual stores or to centrally located distribution centers. These operations became known as *corporate chains* or *integrated wholesale/retail chains* because one firm owned both the retail stores and the wholesale operation. These chains account for nearly 50 percent of total annual retail grocery sales in the United States.

In response to this pressure, many full-service wholesalers and non-chain independent retailers began to form alliances in order to insure their mutual survival. One type of alliance is called the *cooperative affiliated chain*. Here the independent retailers band together as a purchasing cooperative and either acquire or form a wholesaling operation. Through pooled purchasing they gain the same benefits of high-volume buying that are available to the larger chain stores. This cooperative affiliated chain approach is the one adopted by many IGA food stores.

A second type of alliance is the *voluntary affiliated chain*. In this arrangement a food wholesaler seeks out a number of independent retailers who agree to buy products for resale from him. This loosely organized arrangement of independently owned retailers and a wholesaler is used by firms such as Thriftway, United Supers, and Piggly Wiggly. These two affiliated arrangements, cooperative and voluntary, account for about 40 percent of total retail grocery sales.

The remaining 10 percent of the trade between wholesalers and retailers is done by independent wholesalers and independent retailers. The small portion of market share may understate the importance of the independents. Independent retailers may well dominate their local markets despite the efforts of the chain stores. The independents may be more flexible than their large national chain competitors in developing promotional programs and offering special services to customers, and on certain items may even beat them on price. The key to success for independent retail grocers is their ability to find and exploit a niche in a local market. The niche may be extended hours, higher-quality products and services, friendlier help, free coffee for shoppers, check cashing, or carpeted aisles. Whatever it is, it can give them a competitive edge in their market.

FOOD MERCHANDISING TECHNIQUES

The success of food retailers comes in part from the application of good merchandising practices. *Merchandising* is how products are presented to consumers for sale. It includes store layout, the use of displays, allocation of shelf space, and so on. The basic concept behind good merchandising is to design everything in the store to make it easy for the customer to buy. The process begins with locating the store at a place that is convenient to the shopper. The parking lot should be arranged to make parking convenient, with all spaces as close as possible to store entrances and exits.

When the customer enters the store, well-maintained and clean shopping carts should be readily available. Research has shown that once shoppers have a cart, many feel compelled to put items into it. Small hand-carried baskets should also be available for those interested in "just a few things." Without them most people will buy only what they can easily carry in their hands.

The store layout should direct customers through the store. The aisles should be arranged to allow a customer to progress through the store in a logical manner and emerge at the checkout area. One standard arrangement is to begin with fresh fruits and vegetables, move on to meats, then canned and boxed foods, frozen foods, dairy, beverages, and finally bakery and deli items. Another approach is to put deli and bakery departments near the entrance so customers will stop in to buy ready-to-eat items. In this way supermarkets can compete with fast-food restaurants. Nonfood products may be scattered throughout the store or located adjacent to the food portion of the store.

Product Location

Where a product is located in the store and on what level of shelf it is placed can greatly influence volume of sales. This is especially true for items that have many substitutes. Eye level is considered the best location. Slightly above eye level is the second most preferred spot, while the bottom shelf is considered the worst location. Sales can also be increased if an "As Advertised" or other form of "shelf talker" sign is used to attract attention to the product. Regarding product location, colorful end-of-the-aisle product displays and in-the-aisle pyramids can bring about 200–500 percent increases in sales.

The preference for eye-level shelves is why retailers attempt to put their most profitable items there. It is also why food manufacturers' sales representatives are always willing to "help out" store managers by arranging attractive displays of their company's products as a "favor" to the retailer. Because of the inevitable disputes among competitors for prime shelf space, the retail store manager assigns shelf space after consulting the store's computer program. The program allocates shelf space so that it maximizes the *store's* profits after taking into account recent sales data collected by the electronic check-out system. Food manufacturers continually offer special promotions, discounts, and other incentives to secure shelf space and other merchandising advantages from a retailer. Such promotions are also useful to the retailer since they attract new customers to the store which can increase sales and profits.

Price Incentives

Food retailers also use price as part of their promotional campaigns. They typically advertise heavily in the Wednesday, Thursday, and Friday local newspapers since that is when and where most shoppers look for advertised specials before doing their weekly food shopping. These ads emphasize items whose prices are below those of competitors. Retailers may even lower the price of some "big draw" items to below cost in order to entice customers into the store. This marketing tactic is based on the assumption that the shopper will not purchase just the *loss leader* item but will also buy other items on which the store can earn enough profit to more than make up the loss. The process of using loss leader pricing along with regular prices on other items is called *mix pricing*. The use of mix pricing permits the store to hit the typical overall financial goal of a 20 percent gross margin (sales - cost of goods sold) and a 1 percent net profit.

There is one store in the Midwest that makes it a regular policy to have at least six loss leader items advertised each weekend. This includes at least one item in dairy, meat, produce, frozen food, canned food, and nonfood categories. The very real losses on the sale of the loss leaders are made up by either higher sales on all other items with regular profit margins or by temporarily raising the prices on complementary items. For example, if the loss leader is lettuce, then losses may be countered by higher prices on salad dressings displayed next to the lettuce. If the loss leader is hot dogs, losses could be made up by a higher price on hot dog buns. This works because of strong cross price elasticity of demand for these complementary products.

Some shoppers attempt to take advantage of this system by buying only the loss leaders at each market. These people are sometimes referred to as "plum pickers." Retailers have tried to counter this practice by requiring a minimum purchase in order to be eligible to purchase the loss leader. The offer to double or triple the value of manufacturers' cents-off coupons is another price incentive to get shoppers to patronize a particular store.

Other Merchandising Techniques

How can food retailers afford to give away their profits? What they are actually doing is giving up short-term profits to capture a customer for the long run. There is evidence that if a shopper uses a product or patronizes a store three times in a row there is an excellent chance that this person has established a new habit and will continue to purchase the product or patronize the store over the long run. Retailers try to reinforce this relationship by filling as many of a customer's needs as possible. By applying a concept known as one-stop shopping, supermarkets are now offering services like banking, film development, restaurants, garden centers, video rentals, pharmacies, and so on. This concept appeals to many busy consumers especially in two-career families and single-parent households where saving time is of great importance.

Food retailing seems to go through cycles that include various forms of nonprice competition (games, giveaways, trading stamps, and so on). A nonprice promotional program works fine to draw customers into a store, giving it a temporary advantage. But the advantage fades quickly once other stores match it with their own nonprice forms of promotion. These forms of competition can be very expensive. Low margins in food retailing do not allow stores to absorb the increased costs. The costs must eventually be included in the price of food products. As prices rise, an opportunity is created for one store to announce "No more gimmicks! Just low prices!" Customers flock to that store and soon other stores in the area drop their nonprice competition programs in favor of reduced grocery prices. The dilemma is that an individual store cannot use nonprice competition and low prices at the same time. A cycle is created as stores use one tactic and then switch to the other as they try to gain market share.

Food retailers use a variety of merchandising techniques to attract and keep their customers. In addition to the procedures already discussed, they apply a number of rather standard practices such as offering free samples of products, pricing with quantity discounts (2 for 49 cents, 5 for $1.00, and so on), and pricing below the next round number (95 cents or 99 cents rather than $1.00). Because of the frequency of purchases and the amount of money involved, many food shoppers are very price and value conscious. Other food shoppers look for quality and service. People search for a retail grocery store that will satisfy their particular set of needs. The point is that the food retailer who does not focus on the consumer will soon find his customers and profits disappearing.

FOOD RETAILERS AS MARKETING CHANNEL LEADERS

More than 2,000 new food products are introduced by food manufacturers each year, but the amount of supermarket shelf space per store remains fairly stable from year to year. The result is a fierce battle among food manufacturers to get their new products on these already filled shelves when retail grocers control the shelf space allocation. To get a new product on the shelf, a food manufacturer's representative must convince a retail grocer that the product will yield a greater profit per linear foot or cubic foot of shelf space than a product that is already there. The retail grocer has immediate access to sales and profit information from his computer-linked check-out system. If a new product does not sell, a grocery store manager will pull it off the shelf and replace it with another product.

Food manufacturers once had the leadership position in food market channels. Their highly advertised national brand products created sales and profits that retailers could not do without. New products were eagerly anticipated by retail grocers and customers. But the competitive battle among food manufacturers for shelf space and the "gatekeeper" role of retail grocers have combined to shift market power to the grocers. Grocers have increased their market power even more by integrating into wholesaling and even food manufacturing. Retailers use the leverage that this market power gives them to influence the quality, price, and terms of delivery of the products they buy from food manufacturers. Retail grocers as a group say they are the natural choice to be the food marketing channel leaders not only because of their market power but also because they are closer to consumers. Thus, they believe they are in the best position to know the needs of consumers and communicate them to other firms in the food market channel.

SUMMARY

This chapter reviewed the development of the retail food chain stores and supermarkets, and also looked at the relationships between food retailers and wholesalers. A variety of relationships were examined, including direct buying, integrated arrangements, and market nicheing by both food manufacturers and retailers. Various merchandising techniques used by supermarkets were also examined as well as the market channel leadership role that has been assumed by food retailers.

Like many other sectors of the food and fiber system, food wholesaling and retailing are consistently seeking ways to stay abreast of changing consumer preferences. With the growth of single-person households, dual wage earner households, and so on, there is no longer any single "typical consumer." Rather, there exist several forms of typical consumer, each with special needs and desires. Those firms that can best determine and profitably fill these needs are likely to prosper in the future. The guideline to successful food wholesaling and retailing in coming years is change. Those food firms that accept that fact are likely to have a bright future.

QUESTIONS

1. What factors led to the growth of chain stores?
2. What factors led to the growth of supermarkets?
3. What are the differences between a supermarket and a convenience store?
4. What is merchandising and how is it used by food retailers?
5. Define the terms *loss leader* and *mix pricing*, and explain how they are used by food retailers.

12

The Food Service Industry

One of the fastest-growing segments of the agribusiness system is the food service industry. This industry is commonly referred to as the HRI trade: hotels, restaurants, and institutions. It includes all those people and firms involved in serving food at hotels, restaurants, fast-food outlets, schools, hospitals, prisons, military installations, and other away-from-home eating locations. Sales at these outlets represent over one-third of all the money spent on food at the retail level, and the percentage is rising

This growth reflects a change in American lifestyles. Increasing numbers of households include a husband and wife who both work, or a single head of household who must work. There is simply less time for these people to spend on food shopping, preparation, and cleanup. People are willing to substitute money for time by eating away from home. The population is also more mobile. This leads to more people being away from home at mealtime; and even if they are at home, many like to drive to a restaurant to eat. These factors have combined to transform eating out from a luxury to a necessity for many Americans.

FULL-SERVICE RESTAURANTS

The full-service restaurant, where waiters or waitresses serve full meals of breakfast, lunch, and dinner to their customers, has long been a staple of the away-from-home food industry. The secrets to a restaurant's success have always been good food, served in a pleasant environment, with good service and reasonable prices. In addition to meeting the customers' needs outlined above, the operators must accomplish all this at a profit. This means constant attention to cost control, good portion control, and good food-quality control.

The controls are designed to give consumers a consistent quality of product every time they eat at this restaurant. Some people call this "perceived value for the money." This means that each time a customer leaves the restaurant she should feel fully satisfied (that is, her stomach is full and she got her money's worth for the food she bought).

Unfortunately, in today's world this may not be enough. Consumers may face a bewildering number of places to eat when they choose to leave home. In fact, restaurants are the most common type of new business to open *and* close. To counter this, restaurant operators attempt to find a niche in their local market. This accounts for the number of theme restaurants and the amount of "show business" that often accompanies the food. It is important to remember that customers "buy the sizzle, *not* just the steak." This is why they pay extra to get fancy surroundings, waiters with French accents, strolling violin players, and all the rest. Thus, in this highly competitive market, marketing plays a vital role in the success of restaurants.

THE DEVELOPMENT OF THE FAST-FOOD MARKET

As the opportunities for profit in the away-from-home food market became apparent, many well-known food companies became active in this segment of the system by vertically integrating forward into the restaurant business. Examples of this sort of activity are Ralston Purina's operation of the Jack-in-the-Box fast-food chain for a number of years; Pillsbury's ownership of Burger King and Steak'n Ale; and Pepsico's operation of Pizza Hut, Taco Bell, and Kentucky Fried Chicken.

During the past twenty-five years fast food has been a major growth area in agribusiness, especially for places that sell hamburgers, chicken, and pizza. These firms have expanded rapidly through the use of *franchising*. In franchising, the parent firm (the franchiser) sells to others (the franchisees) the right to operate an outlet using the franchiser's name. The franchisee agrees to abide by the franchiser's rules, pay an initial fee, and give the franchiser a royalty on sales. This allows the franchiser to expand very rapidly, with few of the cash flow problems that normally plague rapidly expanding businesses.

The franchisee's fee allows the franchiser to heavily promote its products to the general public, thereby building customer awareness and demand. The continuing royalties, provided the concept is successful, support long-term growth and can make the venture extremely profitable for the original investors. Perhaps most importantly, the franchise approach allows the franchiser to staff the new locations with highly motivated, capable people. It would be difficult if not impossible to hire, train, and motivate the large number of employees required by the rapid expansion of company-owned outlets. Since the purchasers of the franchise own their own businesses, the potential for financial success will motivate them to work many more than eight hours a day if necessary. Initially, they may take little or no money out of the business for themselves in order to establish the new business. Few hired employees are willing to make such sacrifices.

For the franchise fee, the new small business owner (the franchisee) gains the right to start a business that may make him or her a millionaire with little risk of failure. Well-known franchised retail food stores have a very low failure rate compared to that of all new businesses in the United States This is because the franchisee is using a proven business formula. If it is successful for others it has a very high probability of being successful for the new franchisee.

To help insure success, the franchiser provides valuable ongoing business-management help and national advertising. The royalty fees help to pay for these services. New franchisees may find their freedom somewhat restricted by the franchise agreement in which they contract to follow certain business procedures, to be inspected periodically by the franchiser, and to use approved products in operating the business. But the previous success of the franchiser's business formula normally shows that it is wise to adhere to the conditions of the franchise agreement. (The franchiser can set standards and recommend suppliers but cannot require the franchisee to purchase products such as bread, napkins, paper bags, and so on from the franchiser or a specified supplier.)

Franchising in the retail food business has been spectacularly successful because the franchiser gains an inexpensive way to expand the number of outlets quite rapidly. The franchisee realizes the American dream of business ownership, and through hard work is almost guaranteed success because of the proven track record. The consumer is also a winner. Because of the efficient and controlled manner in which franchises operate, the consumer gets consistently good quality food products at convenient locations and at affordable prices.

Pizza Hut

One of the most successful fast-food firms is Pizza Hut. It was begun in 1958 by two college-age brothers who opened the first restaurant around the corner from their family's grocery store in Wichita, Kansas. Within ten years the company had grown to 135 outlets.

To be part of the system, then and now, franchisees pay Pizza Hut an initial franchise fee plus a small percentage of their gross sales. In addition, they are assessed a percentage of their gross sales for national advertising and other services. The franchisees must provide the investment funds for the familiar red-roofed buildings that are built to Pizza Hut specifications.

By 1978 the firm had grown to be the largest pizza seller in the United States with 2,850 outlets. Half of these outlets were company owned and the other half were owned by the franchisees. It was around this time that the parent firm was sold to Pepsico for approximately $300 million. Although Pizza Hut has continued to expand domestically, most of the expansion has been into foreign countries. It is expected that in ten years foreign sales will exceed domestic sales.

To achieve this level of success, Pizza Hut has had to adapt operating procedures and products to changing customer needs. For example, when it entered the German market it encountered several unexpected problems. First, labor costs were high. Second, local custom dictated that managers did not do physical labor in preparing and serving food. These factors raised the costs of operation and reduced the outlets' productivity. Third, the chain found that German people would not eat pizza with their fingers as Americans do. This meant that it had to provide flatware, which it did not do in the United States. (Americans can now get flatware too.)

Pizza Hut has also successfully dealt with changing customer needs here in the United States. Customers had always complained about how long it took to get a pizza after it was ordered. Waits of up to thirty minutes were not uncommon. This is why many consumers have not perceived pizza as a fast food. Lengthy preparation time, especially at lunch, was restricting sales growth. Pizza Hut responded by finding ways to reduce the preparation time and by developing new products that could be prepared quickly. During peak lunch hours Pizza Hut now guarantees that a pizza will be ready in five minutes or the next pizza is free.

Pizza Hut also developed the personal pan pizza so a customer can order a pizza without being part of a group. In addition, the nature of the product was changed to give customers more of what they want—more toppings and cheese. The crust was made thicker to enhance "mouth feel." The physical appearance of Pizza Hut facilities was subtly changed to give a higher-quality image, and more attention was given to providing a spotlessly clean, attractive place to eat.

To maintain customer interest and broaden its customer base, Pizza Hut developed a number of new products and expanded its menus to include salads and other related items. By striving to give customers good value for their money and keeping on top of changing consumer needs, Pizza Hut has prospered.

Kentucky Fried Chicken

Kentucky Fried Chicken (KFC) is another fast-food franchiser that has been successful. The firm was established by a sixty-five-year-old man named Harlan Sanders who hit upon a special mixture of spices and combined it with a method of deep-fat frying of chicken under pressure that people liked. Within a few years he became a millionaire by selling his firm to a group of investors that retained the image of Colonel Sanders and relied on franchising for rapid growth. Because of their aggressive marketing, sales exploded and Kentucky-style fried chicken became very popular. In 1972, this group of investors sold out to Heublein, Inc. for approximately $280 million.

Under Heublein, sales and profits fell. In the opinion of many, both the quality of the food and the appearance of the restaurants began to suffer. The quality of the food reached the point where even the Colonel said publicly that it was terrible. Beginning in 1977 Heublein began to turn things around. Renewed emphasis was placed on value and quality. This culminated in a new program and a slogan for employees called "QUSCVOOFAMP," which stands for quality, service, cleanliness, value, other operating factors, advertising, merchandising, and promotion.

KFC launched a major advertising campaign aimed at removing doubts consumers were thought to have had about the nutritional value of its foods. The campaign included the theme "It's so nice to feel so good about a meal." To remind consumers of KFC's commitment to chicken and quality it later adopted the theme "We do chicken right." The QUSCVOOFAMP program brought increased sales and profits to the firm.

In 1986, Heublein sold KFC to Pepsico. The addition of KFC to its Pizza Hut and Taco Bell chains made Pepsico the largest fast-food company in the United States.

McDonald's

McDonald's is one of the best-known success stories in fast-food franchising. The firm began when the two McDonald brothers migrated to California in the 1930s hoping to become movie stars. While they waited for their big break in the movies, Richard and Maurice McDonald purchased a movie theater and became successful businessmen. They later opened a drive-in restaurant in Pasadena that was so successful that it used six multiple-station milk shake machines. This unheard of level of milkshake sales caught the eye of Ray Kroc a former paper-cup-salesman who had purchased the exclusive sales rights to this type of shake mixer with $10,000 of borrowed money. While investigating the milkshake mixer order, Kroc discovered that the McDonald's drive-in restaurant was packing people in. He negotiated on the spot with the McDonald brothers to let him franchise outlets nationwide.

The number of outlets grew slowly at first, but McDonald's restaurants can now be found all over the world. Franchisees must pay a franchise fee plus royalties on sales to operate at a specific location chosen by the parent company. McDonald's will finance the land and building if the franchisee is unable to do so. Payback is based on a percentage of sales. McDonald's requires all franchise owners to be actively involved in running their outlets. It also requires strict adherence to company standards in all areas, with emphasis on quality of the food, speed and friendliness of service, and cleanliness of the buildings and grounds. How well owners meet the standards determines to a great extent if and when they will be allowed to purchase another franchise. Since McDonald's outlets normally prove quite profitable, the opportunity for multiple franchises is a definite incentive to perform well.

Although known for hamburgers, McDonald's has had great success with french fries. Approximately 70 percent of all customers order french fries, and they account for 20 percent of total sales. Beginning with the original McDonald brothers, french fries were always treated as an important product at McDonald's. For many years they were made each day from freshly peeled potatoes. Franchise owners came to dread this daily chore because of all the problems it involved, including the time required and the disposal of the peels. Today J.R. Simplot in Idaho, a major supplier of frozen prepared french fries for the fast-food industry, provides McDonald's potatoes. However, for McDonald's, J.R. Simplot follows rigid product specifications and a patented process.

The Future

After experiencing strong growth for the past twenty-five years, firms in the fast-food industry are experiencing a maturing of their market and of customer tastes. Fast-food franchising grew up along with the people born in the baby boom era. The last of the baby boomers are out of college while the older ones are now entering middle age. The idea of a burger, fries, and a milkshake served in a paper bag may not have the same appeal that it once did.

Fast-food operators have responded to the changing food preferences of their customers by expanding their menus. First, they brought breakfast back into style. This helped their profits since breakfast is normally a high-profit meal. It also helped to spread their overhead over greater volume. Second, many fast-food restaurants offer "health conscious" or "lite" menu items such as salads, baked potatoes, fish, chicken, and so on. Third, they have upgraded their dinner menus to more closely resemble full-service restaurants in order to attract a larger share of this market. Fourth, they have replaced the flashy, bright, plastic decor with classier surroundings by using wood, plants, and soft lights to imitate the appearance of full-service restaurants. With these types of changes the fast-food chains hope to retain long-time customers by continuing to meet their needs.

THE INSTITUTIONAL FOOD BUSINESS

Another fast-growing segment of this industry is the institutional food business. It includes all those who prepare and sell food to schools, hospitals, and military installations, as well as office buildings and manufacturing plants. Here food is normally prepared in large central kitchens. While much maligned in the past, institutional food has improved dramatically as a result of a variety of technological improvements as well as better professional training. Famous schools such as the Culinary Institute of America in Hyde Park, New York turn out highly trained and respected chefs some of whom are entering the institutional food service industry. With all these advances there is little excuse for poor quality food in an institutional setting.

SUMMARY

The food service industry is one of the fastest-growing segments of the agribusiness system as the trend toward increased consumption of food away from home continues to grow. The most visible aspects of this growth are the increased ownership of retail food outlets by major commodity-processing and food-manufacturing firms and the proliferation of fast-food restaurants. In recent years the entire industry has grown and matured to where it is possible to obtain a quality meal at restaurants at all levels of price. This level of quality and professionalism also extends to the much maligned institutional food market.

The maturation of the HRI industry provides it with a number of new challenges as it attempts to stay abreast of changes in consumer preferences. Concern about the healthiness of foods and the seeming reduction in the amount of time available for eating are affecting the firms in this industry. These changes offer special opportunities to those entrepreneurs with vision. These are being reflected in the greater availability of salads, poultry products, broiled rather than fried foods, and so on, seen in many food-away-from-home outlets today. Success will come to those that can translate changing consumer food preferences to appealing, healthy, well-marketed food products.

QUESTIONS

1. Describe the factors that have influenced the growth of the food service industry.
2. What are the advantages and disadvantages of using the franchise method of growth for both the operator and franchiser?
3. Is the growth of the food service industry likely to continue? Why or why not? What factors are likely to affect future growth?

13

Cooperative Agribusiness

Cooperatives play a major role in agribusiness. That role, as well as the origins and unique features of these organizations, are the subject of this chapter. The interest in cooperatives is twofold. First, cooperatives are a significant part of agribusiness. Second, they represent a challenging area for agribusiness marketing managers.*

BACKGROUND

Farmers own and operate a distinctive form of agribusiness called agricultural cooperatives. An individual cooperative may be referred to as a farmers', growers', or producers' association. If it is affiliated with a major farm organization, it often has Grange, Farmers' Union, Farm Bureau, or Farmers' Equity in its name. Regardless of what it is called, the purpose of a cooperative is to help farmers reduce the prices paid for inputs and to improve the prices received for outputs.

*Portions of this chapter are drawn from James G. Beierlein, Kenneth C. Schneeberger, and Donald D. Osburn, *Principles of Agribusiness Management* (Englewood Cliffs, NJ: Prentice Hall, © 1986; a Reston book). Reprinted by permission of Prentice Hall, Inc., Englewood Cliffs, New Jersey.

Cooperatives play a major role in agribusiness by providing the farmer with the means to integrate vertically backward into the agricultural input sector with *farm supply cooperatives*, and forward into the processing-manufacturing sector through *farm marketing cooperatives*. Many cooperatives perform both types of activities.

Farm marketing cooperatives assist members with the marketing of their products. In 1986 there were over 3,800 such organizations in the United States whose combined net sales were almost $56 billion. As can be seen from Figure 13–1, farm marketing cooperatives have a significant market share of many farm products, and are particularly strong in dairy and grains.

Farm supply cooperatives help members with the purchase of production inputs, such as feed, fertilizer, and fuel. In 1986 there were 2,300 such organizations whose combined net sales were over $15 billion. As can be seen in Figure 13–2, the share of farm inputs purchased through farm supply cooperatives is substantial, and is particularly strong in fertilizer, petroleum products, and farm chemicals.

Despite a decline in the total number of cooperatives, the 5.3 million cooperative members in the United States have seen a steady increase in

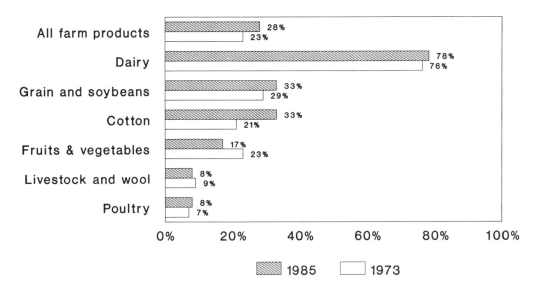

FIGURE 13–1
Cooperatives' Share of Agribusiness Marketing Activity

Source: USDA, *1988 Agricultural Chartbook.*

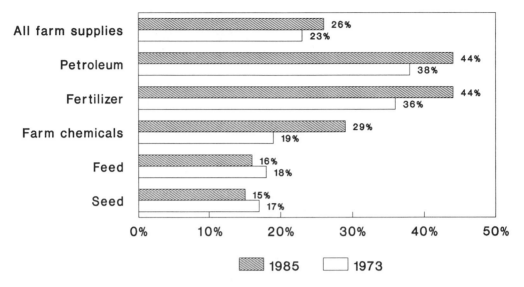

FIGURE 13–2
Cooperatives' Share of Agribusiness Purchasing Activity

Source: USDA, *1988 Agricultural Chartbook.*

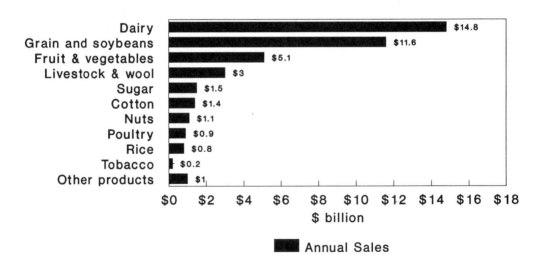

1986 data. Total net marketing
business ▪ $41.5 billion.
Total may not add due to rounding.

FIGURE 13–3
Farm Products Marketing by Farmer Cooperatives

Source: USDA, *1988 Agricultural Chartbook.*

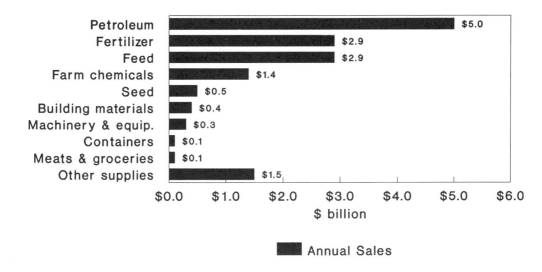

Annual Sales

1986 data. Total net farm
supply business = $15.1 billion.
Total may not add due to rounding.

FIGURE 13–4
Farm Supplies Handled by Farmer Cooperatives

Source: USDA, *1988 Agricultural Chartbook.*

business volume that reached $66 billion in 1986 (Figures 13–3 and 13–4). The reduction in the number of cooperatives has come largely from merger or acquisition activity of individual cooperatives, and from the formation of state and regional cooperatives made up of many local organizations. On the basis of sales, twenty-two of the larger cooperatives would have qualified for *Fortune* magazine's listing of the 500 largest businesses in America, and would include such well-known cooperatives as Land O'Lakes, Sunkist Growers, and Sun-Diamond Growers (Table 13–1).

There is also a third form of agricultural cooperative, called the *service cooperative*, which benefits the agribusiness community. This group of cooperatives includes the Federal Land Banks, Production Credit Associations, Banks for Cooperatives, rural credit unions, rural telephone cooperatives, rural water districts, artificial breeding associations, and dairy herd improvement associations. These service cooperatives also play a vital role in helping America's farmers improve the profitability of their farm businesses and standard of living. Cooperative forms of business have been a major contributor to the success of American agribusiness.

TABLE 13–1   **Agricultural Cooperatives with Annual Sales Large Enough to Be Listed by** *Fortune* **Magazine**

Farmland Industries, Inc.
Agway Inc.
Land O'Lakes, Inc.
AGRI Industries
Associated Milk Producers, Inc.
Grain Terminal Association
GROWMARK, Inc.
Gold Kist, Inc.
Indiana Farm Bureau Cooperative Association, Inc.
Farmers Union Central Exchange, Inc.
Mid-America Dairymen, Inc.
Dairymen, Inc.
CF Industries, Inc.
Landmark, Inc.
MFA Incorporated
Union Equity Cooperative Exchange
National Cooperative Refinery Association
Southern States Cooperative, Inc.
Sunkist Growers, Inc.
Riceland Foods, Inc.
Michigan Milk Producers Association
Sun-Diamond Growers of California

Source: American Institute of Cooperation, *Newsletter*, June 1982.

THE ORIGINS OF COOPERATIVES

Agricultural cooperatives grew in large part out of the dissatisfaction many farmers felt with the way their special needs were being met by input suppliers and processors. In response to this situation, groups of farmers formed cooperatives to do some of these things for themselves.

The objectives of farmer cooperatives have changed little over the past century. Cooperatives continue to seek ways to improve the economic welfare of their members. Their fundamental objectives are:

1. To provide farmers with a dependable, honest, and accurate market for the products they sell and for the supplies they purchase. Farmers want a business that will give them a fair price for products throughout the year and one that will provide them with supplies and services that are properly adapted to their special needs.

2. To increase the farmers' returns for farm products, and to reduce the cost of farm supplies and services.

These two objectives are accomplished primarily by banding together in order to obtain sufficient volume to purchase and sell more efficiently, and by returning all net income above expenses back to the member-patrons of the cooperative.

In addition to the two specific objectives, many feel that cooperatives also provide: (1) a competitive yardstick by which other businesses that serve production agriculture can be measured for the quality, price, and type of service they provide; (2) a way to improve farmers' bargaining power in marketing their products and purchasing their supplies; and (3) a means to maintain the position of the family farm as the primary production unit in agriculture. Through these cooperative efforts, farmers have been able to increase their economic welfare by more efficiently meeting their own needs.

PRINCIPLES OF COOPERATIVES

Cooperation among farmers has been practiced since colonial times when barn raisings, corn-husking bees, and other such events were held. Today's farmer cooperatives incorporate much of this same spirit in the way in which they conduct their business. This is particularly apparent in the principles that these firms use.

Agricultural cooperatives in the United States are organized or chartered by state laws that permit each cooperative to adopt its own special bylaws. These state statutes, however, normally specify that the following general principles of control and operation must be part of the bylaws:

1. *Ownership and control by the producers of agricultural products.* This principle insures that farmers are the beneficiaries of these organizations. Some regulations do permit a small percentage of membership control by non-producers, such as estates and farmers who have recently left farming or have moved out of the trading area.
2. *Voting is limited to one vote per member regardless of the amount of money invested or business done with the cooperative.* This principle insures that all users are given fair treatment by the organization and that large investors or users do not dominate the organization.
3. *The return on capital invested cannot exceed 8 percent or the legal rate of interest in a state (whichever is higher).* This insures that emphasis is placed on improving the efficiency of the marketing or buying

activities rather than on capital appreciation or return from cooperative investment.

4. *At least 50 percent of the cooperative's business must be done with members.* Like the first principle, this helps keep the benefits in the hands of the producers.

5. *The cooperative must distribute most of its net income (net savings) back to the producers based on the amount of business done with the cooperative.* This principle insures that the organization operates for the mutual benefit of the farmers since most income above costs is returned to the members.

In addition to these more specific principles, cooperatives also endorse the ideas of open membership, neutrality in politics, and continual member education. These principles of control and operation distinguish them from other forms of business.

COOPERATIVES AND ANTITRUST LAWS[*]

History

During the latter part of the nineteenth century the rural viewpoint was politically dominant in most states and at the federal level. Many economic conditions that were creating problems for farmers were blamed on such developments as the growth and abuse of economic power wielded by railroads and others. Toward the end of the century mergers of steel companies and firms in other basic industries concerned much of the public. Various political movements developed, and legislation was proposed and adopted to slow the concentration and prevent some of the abuses from recurring.

Interestingly enough, labor felt much the same as agriculture about these giants of industry. While farmers were forming cooperatives and general farm organizations to combat or gain equality with them, labor was organizing unions. The antitrust laws left marketing cooperatives unsure of their legal status and made formation of labor unions almost impossible. Federal legislation affecting cooperatives and labor unions was for the most part identical during the period from 1890 to the early 1920s. From that time on each group received special legislative attention. Farmer cooperatives and labor unions were attempting to correct what they believed were economic

[*]The material in this section is from Thomas A. Brewer, "Farmer Cooperatives and the Struggle for Market Power," *Farm Economics*, Department of Agricultural Economics and Rural Sociology, Pennsylvania State University, November 1974, pp. 2–3.

injustices for their members. To be effective, each group had to unite. The antitrust laws were opposed to the uniting of business firms to gain economic power. It took thirty years of legislation and court actions to differentiate between combinations of farmers or laborers and those of business firms.

The Capper-Volstead Act

The Capper-Volstead Act of 1922 is the primary federal act that establishes the status of farmer marketing cooperatives with respect to antitrust laws. Before the Capper-Volstead Act it was not clear whether farmers combining to form marketing cooperatives were, at the same time, violating antitrust laws. The Capper-Volstead Act authorizes and sanctions the elimination of competition among independent farmers.

It should be observed that the law does not permit cooperatives to operate in ways or indulge in activities that would be illegal for noncooperative forms of business. In a sense, all the legislative and court battles were fought to allow farmers and laborers to achieve organizational parity with noncooperative forms of business organization. The laws do not allow cooperatives to operate any differently than other forms of business.

The act reads in part:

> Be it enacted...that persons engaged in the production of agricultural products as farmers, planters, dairymen, nut or fruit growers may act together in associations...in collectively processing, preparing for market, handling, and marketing in interstate and foreign commerce, such products of persons so engaged. Such associations may have marketing agencies in common; and such associations and their members may make the necessary contracts and agreements to effect such purposes: Provided...that such associations are operated for the mutual benefit of the members thereof... .

It further requires that no member be allowed more than one vote because of the amount of stock or membership capital that he or she may own, and that the associations not pay dividends on stock or membership capital at a rate greater than 8 percent per annum if voting on number of shares of stock or volume of business is permitted. In addition, it is required that every association not deal in the products of nonmembers to such an extent that the value of nonmember products is greater than the value of those handled for members.

The act permits cooperatives to finance their operations with capital stock. Section 2 of the act states that the U.S. Secretary of Agriculture, if he has reason to believe that any association monopolizes or restrains trade in interstate or foreign commerce to such an extent that the price of any agricultural product is unduly enhanced, can serve a complaint on the alleged offender and initiate an inquiry into the matter. If after hearing the evidence he believes that the allegations are true, he may issue a cease-and-desist order to the cooperative. The cooperative has access to the courts for modification or possible set-aside of the order. The Secretary of Agriculture can petition the court to enforce his order. The Department of Justice enforces the order or its modified version. Cooperatives are given no special privileges under this law. It simply allows one group of independent business owners (farmers) to act collectively in marketing without fear of prosecution under the antitrust statutes as long as those combinations do not violate the laws as they apply to actions of other business organizations.

Farmers won legislative permission to organize for marketing purposes without fear of being prosecuted under the antitrust laws. They were now free to make their weight felt in the marketplace and obtain more equitable treatment for farmers.

When one remembers that the legislative posture of the country from the late nineteenth century through the 1920s was inclined toward the rural point of view, it is surprising that the battle was so long and difficult. One can wonder whether today's Congress, with its more urban views, would pass such legislation. The legislation was difficult to achieve but it may be more difficult to keep. Without it, the opportunities afforded individual farmers to achieve economic equality in the marketplace would be seriously hampered.

CLASSIFYING COOPERATIVES

There are several ways to classify farmer cooperatives. Classification can be made by (1) the type of commodity handled, (2) the organizational structure employed, (3) the geographic area covered, and (4) the type of function performed. Each category highlights a different way that cooperatives can go about meeting the needs of their members.

1. Type of Commodity Handled.   The first classification is by type of commodity or product handled. Examples are cooperatives that specialize in marketing grain or cotton, or in purchasing feed or fertilizer. Often a cooperative begins with a single commodity but later finds itself handling others. This sort of diversification is also found in organizations that began by marketing products but now find themselves purchasing inputs. Many cooperatives that predominantly deal with supplies also market grain. In fact, there are more marketing cooperatives handling farm supplies than there are pure farm supply associations.

2. Organizational Structure Employed.   Most farmer cooperatives are owned directly by their farmer members. This form of structure is called a *centralized association*. It operates local facilities that serve local farmers. Throughout the country, the trend in recent years is for local or countrywide cooperatives to organize on a statewide or regionwide basis to perform central or terminal marketing functions such as selling the products, processing of products, and so on. In addition, some regional cooperatives have formed national cooperatives for similar purposes. These cooperatives are made up exclusively of other cooperatives, and this type of organizational structure is called a *federated structure*.

There are also examples of groups that use a combination of the centralized structure and the federated structure, and these are referred to as having a *mixed structure*. In 1977 there were 6,125 centralized local cooperatives, 360 centralized regional, 87 federated regional, 77 mixed regional, and 37 interregional federated cooperatives. Thus cooperatives use a variety of organizational structures to accomplish their objectives.

3. Geographic Area Covered.   Cooperatives may serve more than a single community, county, or region and may find it necessary to divide their organization into different parts in order to serve each part efficiently. To accomplish this, they use either a centralized or federated organizational structure where each part serves a particular geographic area.

4. Type of Function Performed.   Local marketing cooperatives are first handlers of the farmers' products, and local supply cooperatives provide input products and retail services to farmers. But each represents just a single marketing function that must be done to get farm products to the ultimate consumers and farm supplies to the producers. These additional marketing functions, such as finding a place to store grain and trains to haul it, or building a plant to produce fertilizer or petroleum, are normally handled by other parts of a federated cooperative. The forward vertical integration of marketing functions toward the consumer, and backward vertical integration of supply functions to the actual production of farm inputs, can each be handled by a different unit of the cooperative. This approach can also serve as a means to organize the cooperative.

There is no one organizational approach that is always preferred to every other. The organization of any particular cooperative depends in large measure on the situation. The best organizational structure is normally the one that permits most efficient accomplishment of the critical tasks.

THE MANAGEMENT CHALLENGE

The tremendous growth in size and complexity of agricultural cooperatives provides a big challenge to both members and management. Cooperatives have succeeded thus far by efficiently meeting the needs of their members. This task grows exceedingly more difficult as the organization grows larger. Thus, the major challenge facing cooperative managers is to meet the needs of the members, operate efficiently, and keep in mind the cooperative principles upon which they were founded. To accomplish this requires capable managers and boards of directors.

Agribusiness has changed drastically in recent years. Many of today's farmers do not have the same blind loyalty to the cooperative that was present in earlier years. They want to see definite benefits from cooperative membership. For the cooperative to attract and keep its members, it must be constantly searching for better, more efficient ways to serve the needs of all its members.

Having an efficiently-run cooperative requires a well-trained and involved board of directors that sets direction and establishes general policies. All too often boards of directors have been reluctant to give the adequate pay and sufficient decision-making latitude necessary to recruit and keep a strong management team. Continued success, however, will require boards to move more in this direction. This is particularly the case where cooperatives have grown to the point where they can no longer be handled as a small business.

Management Challenges Facing Agricultural Cooperatives

- The need to demonstrate the economic value of the cooperative and its principles to the users
- The ability to attract qualified, well-trained boards of directors who can effectively set the direction and the general policies of the cooperative
- The ability to attract qualified, well-trained managers who can effectively manage the cooperative
- The ability to meet the needs of all the members both young and old, and large and small
- The need to develop a more stable and equitable capital base

Boards of directors must also see to it that the needs of *all* the members are given attention. This is particularly true for young farmers who often have capital constraints and cash flow needs that differ markedly from those of older, more established operators. It is through the process of self-examination and self-renewal that cooperatives can insure their own future.

Another issue challenging cooperatives is the need to develop a more stable and equitable capital base. This implies less use of revolving fund and debt, and more use of permanent forms of capital such as stock.

SUMMARY

The cooperative method of business has been an important way for an individual farmer to join with other farmers to improve their economic well-being. Cooperatives enable farmers to obtain products and services that are properly adapted to their special needs at fair prices throughout the year. The tremendous growth and success of agricultural cooperatives in recent years reflects not only the evolution of agribusiness, but also their ability to efficiently meet the needs of their members.

The principles surrounding the operation of cooperatives have changed very little throughout their history. They continue to be (1) control and membership limited to active producers; (2) one person, one vote; (3) limited return on capital; and (4) operation at cost. These principles of operation are unique to cooperatives and distinguish them from other forms of business. The challenge facing cooperative leadership is how to continue to effectively manage the large complex organizations that have emerged. Continued success requires adherence to the principles of cooperation, as well as strong boards of directors and teams of managers that are always looking for more efficient ways to meet their members' needs in the future.

QUESTIONS

1. Why did agricultural cooperatives develop?
2. How does a cooperative differ from a corporation?
3. What are the major types of cooperatives, and how do they differ?
4. What are the major types of financing used by cooperatives?
5. Describe the challenges facing cooperative managers and directors.

PART FOUR

Agribusiness Marketing Management

The management of the marketing function within an agribusiness firm is the subject of the eight chapters found in this section. Each deals with a separate issue in this area. Chapter 14 develops the need for a marketing plan and outlines the essential elements. Chapter 15 deals with how the needs of consumers should be analyzed and evaluated to determine just which consumer needs the firm feels it can fill the most profitably. The next four chapters discuss how to manage the marketing mix of price, product, place, and promotion to accomplish the marketing and financial objectives established in the firm's marketing plan.

Chapter 20 examines the role that personal selling and merchandising play in successful marketing management. The final chapter in the section examines how an agribusiness firm can reduce its market risk through the use of the commodity futures markets and the options markets. Each offers the firm a way to minimize its exposure to adverse price fluctuations.

14

Developing the Marketing Plan

The first step in the marketing management process is the development of a marketing plan. It sets the direction and tone of the business's marketing efforts. The marketing plan is a part of and in turn influences the firm's total business plan which also includes an organizational plan, a production plan, and a financial plan. Before a firm writes a marketing plan it should decide upon an overall business plan. The *business plan* describes the company's overall approach to its business and how it is going to gain a successful competitive edge in the market. It also includes a clear and concise statement of the firm's purpose and objectives.

While this type of business planning is critical, a formal planning process is a relatively new activity to many agribusinesses. A business plan is required because of today's more complex and competitive business environment. But more importantly it is needed because of the evolution of the food and fiber system from a production-oriented system to a marketing-oriented system. Success in agribusiness in the future will likely depend more heavily on a firm's marketing skills than on its production skills.

Planning is also important because it forces the organization to examine vital issues and encourages systematic thinking about what it will do and how it is going to do it. Many times managers are so involved in doing things necessary for the moment that they fail to deal with what is really important in the long run. The very act of writing out the firm's purpose and objectives on paper makes managers think more clearly about what their firm does.

THE BUSINESS PLAN

The success of many businesses can be traced to a good business plan. The plan tells the managers who wrote it and all others who read it how this firm intends to be successful. It explains what the firm is going to do and how it will do it.

The Firm's Purpose

The business plan begins with a clear, concise statement of the firm's *purpose* that indicates the specific consumer needs it is going to fill. The purpose must be written down and widely publicized so that the owners, employees, lenders, and even customers know it and understand it. It should be accepted as good and worthwhile by all that work for the firm. When all employees know and accept the purpose it gives them a common sense of purpose in their work. This is the first element in forming a cohesive team that will focus their efforts toward the accomplishment of a common goal.

A recent advertisement for a chemical company shared the firm's purpose with potential customers and employees by stating that the firm's purpose is to solve the chemical mysteries that stand in the way of an adequate world food supply. It is hard not to get excited about joining a firm on such a worthy mission.

The Firm's Objective

The next step is to establish the firm's *objective*, which indicates how the firm is going to accomplish its purpose. This is what gives the business its competitive edge. It describes what this firm will do better, cheaper, faster that its competitors, and will cause a consumer to buy this company's products rather than someone else's. The objective could be to have the lowest prices, the highest quality, the largest selection, the fastest service, and so on. Regardless of what it is, the objective is what separates this firm from all of its competitors. The objective should always be built around the efficient, effective, and profitable satisfaction of consumer needs. If a firm fails to put customers and their needs first, customers will buy from another firm which does.

The task of developing a firm's purpose and objective is the responsibility of top management, which sets the broad directions for the firm. The plan will succeed only if top management makes a strong commitment to it and exerts strong leadership to motivate others in the firm toward its accomplishment. Many firms use a system where top management sets the purpose and objective and then middle- and lower-level managers develop the plans necessary for implementation. In this way each manager in the organization feels that his or her efforts contribute toward the accomplishment of the overall, common corporate goal. This helps to keep everyone moving in the same direction.

The planning process should not only include an analysis of existing lines of business, but should also help select which businesses and products should be terminated and which new businesses should be entered. This type of planning is called *strategic planning*. The goal of strategic planning is to match profitable business opportunities with the firm's resource base (people, equipment, technology, and so on).

Analysis of the Market

The business plan is composed of separate subplans that deal with organizational structure, production, and marketing (Figure 14–1). Despite differences, these separate plans have at least two things in common. First, they must all include a financial analysis section so that all the different pieces can be reassembled using common measures of income and expense. Second, each of these plans must include a clear and thorough statement of the consumer needs and preferences the firm intends to fill.

A firm's purpose can be stated without a great deal of consumer input. It can, for instance, be based on an analyst's assessment of what consumers seem to need. But if the assessment process ends here, it may be doomed to failure. Success requires that the firm adopt the proper marketing mix of price, product, place, and promotion. This can only be accomplished after consumer preferences and needs have been thoroughly researched through a *market analysis*. This process permits the clear identification of a firm's objectives since it clarifies the precise needs and consumer groups the company will service, as well as how the needs will be filled. This process is the subject of the next chapter.

Once the market analysis process is complete, the firm should have enough information to begin planning the proper marketing mix. This is why marketing normally takes priority over all other activities in the firm's planning process. Marketing people are responsible for identifying, analyz-

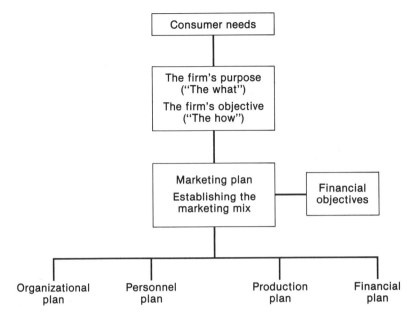

FIGURE 14–1
The Business Planning Process

ing, and understanding the consumer needs that the rest of the firm is being organized to fill. Finance tells the firm whether it can be done profitably. Production tells the firm whether it can be done technically. Personnel tells the firm whether the right people can be found to accomplish it. But the decisions about what the "it" is and how "it" should be done are determined by the marketing people after careful analysis of consumers in the marketplace.

Marketing is a central player in this process, but it does not act alone. It takes all those people in finance, production, personnel, and so on working in concert with marketing to profitably meet the consumer needs identified by marketing. Some have likened marketing to the engine of a car, with finance supplying the fuel to operate it. If everyone in the firm accepts a marketing approach to the activities of the firm, it can lead to a more effective meeting of consumer needs, which translates into higher profits for the firm. With these ideas firmly in place, let's turn our attention to a more detailed discussion of the marketing plan which is the starting point of all the other business planning activities.

THE MARKETING PLAN

After establishing the firm's purpose and objective, the marketing plan becomes the starting point for the rest of the planning process. The marketing plan gives a complete assessment of all the factors surrounding the consumer needs the firm hopes to fill. Most plans involve either single products or lines of products. Philip Kotler has developed a rather complete outline of what such a plan should include. The plan covers the following topics: the current situation, opportunity and issue analysis, objectives, marketing strategies, implementation plans, financial analysis, and needed controls.[*]

The Current Market Situation

The first step in developing the marketing plan is to correctly assess the current situation of the firm and its products.

1. The Market Situation. This section gives the background and current situation on consumer needs, perceptions, and buying trends. It should include data on the current size and past growth of the market in total, by submarkets, and by geographic area.

2. The Product Situation. For a current product, the recent history of its sales, revenues, costs, and profits should be presented.

3. The Competitive Situation. The major competitors are identified in this section and described in terms of their size, goals, market share, product quality, marketing strategies, and anything else that is appropriate to understanding their position in the market or their intentions.

4. The Distribution Situation. The sales made through each type of middleman in the distribution channel (such as brokers, direct sales, wholesalers, and retailers) and the level of importance attached to each should be identified. This section should also cover the prices, practices, and trade terms currently used to motivate these groups of firms to do a good job.

5. The Macroeconomic Environment. The relevant general economic situation that has a bearing on sales of the firm's product is discussed

[*]Phillip Kotler, *Marketing Management: Analysis, Planning, Implementation, and Control*, 6th ed. (Englewood Cliffs, N.J.: Prentice Hall, •1988), p. 77. Used by permission of Prentice Hall.

here. Such a discussion should include factors such as demographics, the economic climate, technology, the political situation, legal issues, social issues, cultural issues, etc.

Opportunities and Issue Analysis

Based on the analysis of the current situation, the marketing manager needs to identify the market opportunities and issues the firm and its products are likely to encounter.

1. Opportunities and Threats Analysis.   This part deals with the main opportunities and threats that face the business in general and the product in particular from factors *outside the firm*. These items should be placed in order of importance so that the more important ones can be given greater attention. Each should be accompanied by a suggested response by the firm.

2. Strength and Weakness Analysis.   The main strengths and weaknesses of the company and the product should be discussed here. These are the factors *within the firm* that can be built upon or need to be corrected.

3. Issues Analysis.   Using the findings from the analysis section helps the firm define the main issues that should be addressed in the marketing plan. The identification of issues is important because certain issues may limit the choices the firm has as it sets its marketing objectives and establishes marketing strategies. The types of issues that should be analyzed include such strategic matters as types of new products the firm should produce and whether it should continue to produce existing products.

4. The Objectives.   Now that the market situation and issues are clearly defined, the firm needs to establish both its financial and marketing objectives. The *financial objectives* are normally established first and are typically set for one year or longer. Financial objectives can be items such as "an average return on investment of 20 percent per year" or "a profit of at least $250,000 per year." They must be established using some measurable criteria such as dollars or percentages, and be internally consistent (for example, dollar profit figures should be possible given the level of investment and sales).

The *marketing objectives* are based on the financial objectives but must be converted into marketing terms. For example, to achieve the minimum profit levels set in the financial objectives, the firm must convert these to sales goals in terms of units sold, dollars, and prices. These goals should then be given some ranking so that the manager will know, for example, whether it is more important to meet the unit sales or the dollar sales objective.

5. The Marketing Strategy. This is where the firm sets its basic approach to achieving its objectives. It includes broad decisions on the selection of target markets, market positioning, marketing mix, and marketing expenditure levels. What the manager is looking for is the best combination of the 4 Ps that will enable him or her to achieve the financial and marketing objectives set forth above.

The specific items that must be covered by this section include:

- *Identification of target markets.* Exactly what consumer needs the firm is going to fill and for which groups of consumers.
- *Product positioning.* What thoughts your product brings to the mind of the consumer (for example, best quality available, lowest price, best service around).
- *Size of the product line.* The number and types of products the firm will offer.
- *Price.* The product's price relative to that of competitors' prices for similar products.
- *The number and types of distribution outlets.* How, where, and by whom products will be distributed to consumers.
- *The size and type of sales force.* What size, type, and quality of sales force is needed to accomplish the objectives.
- *The level and quality of service.* The type and number of service facilities and the level of service offered by each type.
- *Advertising.* The amount of advertising and which media to be used in reaching the firm's marketing and financial objectives, as well as an evaluation of the success of previous advertising efforts.
- *Sales Promotion.* The amount and types of sales promotions that will be used to reach the firm's marketing and financial objectives, as well as an evaluation of the success of previous sales promotion efforts.
- *Research and Development.* The amount, types, timing, and expected success of research and development efforts.
- *Market Research.* The amount and types of market research that is being undertaken to help the firm accomplish its marketing and financial objectives.

Each of these items deals with factors that the firm has control over and that can be made part of its marketing mix of product, price, place, and promotion. To be successful these marketing plans must be coordinated with all the other activities of the company to insure that the timing is correct and the resources needed to support these efforts are available.

6. The Implementation Program.   Once the marketing plan is approved, the marketing manager needs to have an implementation program that will effectively and efficiently turn the plan into reality. Poor implementation is the cause of more failure than poor plans. The implementation plan should include clear statements as to who is to do what, by when, for whom, and for how much.

7. Financial Analysis.   This section translates the marketing plan and the implementation program into revenues and expenses. On the revenue side, the impacts of decisions on price, product positioning, changes in sales force, changes in distribution channels, level of service, and so forth are all incorporated into the forecast of future sales and revenue levels. On the expense side, the cost of additional service facilities, sales personnel, advertising, and so on are also tallied. Revenues and expenses are combined to show how the marketing plan will contribute to the attainment of the financial and marketing objectives established earlier. This final step of putting the plans and strategies into financial terms helps marketing managers see the consequences of their decisions and how all the pieces fit together.

8. The Controls.   The next step is to decide what types of control or feedback mechanisms are needed to measure the firm's and the product's progress toward the accomplishment of the objectives. Controls often take the form of quarterly or monthly reports. These reports should help managers spot any serious deviations from expectations early on so corrective action can be taken before things get seriously out of hand.

Through use of the marketing plan a company is able to develop a systematic way to analyze the market it hopes to serve and to map out a route to success. The subject of market analysis is treated in greater detail in the next chapter. The selection of a successful marketing mix is also covered in greater detail in subsequent chapters in this section.

THE RELATIONSHIP OF THE MARKETING MIX TO SALES AND PROFITS

In order to develop an effective marketing plan, a marketing manager must first understand the relationships among the four elements of the marketing mix and their effects on sales and profits. The goal is to find just the right mix of product, price, place, and promotion that will generate the sales needed to maximize profits. There are a variety of methods that companies use to accomplish this, ranging from large, complex computer models to simple judgment models. The more complex models are beyond the scope of this text, but the judgment models are quite useful and are easy to understand and use.

The *judgment model* establishes profit and sales estimates based on the judgment of experts in the area regarding the response of sales and profits to given changes in the marketing mix. Let's begin by using the profit equation discussed in Chapter 5. In it profit (π) is equal to total revenue (TR) minus total cost (TC) or

$$\pi = TR - TC$$

Total revenue is determined by the multiplication of product price per unit (P_y) by quantity sold (Y) or

$$TR = P_y \cdot Y$$

Total cost is assumed to be equal to the sum of the total fixed costs (TFC) (for example, the cost of the buildings, property, and equipment) plus total variable costs (TVC) plus the cost of marketing in the form of advertising (A) and promotion (M) or

$$TC = TVC + TFC + A + M$$

Total variable costs can be redefined to be

$$TVC = R \cdot Y$$

where

$$
\begin{aligned}
R &= \text{variable costs per unit of output} \\
Y &= \text{number of units of output}
\end{aligned}
$$

Recombining these terms gives:

$$
\begin{aligned}
\pi &= TR - TC \\
&= P_y Y - RY - TFC - A - M \\
&= (P_y - R)Y - TFC - A - M
\end{aligned}
$$

This profit equation is then combined with data from a hypothetical firm in Table 14–1 where total variable costs per unit (R) are equal to $10/unit and total fixed costs (TFC) are equal to $100,000. A group of experts within the firm are then asked to estimate the level of sales that they feel would be generated from changes in one item of the marketing mix when all others are held constant. For example, if the level of expenditure for advertising and promotion is held constant while the price is changed (marketing mix #5), the new estimated level of profits is $50,000.

This same procedure can be done while holding price constant and adjusting either the level of expenditure for advertising or promotion or both. The results of this process can be put in table form as shown in Table 14–1 to determine the highest levels of profit from the various marketing mixes numbered 1 through 8. Based on this table from the judgment sample, the largest profits should occur using marketing mix #3 where the price is set at $25 with $50,000 spent on advertising and $25,000 spent on promotion. So it is possible, by using a judgment model based on the opinion of experts in the field and a simple profit equation, to make decisions based on the relationship that exists among the different marketing mixes and the level of sales and profits.

ADDING AN INTERNATIONAL DIMENSION TO THE MARKETING PLAN

In today's world the successful agribusiness firm thinks in terms of markets that extend beyond national borders. The growth and development of many countries around the world have made them potential consumers of many of

TABLE 14–1   Hypothetical Marketing Mixes

Marketing Mix No.	Price	Quantity	Advertising Expenditure	Promotion Expenditure	Profit
1	$25	20,000	$25,000	$25,000	$150,000
2	25	21,000	25,000	50,000	140,000
3	25	22,000	50,000	25,000	155,000
4	25	23,000	50,000	50,000	145,000
5	50	5,000	25,000	25,000	50,000
6	50	6,000	25,000	50,000	65,000
7	50	7,000	50,000	25,000	105,000
8	50	8,000	50,000	50,000	120,000

$\pi = (Py - R)Y - TFC - A - M$
$R = \$10/\text{unit}$
$TFC = \$100,000$

our products. However, these foreign markets need to be examined and approached with the same careful analysis that is used for domestic markets.

A number of leading agribusiness firms such as Coca-Cola, H.J. Heinz, McDonald's, Kentucky Fried Chicken, Pizza Hut, and others have had great success from foreign expansion. Many foreign firms sell their products in the United States. The United States is one of the largest and richest markets in the world for agribusiness products. Some foreign agribusiness firms have been very successful here, for example, Nestlé, Ciba-Geigy, Massey-Ferguson. The result is a new breed of firm called a *multinational corporation* which markets products worldwide. These companies look to world markets for both purchases and sales. A multinational corporation may purchase raw materials in South America for a production facility in Asia whose output is destined to be sold in Europe.

The addition of an international dimension to a company's marketing plan may be exciting, but it can also be filled with problems. For this reason the market analysis for international sales requires greater precision. Strong use of foreign national marketing and management talent may be called for to insure that no big blunders are made and to give the company more understanding of foreign markets. For example, Coca-Cola found that before it sold its soft drink in China it had to change its name. It did this after finding out that in Chinese, Coca-Cola means "bite the wax tadpole." A new name was selected that translates to "may the mouth rejoice."

The market analysis process for international markets must be expanded. First, what is the attitude of consumers in each country to foreign-produced goods, especially those made in the United States? If the attitude is not friendly, the company should look elsewhere. Second, what is the attitude of the government of the country to imports, and how efficient is its bureaucracy at handling the regulations that affect the conduct of business? If the country has many barriers to imports or if the bureaucracy is cumber-

---

Questions Companies Should Ask
Before Expanding into Foreign Markets

- What is the people's attitude in the country toward foreign-produced goods?
- What is the attitude of the government of the country to imports? How efficient is its bureaucracy at handling regulations affecting the conduct of business?
- What type of monetary stability and currency controls exist?
- How stable is the political system?

some, it may pay to look elsewhere. Third, what type of monetary stability and currency controls exist that may limit a firm's profit potential and control of its own financial affairs? Fourth, how stable is the political system? Wide swings in a country's enthusiasm for foreign investment can leave a multinational firm at great peril.

These factors are often hard to evaluate, especially if a firm has never been involved in foreign markets before. The commonsense response of many firms has been to take a go-slow approach to international markets. The first attempt might be to find new markets for existing products in foreign countries. The firms can then fill the needs of these new customers in much the same way that they satisfy domestic customers except that their regular products are exported to foreign countries. This straight extension of product marketing to international markets is fairly inexpensive and less risky than some other approaches. The situation does, however, normally call for the adoption of a slightly different marketing mix to fit the special needs of the foreign consumer. For example, advertising is normally changed to fit the country. Often, after the firm has been successful at this level and feels comfortable in the new foreign environment, it may seek to develop new products or adapt existing products to meet the specific needs of foreign consumers.

To be successful in any market, foreign or domestic, requires that the firm understand the workings of the market as well as the needs of the consumers in it. If the firm tries to lump all foreigners together it will fail. Again, careful market analysis and attention to meeting consumers' needs efficiently and effectively are the secrets to success.

THE RELATIONSHIP BETWEEN WELL-DEFINED MARKETING GOALS AND LONG-RUN PROFITS

There is evidence that firms achieve higher rates of return on invested capital when they have a clearly focused marketing objective. The objective might be to be the lowest-cost producer in the industry, the dominant seller in a clearly segmented customer market, or to sell highly differentiated, high-priced products that emphasize quality. Those firms that do not have a well-defined marketing objective or just copy the actions of competitors in the marketplace often have returns on investment that are average or below average. Without a well-defined marketing objective the firm has no competitive edge in the marketplace.

Consumers see little reason to buy an average product from an average firm when they can get exactly what they want from a firm that gives them special attention. It is clear that consumer market analysis and goal setting is worth the effort when viewed from the standpoint of return on investment.

MARKET STRUCTURE AND THE MARKETING PLAN

The structure of a market can also be a major factor in the development of a successful marketing plan. The structure of the market here means the number and size of firms in a market. The size of firm refers to its share of the total market. A relatively small firm may be the dominant player in a specific market if it has a large share of the total market. The firm's size and its objectives relative to a particular market and competitors can have a great influence on the firm's marketing plan.

As was seen in the dominant core–competitive fringe model, marketing channel leaders tend to dominate an industry. A firm may attempt to become a dominant marketer in a number of ways. First, it can seek to expand the total market for its products by searching for new users and new uses for its products. Second, it can develop new products that will allow it to gain a greater share of the total product market at the expense of its competitors. Third, it can do everything possible to protect the market share it already has while trying to find new ways to expand it.

By being aggressive and following a well-thought-out marketing plan, a market leader can keep competitors at bay. By seeking a larger market share a firm hopes to enjoy higher profits. Research has shown that larger market shares generally lead to higher profits and higher returns on investment. The higher profits come primarily from lower costs per unit due to economies of size as sales volume rises, but may also come from the firm's ability to charge slightly higher prices than competitors because customers perceive its product to be more desirable.

How a Firm Can Become a Market Leader

1. Expand the total market for its product by searching for new uses and new users.
2. Develop new products that will allow it to gain a greater share of the total market.
3. Do everything possible to protect its existing market share while looking for ways to expand.

Firms on the competitive fringe can adopt a high-risk marketing strategy of challenging those firms in the dominant core for leadership or a low-risk marketing strategy of being content to be merely an industry follower. If the firm aspires to industry leadership it must take some risks. The firm must develop a solid, well-focused marketing plan that has as its major objective the attacking of dominant core firms.

When a firm does this it usually develops a slightly better product or starts a large-scale advertising campaign, both of which can be expensive. Another approach for a competitive fringe firm that wants to grow is to take market share away from other competitive fringe firms. This is usually a less costly, less risky route to growth. But at some point the large dominant core firms will notice the upstart firm and fight back. That is where the risk comes. Of course the least risky course of action is to continue as a competitive fringe firm and remain content with a small market share and correspondingly small profits. Even this marketing strategy is not risk free. A new development in product technology or aggressive marketing by a dominant core firm can put a timid firm's future in jeopardy.

Another strategy that has proven profitable for small firms is to find a market niche and forget about the size of the firm's share of the total market. A market niche is a small segment of the total market that is being ignored by other firms in the market. The special needs of customers in the market niche or the size of the market niche in terms of sales potential may not be of interest to a large firm. Ideally, a market niche is easily defined, offers profit to a firm willing to serve it, and has growth potential (although by definition market niches are small relative to the total market). Unfortunately, all too often successful marketing within a niche attracts competitors.

It is clear from this discussion that firm size and marketing objectives do influence the marketing plan. The marketing plan should reflect industry structure and a firm's place in the industry if the firm wishes to be successful.

SUMMARY

This chapter outlined the need for a marketing plan as part of a company's overall business plan. Marketing planning is shown to be important because it often forces an organization to examine vital issues and encourages systematic thinking about what the firm is to do and how it is to do it. Often just the act of writing out the firm's purpose and objectives makes managers think more clearly about the future.

The first step in the market planning process is the business plan. The business plan includes the firm's purpose (that is, what consumer needs the firm is going to fill) and objectives (that is, how the firm is going to gain its competitive edge in the market). The process begins with a clear definition of consumer needs. This helps the firm to better define its purpose and objectives. These are combined with the business's financial objectives in the marketing plan. The marketing plan is the centerpiece of this planning process, with the four Ps of the marketing mix being the instruments that are employed to transform this plan into reality. The marketing plan establishes the parameters needed to develop the organizational, personnel, and other subplans.

The marketing plan is a complete assessment of all the factors surrounding the firm's ability to fill the consumer needs specified earlier. There is growing evidence that attention to this type of market planning leads to greater profits and higher financial returns. This method is successful because in today's highly competitive markets consumers can see little reason to buy an average product from an average firm when they can get exactly what they want from a firm that gives them special attention.

QUESTIONS

1. Why is it important for the firm to have a detailed business plan?
2. What is the difference between the firm's purpose and objectives, and why must they be decided upon by top management?
3. Why does marketing take priority over production, finance, and all other activities in the firm during the development of the business plan?
4. Outline the major parts of the marketing plan, and explain how financial objectives are related to marketing objectives.
5. What is a judgment model and why is it valuable to marketing managers?

15

Analyzing the Market

One of the most important tasks in developing a marketing plan is the analysis of markets. It is a critical part of the firm's strategic plan whose goal is to match the company's resources with profitable business opportunities. This planning process becomes a good deal easier when a number of solid business opportunities have been clearly identified. Market analysis is devoted to the identification and evaluation of business opportunities. It is also concerned with how target markets are identified and segmented, and how a product is positioned in the mind of the consumer. It is to these tasks that this chapter is devoted.

Successful marketing requires a great deal of information about consumer needs. It is the responsibility of marketing research to provide the marketing manager with the data needed to make these types of decisions. This is especially true today when marketing managers are usually physically separated by many miles from the consumers of their products. Market analysis is the only way the firm can stay in touch with consumer preferences.

IDENTIFYING MARKET OPPORTUNITIES

Firms in the food and fiber system are in the process of transforming their approach to the market from a mass marketing to a target marketing approach. Mass marketing most closely resembles the production approach to the market discussed in Chapter 3. In *mass marketing* all consumers are assumed to have the same set of needs, so a firm needs only to produce a single product and use a single marketing approach to meet the needs of each consumer. For example, if a firm sells hamburgers and *most* people prefer a well-done burger with ketchup, a little mustard, pickle, and onion, it will offer only that one product since that is what will satisfy most people. Promotion is standardized so that the same advertisements, coupons, and so on are used in all geographic markets because it is assumed that the response of all potential customers will be the same.

Mass marketing is the perfect counterpart to mass production. From the perspective of the firm, it has a number of attractive advantages. Mass marketing is low-cost, efficient and easy to do. It fits in nicely with the misconception many people have that marketing is the disposal activity of production. But in today's market the "one size fits all" approach to marketing generally leaves many consumers at least a little bit unsatisfied.

Target Marketing

In recent years agribusiness firms have come to appreciate the added profits possible from target marketing. Under the *target marketing* approach, consumer needs determine the product characteristics and marketing programs. Firms adjust their production and marketing efforts to produce and sell goods that are designed to fill the specific needs of targeted groups of consumers. Firms produce a product *for* a specific market under the target marketing approach, not *to* a general market as is done under the mass marketing approach.

Let's continue the hamburger example and assume that the firm conducts some market research and finds that consumers like burgers prepared a number of ways. The firm responds to this situation by giving the customer a choice as to how well done the burger should be, what types of toppings to add, what type of bun to use, and so on. The firm could advertise "we do it your way" in an attempt to attract more of the targeted consumer audience. This leads to greater satisfaction on the part of consumers since they are more likely to get a product that will exactly fill their needs rather than having to settle for what is available.

Under the target marketing approach marketing is no longer the disposal activity of production. Market research provides producers with the information they need to better understand their consumers so that they can better serve them. Marketing costs may increase, but in return for the higher level of satisfaction consumers are often willing to pay higher prices and buy more of these products.

Target marketing is more expensive and difficult to manage, but it is also generally more profitable to the producer and more satisfying to the consumer. If a company chooses not to adopt the target marketing approach it does so at its own peril since there are competitors who will. Consumers quickly learn which firms do the most to satisfy their needs and will buy accordingly.

The objective of target marketing is to develop a unique and effective marketing mix that will completely satisfy a previously unmet or only partially met set of consumer needs. This permits a company to develop a monopolistically competitive situation where it may be able to increase profits by offering consumers something no other firm has and that cannot be easily copied by competitors. To accomplish this requires that producers increase their understanding of consumers and consumer buying habits.

What Is a Market?

This leads to the definition of a market. *A market is a group of current or potential consumers with similar unmet needs and purchasing power*. This definition is given in terms of consumer needs, not in terms of a product. This is important because basic consumer needs tend to change slowly if at all, while products come and go. It is the satisfaction of consumer needs rather than the development of a particular product that makes target marketing work. For example, when it was found through market research that consumers were seeking quick, nutritious, high-quality prepared dinners, firms responded with shrimp florentine, beef stroganoff, lobster thermidor, and other frozen dinners that can be cooked quickly in a microwave oven. These meals were more interesting than the traditional TV dinners, and they filled a need that previously had been inadequately met. Firms that responded to the need found that the target market was enormous and highly profitable, and a whole new dimension was added to the market for frozen dinners.

Markets also have geographic boundaries. While it is commendable to have as a goal the satisfaction of consumer needs worldwide, it is more practical to think of more geographically limited markets. First, target marketing is based on the idea of that there are individual differences in consumer needs. These differences are often quite large even within seemingly homogeneous geographic areas such as the United States. Imagine the differences in needs around the world with all the different cultures, religions, customs, and so forth. Second, even if these needs could be properly identified, it would be extremely difficult to fill them all profitably.

Within a limited geographic area the needs of consumers are often best defined after separating consumers into groups according to common demographic characteristics such as age, sex, household size, level of education, and marital status. Demographic characteristics are used for two reasons. First, they are usually closely associated with specific sets of consumer needs. Second, these data are fairly easy to obtain for specific geographic areas. By tying consumer needs to demographic information it is possible to more clearly identify specific groups of consumers and their desires—in other words, target markets.

There are a variety of ways in which marketers can group consumers. Kotler offers several interesting approaches. The first is to separate consumers according to social class (Table 15–1). The second is by stage in the family life cycle (Table 15–2). Table 15–3 offers a summary of the typical variables and breakdowns used in consumer markets.

Identifying Target Markets

The market identification process begins with the identification of consumer needs, benefits sought, and preferences. These have to be narrowed down to something fairly specific so the identified needs can be met by a single product. While the identification process should not be tied to any existing product, it should be conducted using productlike terms. The needs of consumers are then matched on several sought-after productlike characteristics to see if any patterns emerge.

For example, let's assume a number of consumers are interviewed about the characteristics of soft drinks they like best for a potential new product. As part of this interview they are asked to give their preferences on the levels of product sweetness and carbonation. When these responses are graphed they may give results that look like those found in Figure 15–1A, B, and C on page 195. In graph A no pattern of preferences emerges. The appropriate marketing response is to select any combination of these two preferences for incorporation into the new product. If the results are like those found in graph B, then some moderate amount of sweetness and carbonation are called for. To deviate from this strong consumer preference would be too risky. If the results are like those found in graph C, there appears to be three distinct combinations of product characteristics that appeal to consumers. In Group I the preference is for high sweetness and low carbonation. In Group II the preference is for high levels of both. In Group III the preference is for low sweetness but high carbonation.

Let's assume that the results of the consumer interviews are those from Figure 15–1C and that three groups of consumer preferences have been discovered. The next step is to match these preference groups with demographic information. The people in Group III may tend to be highly educated

TABLE 15–1   Characteristics of Seven Major American Social Classes

1. *Upper uppers (less than 1 percent).* Upper uppers are the social elite who live on inherited wealth and have a well-known family background. They give large sums to charity, run the debutante balls, maintain more than one home, and send their children to the finest schools. They are a market for jewelry, antiques, homes, and vacations. They often buy and dress conservatively, not being interested in ostentation. While small as a group, they serve as a reference group for others to the extent that their consumption decisions trickle down and are imitated by the other social classes.

2. *Lower uppers (about 2 percent).* Lower uppers are persons who have earned high income or wealth through exceptional ability in the professions or business. They usually come from the middle class. They tend to be active in social and civic affairs and seek to buy the symbols of status for themselves and their children, such as expensive homes, schools, yachts, swimming pools, and automobiles. They include the nouveaux riches, whose pattern of conspicuous consumption is designed to impress those below them. The ambition of lower uppers is to be accepted in the upper-upper stratum, a status that is more likely to be achieved by their children than themselves.

3. *Upper middles (12 percent).* Upper middles possess neither family status nor unusual wealth. They are primarily concerned with "career." They have attained positions as professionals, independent businesspersons, and corporate managers. They believe in education and want their children to develop professional or administrative skills so that they will not drop into a lower stratum. Members of this class like to deal in ideas and "high culture." They are joiners and highly civic minded. They are the quality market for good homes, clothes, furniture, and appliances. They seek to run a gracious home, entertaining friends and clients.

4. *Middle class (31 percent).* The middle class are average-pay white- and blue-collar workers who live on "the better side of town" and try to "do the proper things." Often, they buy products that are popular "to keep up with the trends."Twenty-five percent own imported cars while most are concerned with fashion, seeking "one of the better brand names." Better living means "a nicer home" in a "nice neighborhood on the better side of town" with "good schools." The middle class believes in spending more money on "worthwhile experiences" for their children and aiming them toward a college education.

5. *Working class (38 percent).* The working class consists of average-pay blue-collar workers and those who lead a "working class lifestyle," whatever their income, school background, or job. The working class depends heavily on relatives for economic and emotional support, for tips on job opportunities, for advice on purchases, and for assistance in times of trouble. A working class vacation means "staying in town," and "going away" means to a lake or resort no more than two hours away. The working class maintains sharp sex role division and stereotyping. Car preferences include standard size and larger cars, rejecting domestic and foreign compacts.

6. *Upper lowers (9 percent).* Upper lowers are working, not on welfare, although their living standard is just above poverty. They perform unskilled work and are very poorly paid, although they are striving toward a higher class. Often, upper lowers are educationally deficient. Although they fall near the poverty line financially, they manage to "present a picture of self-discipline" and "maintain some ei. .rt at cleanliness."

7. *Lower lowers (7 percent).* Lower lowers are on welfare, visibly poverty stricken, and usually out of work or have "the dirtiest jobs." They are seldom interested in finding a job and are permanently dependent on public aid or charity for income. Their homes, clothes, and possessions are "dirty," "raggedy," and "broken-down."

Source: Philip Kotler, *Marketing Management: Analysis, Planning, Implementation, and Control,* 6th ed. (Englewood Cliffs, NJ: Prentice Hall, © 1988), p. 178. Reprinted by permission of Prentice Hall, Inc., Englewood Cliffs, New Jersey.

FIGURE 15–2   An Overview of the Family Life Cycle and Buying Behavior

Stage in Family Life Cycle	Buying or Behavioral Pattern
1. Bachelor stage: young, single people not living at home.	Few financial burdens. Fashion opinion leaders. Recreation oriented. Buy: basic kitchen equipment, basic furniture, cars, equipment for the mating game, vacations.
2. Newly married couples: young, no children.	Better off financially than they will be in near future. Highest purchase rate and highest average purchase of durables. Buy: cars, refrigerators, stoves, sensible and durable furniture, vacations.
3. Full nest I: Youngest child under six.	Home purchasing at peak. Liquid assets low. Dissatisfied with financial position and amount of money saved. Interested in new products. Like advertised products. Buy: washers, dryers, TV, baby food, chest rubs and cough medicines, vitamins, dolls, wagons, sleds, skates.
4. Full nest II: Youngest child six or over.	Financial position better. Some wives work. Less influenced by advertising. Buy larger-sized packages, multiple-unit deals. Buy: many foods, cleaning materials, bicycles, music lessons, pianos.
5. Full nest III: Older married couples with dependent children.	Financial position still better. More wives work. Some children get jobs. Hard to influence with advertising. High average purchase of durables. Buy: new, more tasteful furniture, auto travel, unnecessary appliances, boats, dental services, magazines.
6. Empty nest I: Older married couples, no children living with them, head in labor force.	Home ownership at peak. Most satisfied with financial position and money saved. Interested in travel, recreation, self-education. Make gifts and contributions. Not interested in new products. Buy: vacations, luxuries, home improvements.
7. Empty nest II: Older married. No children living at home, head retired.	Drastic cut in income. Keep home. Buy: medical appliances, medical-care products that aid health, sleep, and digestion.
8. Solitary survivor, in labor force.	Income still good but likely to sell home.
9. Solitary survivor, retired.	Same medical and product needs as other retired group; drastic cut in income. Special need for attention, affection, and security.

Source: Philip Kotler, *Marketing Management: Analysis, Planning, Implementation, and Control,* 6th ed. (Englewood Cliffs, NJ: Prentice Hall, © 1988), p. 182. Kotler lists as his sources: William D. Wells and George Gubar, "Life-Cycle Concepts in Marketing Research," *Journal of Marketing Research,* November 1966, pp. 355–63; also see Patrick E. Murphy and William A. Staples, "A Modernized Family Life Cycle," *Journal of Consumer Research,* June 1979, pp. 12–22; and Frederick W. Derrick and Alane E. Linfield, "The Family Life Cycle: An Alternative Approach," *Journal of Consumer Research,* September 1980, pp. 214–17. Reprinted by permission of Prentice Hall, Inc., Englewood Cliffs, New Jersey.

TABLE 15–3   Major Segmentation Variables for Consumer Markets

Variable	Typical Breakdowns
Geographic	
Region	Pacific, Mountain, West North Central, West South Central, East North Central, East South Central, South Atlantic, Middle Atlantic, New England
County size	A, B, C, D
City or SMSA size	Under 5,000; 5,000–20,000; 20,000–50,000; 50,000–100,000; 100,000–250,000; 250,000–500,000; 500,000–1,000,000; 1,000,000–4,000,000; 4,000,000 or over
Density	Urban, suburban, rural
Climate	Northern, southern
Demographic	
Age	Under 6, 6–11, 12–19, 20–34, 35–49, 50–64, 65+
Sex	Male, female
Family Size	1–2, 3–4, 5+
Family Life Cycle	Young, single; young, married, no children; young, married, youngest child under 6; young, married, youngest child 6 or over; older, married, with children; older, married, no children under 18; older, single; other
Income	Under $5,000; $5,000–$10,000; $10,000–$15,000; $15,000–$20,000; $20,000–$25,000; $25,000–$30,000; $30,000–$50,000; $50,000 and over
Occupation	Professional and technical; managers, officials, and proprietors; clerical, sales; craftsmen, foremen; operatives; farmers; retired; students; housewives; unemployed
Education	Grade school or less; some high school; high school graduate; some college; college graduate
Religion	Catholic, Protestant, Jewish, other
Race	White, black, oriental
Nationality	American, British, French, German, Scandinavian, Italian, Latin American, Middle Eastern, Japanese
Psychographic	
Social Class	Lower lowers, upper lowers, working class, middle class, upper middles, lower uppers, upper uppers
Lifestyle	Straights, swingers, longhairs
Personality	Compulsive, gregarious, authoritarian, ambitious
Behavioral	
Occasions	Regular occasion, special occasion
Benefits	Quality, service, economy
User Status	Nonuser, ex-user, potential user, first-time user, regular user
Usage rate	Light user, medium user, heavy user
Loyalty status	None, medium, strong, absolute
Readiness stage	Unaware, aware, informed, interested, desirous, intending to buy
Attitude toward product	Enthusiastic, positive, indifferent, negative, hostile

Source: Philip Kotler, *Marketing Management: Analysis, Planning, Implementation, and Control,* 6th ed. (Englewood Cliffs, NJ: Prentice Hall, © 1988), p. 287. Reprinted by permission of Prentice Hall, Inc., Englewood Cliffs, New Jersey.

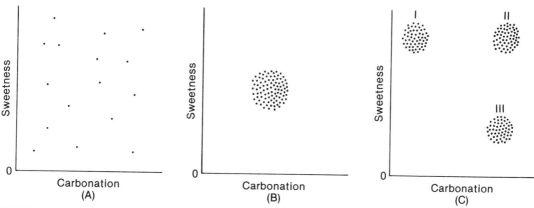

FIGURE 15–1
Hypothetical Consumer Preferences for a Soft Drink

males who have high incomes, live in large cities in the Southwest, and are between 45 and 60 years of age. These characteristics tell the firm quite a bit about the type of consumer this product appeals to. The producer can better define the needs of this group of consumers with this information.

By contrast, the people in Group I might be high-school-age females who live in small towns in the Midwest and come from families that have below-average incomes. The characteristics of this group are quite different from that of Group III.

The consumers in Group II, who prefer both high sweetness and high carbonation, might include equal numbers of men and women, 18–45 years of age, with average to slightly above-average incomes. There may be equal numbers of urban and rural consumers and there may be no regional dominance for location. Group II may be called the "middle America group."

Deciding Which Target Group to Pursue

To which group of consumers should the soft drink company try to target the appeal of its product? One approach is to sell a single product to all soft drink consumers with just an average amount of sweetness and carbonation. This mass marketing approach may work, but not very well, since it would not exactly meet the needs of any one of these three groups. What is called for are three different products each formulated to meet the preferences of each specific group of consumers. This is called *market niching*, where a market niche is an identifiable segment of a larger market. If the firm feels it does not have the resources to go after all three market niches, the decision becomes which market niche to pursue. This calls for an evaluation of the three market niches to determine which can be most profitably served by the firm.

To successfully segment the soft drink market into the three separate niches proposed here requires that a number of conditions be met. First, the products offered to each segment must have clearly distinguishable differences so consumers will perceive them to be different products. Second, there must be a large enough number of potential consumers of each product who have sufficient incomes and are geographically concentrated enough to be served profitably. Third, the producers must have access to the potential consumers by way of television, radio, and other forms of promotion. Fourth, the customers' need must be long-lasting enough to warrant the investment in filling it. If the need is highly seasonal or just part of a fast-moving fad it may not be worth the effort. Meeting these four conditions determines whether it is economically feasible to segment the market into three profitable niches each with its own specially formulated soft drink.

An evaluation of the three preference groups would show that each has some promise. Group I (the high-school-age females) is certainly a large enough group. But if other consumer research shows that they spend a large portion of their limited incomes on clothing and cosmetics this may limit sales potential. Combining this with information that they live in widely dispersed small midwestern towns and that they tend to be followers of fads may lead the firm to feel this is not the consumer group to which it wishes to appeal.

Group II (the middle America group) looks very promising. Members have average to above-average incomes; there are equal numbers of men and women; and there are large numbers of people with these characteristics nationwide. However, to service this group would put the firm's product in direct competition with a number of large national soft drink firms. This may make it difficult to succeed on a national level. Because of the competition, our firm may not be able to achieve reasonable profits without a long uphill struggle.

Group III (the high-income males in the Southwest) may be the best choice. Market research shows that they have a strong preference for a particular sweetness and carbonation combination. Consumers in this group felt the proposed soft drink provided a "rugged taste" that was not like those "sissy drinks" that kids gulp down. This may be the firm's market niche. The consumers are geographically concentrated, are accessible for advertising, and have adequate purchasing power. There are enough of them to make the sales and profit potential interesting; they are in some of the fastest-growing cities in the country; and their tastes are fairly stable. Based on the data this appears to be the best target market since it meets most of the market evaluation criteria.

The Market Segmentation Process

The market segmentation process can be summarized in the following seven-step procedure offered by McCarthy:[*]

1. Select the product and market area. Determine the business the firm is really in. Hopefully it will be one where the firm is very strong and the competition is weak. The definition of both the product and the market should be focused on consumer needs and not be defined in terms of a specific product.
2. Determine all the needs that all the potential customers may have in the product and market area.
3. Form at least three possible market segments. Describe at least three groups of consumers of this product and the specific needs of each group.
4. Determine the dimensions of the product that affect the consumption decision of the consumer. Remove all the product dimensions (that is, product characteristics) that are common to all products of this type. For example, common product traits for all foods are that they be nutritious and safe. This should be true of all food items and does not affect the selection of any particular food item. Therefore, these traits should be removed from the list of items that influences product selection.
5. Give a name to each possible product market segment.
6. Seek a solid understanding of the factors that motivate the purchase of this product by each possible market segment.
7. Associate each segment with demographic and other possible customer-related characteristics. This will permit the firm to describe the market and each segment within it.

This seven-step procedure will make it possible to develop marketing mixes that will be attractive to each market segment.

DETERMINING MARKETING OBJECTIVES

Once the market segments have been identified from patterns of consumer preferences, sharpened through the application of demographics, and evalu-

---

[*]E. Jerome McCarthy and William J. Perreault Jr., *Basic Marketing: A Managerial Approach* (Homewood, Ill.: Richard D. Irwin, Inc., 1987), pp. 83–87.

ated for economic viability, the next step is to match these results to the firm's marketing objectives. The first decision is to determine what the firm's marketing objectives are with respect to this product. One objective could be *market penetration*. This means seeking ways to increase the sales of a current product in the present market areas or capturing a large market share quickly with a new product. This can be done by increasing the firm's efforts with respect to the marketing mix. A stronger promotional effort, making the product available at more outlets within the existing market area, and so forth will lead to greater sales of the product.

Another objective can be *product development*. This means offering users a new or improved product in existing market areas. "New and improved" versions of existing products can also lead to new interest on the part of customers and higher sales. Entirely new products may be developed to bring in new sales. Jello's Pudding Pops are a good example of this.

A third objective can be *market development*. This means developing the sales of existing products in new markets. This normally involves selling in new geographic areas. It can also involve selling an existing product to a new target market group. A good example is Johnson's Baby Shampoo, which is now sold to adults who are frequent shampooers.

A fourth objective can be *diversification*. This means selling new products in new markets. A good example is provided by the Gerber Company. It now sells insurance to senior citizens as well as continuing to sell baby food.

In each instance, the selection of the target market is determined in part by the marketing objective of the firm. Extending the soft drink example used earlier, if the firm already sells this type of soft drink in the northwestern part of the country, the addition of the new southwestern marketing area may be welcomed if the firm is interested in market development. But if the firm's marketing objective is greater market penetration in its current northwestern marketing area, the results of the consumer poll are less interesting.

Strategic Planning

Marketing opportunities must be matched well with the firm's objectives and resources. This is why the firm does strategic planning. In this example the firm may not have the additional resources (people, money, energy, and so on) needed to open a new market area. The firm's objectives may limit its search for business opportunities. If that is the case, the firm may need to reexamine its objectives.

One way to evaluate the market situation and marketing objectives is to look at the potential for market growth and projected market share. This approach was popularized by the Boston Consulting Group to help its clients see the relative attractiveness of various product alternatives. By using a graph divided into quadrants it is possible to identify the best and worst products a firm has to offer (Figure 15–2). This procedure forces firms to confront the results of their past product decisions.

To do this it is necessary to construct a graph where the vertical axis is the product's annual market growth potential. It is suggested that the vertical axis run from zero to 20 percent with 10 percent as the midpoint. On the horizontal axis is a scale from 0.1 to 10, with 10 being at the origin. This gives the firm's sales relative to those of its leading competitors. A 10 means

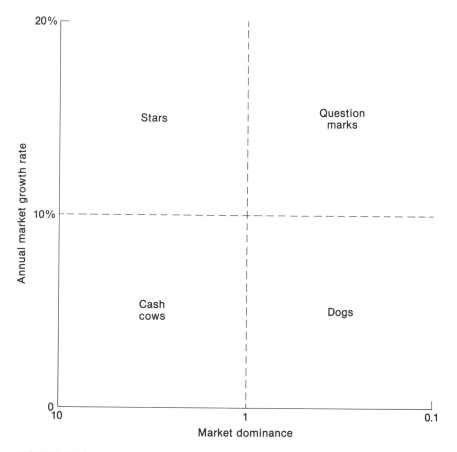

FIGURE 15–2
Boston Consulting Group's Market Evaluation Grid

Source: Arnoldo C. Hax and Nicolas S. Majluf, "The Use of the Growth-Share Matrix in Strategic Planning," *Interfaces*, 13, no. 1 (February 1983), 49. © 1983 The Institute of Management Sciences.

that the firm's sales are 10 times those of the next leading competitor and indicates market dominance. A 0.10 means that the firm's sales are equal to 10 percent of those of the leading competitor and indicates that the firm occupies a relatively small position in this market. A 1.0 is the midpoint of the horizontal axis and indicates the firm's sales are equal to those of the leading competitor.

Cash Cows, Stars, Question Marks, and Dogs

Each of the quadrants is given a name befitting its characteristics. *Cash cows* are products that give the firm a dominant position in the market though the potential for market growth is low. Products in this category normally generate consistent and large profits with little variation from year to year. They are called cash cows because of the consistency of their high profits and the firm's ability to "milk" them to support other products. *Stars* are products that offer not only the potential for high market share and profits but also have high potential for market growth. Successful new products that catch on quickly such as Pudding Pops normally are placed here. The products in this category often become cash cows as their market matures.

Question marks are products that currently do not occupy a dominant position in the market but are in a market that has high growth potential. There are two directions in which a product can go from this category. It can be made into a star, but that may take a major commitment of resources to accomplish. It can also slip down into the dog category if the firm withdraws attention and resources from the product. *Dogs* are those products for which the firm lacks market dominance and for which the market potential for growth is low. Products in this category represent a "cash trap" since they

---

Product Categories

- Cash Cows–Products that generate consistently large profits.
- Stars–Products that offer high market share and profits as well as high potential for market growth.
- Question Marks–Products that currently do not occupy a dominant position in the market, but are in a market that has high growth potential.
- Dogs–Products for which the firm lacks market dominance and for which market growth potential is low.

usually require a significant amount of resources just to maintain the status quo with little or no hope of ever reaping big profits.

Management's goal with respect to its products should be to seek a blend of stars and cash cows. Question marks should be converted into stars or cows. Dogs should be dropped. This approach helps marketing managers visualize their product situation and match it better to their marketing objectives. Regardless of what procedure is used, the firm's selection of the mix of products it will sell should always be the one that maximizes overall profits. This may mean carrying a few dogs if having them in the product line helps the sales of other products and thus leads to higher overall profits.

ESTIMATING MARKET POTENTIAL

There are a number of methods that can be used to estimate the economic potential of a market, but before proceeding it is important to define several important terms. *Market potential* is the total level of sales possible in a target market for all firms. *Sales forecast* is the level of sales a single firm can expect to receive from a target market. *Market share* is the percentage of total sales from the target market achieved by a single firm. Sales forecast divided by market potential gives estimated market share.

The Factor Approach

The first task is to determine the market potential for a product. This can be done using the *factor approach* where the size of the potential market sales for a specific product is determined by using a series of factors to arrive at a sales forecast. For the factor approach to be useful the market analyst needs to know a considerable amount of information about product usage and consumers.

The simplest version of this approach is to express sales in an industry as a percentage of an easily obtainable statistic such as gross national product (GNP), retail sales, or industrial production, and then estimate the firm's percentage of total industry sales. These national economic data are relatively easy to obtain, are calculated monthly, and are widely disseminated in government publications, the business press, or even on the television news.

For example, if total retail food sales are normally 15 percent of the GNP, and GNP is forecast to be $3 trillion next year, retail food sales can be projected to be:

$$\$3 \text{ trillion} \times 0.15 = \$450 \text{ billion}$$

If a particular supermarket chain's sales normally represent 2 percent of national retail food sales, the chain's next year's sales can be estimated to be:

$$\$450 \text{ billion} \times 0.02 = \$9 \text{ billion}$$

If the real concern is with fresh produce sales and they typically account for 10 percent of the chain's total sales, next year's expected fresh produce sales would be:

$$\$9 \text{ billion} \times 0.10 = \$900 \text{ million}$$

Developing Estimates

A second approach for determining market potential is to develop estimates from the consumer side. Let's again use Group III from the hypothetical soft drink example used earlier in the chapter. If the demographics show that people in this group are highly educated (top 25 percent of the population), are males (50 percent of the population), have high incomes (top 25 percent of the population), live in cities (40 percent of the population), in the southwestern United States (20 percent of population), and are between 45 and 60 years of age (10 percent of the population), these factors can be combined to estimate the size of the market for the new soft drink product.

U.S. population	250,000,000	persons
× % males	× 0.50	
	125,000,000	males
× % urban	× 0.40	
	50,000,000	urban males
× % in SW	× 0.20	
	10,000,000	urban males in SW
× % educated	× 0.25	
	2,500,000	urban males in SW with high levels of education
× % income	× 0.25	
	625,000	urban males in SW with high levels of education and income
× % age 45–60	× 0.10	
	62,500	urban males in SW with high levels of education and income who are between 45 and 60

If each of these people consumes the national average of twelve cans (two six-packs) per week (our made-up estimate of national consumption) of only the new soft drink at the projected selling price of $2.00 per six-pack, each person in the target market would spend

$$(2 \text{ six-packs}) \quad \times \quad \$2.00/\text{week} = \$4.00/\text{week/person}$$

Over one year this would amount to:

$$\$4.00/\text{week/person} \quad \times \quad 52 \text{ weeks} = \$208/\text{year/person}$$

Total market potential per year would then be:

$$\$208/\text{year/person} \quad \times \quad 62,500 \text{ people in target market} = \$13,000,000$$

Based on the intensity of the responses in the market research interviews, the firm feels it could expect to get a 20 percent market share (20 percent of the people in the target market would become regular customers of the product) in the first year the product is offered. This leads to a sales forecast for the first year of:

$$\$13,000,000 \quad \times \quad 0.20 = \$2,600,000$$

Sales and Marketing Management Magazine uses this same type of factor analysis to determine the relative level of retail sales activity in specific geographical areas.[*] It develops a buying power index (*BPI*) by assigning separate weights to an area's population (50 percent), income level (30 percent), and amount of retail sales (20 percent). The *BPI* is calculated as follows:

$$BPI = 0.50 \text{ population} + 0.30 \text{ income} + 0.20 \text{ retail sales}$$

where population   = percent of national population in the area
       income   = percent of national household income in the area
       retail sales = percent of national retail sales in the area

To see how the BPI can be used, let's assume that a large metropolitan area had 2 percent of the nation's population, 3 percent of the household income, and 3.5 percent of the retail sales. Its *BPI* would be:

[*]"Annual Survey of Buying Power," *Sales and Marketing Management Magazine,* July issue of each year.

$$BPI = (0.50)(0.02) + (0.30)(0.03) + (0.20)(0.035)$$
$$= \quad 0.010 \quad + \quad 0.009 \quad + \quad 0.007$$
$$= \quad 0.026$$

Since the value of the *BPI* exceeds its percentage of the nation's population in this area, this indicates that people in this market spend more than one would expect based on their population alone. This normally implies that this is a good market for retailers.

Determining Consumption from National Levels

A third approach for projecting market potential is to determine consumption of an item at the national level and then use this to estimate local consumption levels. For example, if the data from the USDA shows that the per capita (per person) consumption of french fries is 2 pounds per year in the United States, then it is possible to forecast the market potential for french fries in Indianapolis by doing the following:

$$\begin{array}{l}\text{market potential} \\ \text{for French Fries} \\ \text{in Indianapolis}\end{array} = 2 \text{ pounds/person} \times \begin{array}{l}\text{population of} \\ \text{Indianapolis}\end{array}$$
$$= \quad 2 \quad \times \quad 700{,}000$$
$$= 1{,}400{,}000 \text{ pounds per year}$$

This can be converted to dollar sales using the average price per serving. If the average serving consists of 1/4 pound and sells for 60 cents this means a selling price of $2.40 per pound ($4 \times 60$ cents). Thus, the value of the market potential for french fries in Indianapolis is:

$$\begin{array}{l}\text{value of} \\ \text{market potential} \\ \text{for French fries} \\ \text{in Indianapolis}\end{array} = \text{price per pound} \times \begin{array}{l}\text{number of pounds} \\ \text{sold per year}\end{array}$$
$$= \quad \$2.40 \quad \times \quad 1{,}400{,}000 \text{ pounds}$$
$$= \$3{,}360{,}000 \text{ per year}$$

This same approach can be applied to nearly any item. However, one should be careful since this method assumes there are no differences in consumer tastes and preferences, or in consumption rates in different parts of the country.

Determining Local Markets from State Averages

Another approach for estimating market potential that is valuable for businesses that serve only a local retail market area is to determine the size of the local market using statewide averages. To illustrate this procedure let's assume a firm is interested in opening a restaurant in Bucks County, Pennsylvania. This county is located just north of Philadelphia. The analysis of market potential is done using data from public data sources (such as state and federal agencies) or from private sources such as *Sales and Marketing Management Magazine* that give yearly data on sales, population, retail sales, household incomes, and so forth.

The first step is to determine the county's per capita *effective buying income (EBI)*. *EBI* is equivalent to take-home pay or the amount of income left after taxes, Social Security, and so on are removed from peoples' income. Per capita *EBI* can be determined by dividing the total amount of the county's *EBI* by the county's population.

$$\text{Bucks County per capita } EBI = \frac{\text{county } EBI}{\text{county population}}$$

$$= \frac{\$6,048,149,000}{511,300}$$

$$= \$11,829$$

The second step is to determine how much of the money spent by Bucks County residents in eating and drinking establishments is spent within the county (population captured = the percentage of total spending by county residents in eating and drinking establishments that is spent in Bucks County). This is done as follows:

$$\text{population captured} = \frac{\text{sales at eating and drinking establishments in Bucks county}}{\text{per capita eating and drinking sales in Penna.}} \times \frac{\text{Bucks County median household income}}{\text{Penna. median household income}}$$

This gives the number of people who do all their restaurant spending at restaurants in Bucks County. This value is adjusted by the ratio of county to state median household income to reflect differences in the local economic situation. In this example the figures would be:

$$\begin{array}{ll} \text{population} \\ \text{captured} \end{array} = \dfrac{\$233{,}161{,}000}{\dfrac{\$445 \times \$32{,}242}{\$25{,}213}}$$

$$= 409{,}773 \text{ people}$$

This means that the restaurant spending of 409,773 people is fully captured within the county. This represents a "pull factor" of:

$$\begin{array}{ll} \text{pull factor} \end{array} = \dfrac{\text{population captured}}{\text{total county population}}$$

$$= \dfrac{409{,}773}{511{,}300}$$

$$= 80 \text{ percent}$$

This means that restaurants located in the county "pull in" 80 percent of all the dollars spent by its residents in eating and drinking establishments.

The next step is to determine the amount of unmet need for restaurants that exists in Bucks County. This begins with a determination of the average number of people needed to support a single restaurant in the state and is calculated as follows:

$$\begin{array}{ll} \text{number of people} \\ \text{per restaurant} \\ \text{in the state} \end{array} = \dfrac{\text{Penna. population}}{\begin{array}{c}\text{no. of restaurants}\\\text{in Penna.}\end{array}}$$

$$= \dfrac{11{,}965{,}400}{14{,}834}$$

$$= 807$$

Next, the estimated number of people in the county who are having their restaurant needs fully met by currently operating restaurants is calculated as follows:

number of people who have their restaurant needs fully met by existing restaurants	=	no. of restaurants currently operating in the county	×	average no. of people per restaurant in Penna.
	=	537	×	807
	=	433,359		

The estimated amount of unmet restaurant need in the county's market is determined by taking the difference between the number of people whose restaurant needs are being fully served and the total county population as follows:

$$
\begin{array}{lll}
\text{amount of} & & \text{no. of people being} \\
\text{unmet need} & = \text{county population} \quad - & \text{served by existing} \\
& & \text{restaurants} \\
& = 511,300 \quad - & 433,359 \\
& = 77,941 \text{ people} & \\
& \quad (15.2 \text{ percent of the county's population}) &
\end{array}
$$

The estimated maximum dollar value of unmet need is determined by multiplying the county's per capita expenditure in eating and drinking establishments times the number of people with unmet needs or:

$$
\begin{array}{llll}
\text{maximum value} & \text{county per capita} & & \text{no. of people} \\
\text{of unmet needs} & = \text{expenditures in} & \times & \text{with unmet} \\
& \quad \text{restaurants} & & \text{needs} \\
& = \$456 & \times & 77,941 \\
& = \$35,541,096 & &
\end{array}
$$

The maximum number of new restaurants needed to completely fill this amount of unmet need would be:

$$
\begin{array}{ll}
\text{maximum no. of} & \dfrac{\text{maximum dollar value of unmet need}}{\text{county's average sales per}} \\
\text{new restaurants} \quad = & \qquad\qquad \text{possible restaurant} \\
& = \dfrac{\$35,541,096}{\$434,192} \\
& = 82 \ (\text{an increase of } 15.3 \text{ percent})
\end{array}
$$

Thus, theoretically there is room for new restaurants in this county. However, there may be some question as to whether a specific area can "pull" more than 80–90 percent of the restaurant sales given today's very mobile population. But procedures such as these help a firm analyze its chances for success before it enters a market. This analysis, along with more detailed financial, competitor, and site analysis would assist a firm in determining market potential and its chances for success.

PRODUCT POSITIONING

One of the responsibilities of marketing managers today is to favorably position a product in the minds of consumers. Products are positioned by adjusting the marketing mix, including the emphasis given in advertising. Several firms have been so successful at this that their brand names are now synonymous with the products they sell. Two of the best-known products are Kleenex and Scotch Tape. These companies have to be careful to preserve their brand name because many people refer to all similar products as Kleenex or Scotch Tape.

7-Up is advertised as "The Uncola" so that any time anyone thinks about purchasing a non-cola soft drink 7-Up should come to mind. In another example, a supermarket that once had a good but expensive image in the minds of many consumers now bills itself as "the price chopper" and states that it will "meet or beat anyone else's price." This store has repositioned itself to appeal to a larger number of customers by promoting itself as a low-price food store. When the consumer thinks about where to purchase food at the lowest prices this store's name immediately comes to mind.

This type of positioning is most effective when it is built around specific product features such as the best, largest, smallest, lowest price, fastest, most dependable, and so on. In the overnight package delivery business, Federal Express positioned itself to be perceived as the fastest, most reliable firm in the market by using the slogan "Why fool around with anyone else?" If the client wants to be "absolutely positive" the package will get to its destination, then he should think of Federal Express.

Through the proper design of the marketing mix a product can be positioned in the consumer's mind to stand apart from competitors' products. It is important to remember that product positioning occurs even when the firm does nothing about it since consumers will form their own opinions about the firm and its products from what they observe.

OTHER MARKET ANALYSIS METHODS

In addition to formal analysis procedures there are a number of other ways to analyze a market that can give the operators of a business some insights. The first place to look is the sales slip. If it is properly filled out it can yield a wealth of information about a firm's customers and the demand for its products.

The sales slip should include the name and address of each customer. These will tell the firm the sex of its customers, where they come from, and how far they have come. This analysis can also help define a firm's marketing area. The slip should also tell what goods were bought, in what quantities, and at what times of year. This can be valuable in planning what to make or stock, and how much to have available for sale at the same time next year.

One firm used sales slip analysis with great success when at the end of each day it wrote down the level of sales that day, the weather, the day of the week, and the most popular items sold. That helped it plan for sales on the same date the following year. The firm's objective was always to sell more on the same day next year than it did this year.

A second valuable form of market information for operating retail agribusinesses is hourly and daily sales and customer counts from the cash register tape. This can help a retailer decide what days and hours it should be open and when it can close with minimal impact on sales. Customer complaint forms and requests for products that are not in stock or produced may give firms some clues as to what new products they should offer. This type of market research can be implemented rather quickly and inexpensively from existing business records. It can be a source of valuable information about a market.

SUMMARY

This chapter, devoted to the topic of market analysis, developed the reasons for conducting market analysis and discussed why a clear understanding of solid business opportunities is the foundation of business planning.

The process of identifying market opportunities is made more difficult today because people's needs and desires are more varied than they have been in the past. When all consumers had more homogeneous needs, a few products could meet the needs of all consumers, and a mass marketing approach was acceptable. In recent years marketers have come to understand the additional profits possible from better meeting the varied needs of different, smaller groups of consumers using target marketing. The shift to a consumer need, target marketing approach has meant a shift to greater attention to understanding consumer demands.

Because of this shift, marketers must be able to quickly and accurately identify their target markets. Once this is done, they must be able to analyze the profit potential of each market segment and relate it to the firm's overall marketing and financial objectives. Several procedures for accomplishing these objectives were discussed.

The conclusions reached from market analysis can serve as valuable information when a firm goes about developing its marketing mix and segmenting its markets. The results of these efforts can be greater satisfaction for the consumer and greater profits for the firm.

QUESTIONS

1. What is the difference between mass marketing and target marketing? Which one holds the promise for greater profits and why?
2. Why is it better to define what the firm is to do in terms of consumer preferences than in terms of specific products?
3. Why are demographic characteristics a good way to separate consumers?
4. Describe some of the basic marketing objectives a firm is likely to have.
5. Briefly describe several methods that an agribusiness firm could use to estimate the potential of a market.

16

Managing the Marketing Mix: The Product

Deciding upon the optimal marketing mix begins with the development of a product that fully satisfies the needs of the members of the target market. Much of the effort involved in writing the marketing plan and in the analysis of the market is directed at identifying these consumer needs. For these efforts to be of any value they must be translated into a product that embodies all the attributes consumers want.

This chapter is devoted to examining the concept of a product—what it is, how it changes over its life cycle, how to evaluate its market performance, and the use of packaging and branding. An understanding of these concepts will give marketing managers a better knowledge of what they are dealing with and should lead to greater success at developing products that completely satisfy consumer needs.

THE PRODUCT

A product is anything that can satisfy a consumer need. The objective is to clearly define the consumer need and then develop a product that is capable of completely filling it. This requires that the product be defined in terms of consumer needs, not producer needs. For example, while in the mind of a fast-food restaurant operator the hamburger going over the counter may be

1/4 pound (pre-cooked weight) of Grade A ground beef surrounded by a 3-inch hamburger bun covered with 1/3 ounce of catsup and 1 slice of a #24-dh style pickle that is served in a #738-R burger box, to the customer it is a way to satisfy noontime hunger. The consumer doesn't particularly care what kind of box the burger comes in, as long as the container keeps the burger hot and doesn't leak.

Consumers are primarily concerned with the satisfaction of their needs and care little about marketing mechanics. This means that to be successful marketers must look at their products the way their consumers do. They must look at the buyers' total consumption pattern in order to correctly determine what consumers are trying to accomplish by using their products.

Consumers seek to satisfy a variety of psychological needs (such as status and self-esteem) as well as physical needs (such as hunger and thirst) through the consumption of products. This is why people dine at elegant restaurants where the waiters wear ruffled shirts and speak with French accents. If they just want to maximize food consumption per dollar spent they can do this at a place with cents-off coupons and a drive-up window. The customers in the French restaurant are buying the atmosphere as well as the food. If marketing managers can keep customer needs and perceived needs in mind they will enhance their chances of developing a successful approach to the market—one that will effectively and profitably fill a consumer need.

Product Classifications

To help marketers understand the product concept a general classification system of products has been developed. It begins by separating products into three groups according to physical characteristics. The first group is referred to as *durable goods*. They are goods that are not immediately consumed in use. They last through several uses and include items such as tractors, clothing, dishwashers, buildings, food-processing equipment, and so forth. The second group is referred to as *non-durable goods*. This group includes goods that are consumed in use and includes items such as food, soap, fertilizer, and so on.

The third group is referred to as *services*. They are non-tangible items that cannot be held, stored, or touched. They include benefits, activities, or satisfactions that are offered for sale. This group includes items like haircuts, taxi rides, concerts, aerial crop spraying, commodity market advice, and so on.

A second classification scheme is to separate products according to use. The major groupings are *consumer goods* and *industrial goods*. Consumer goods are those products that are used by the final consumer. Industrial goods are those products that are used to produce other goods.

The consumer goods group is divided into four categories according to buyer behavior. The first category is *convenience goods*. These are low-cost goods that are purchased frequently with little thought, effort, or comparison shopping. They are usually bought out of habit and require no servicing in their use.

Within the convenience goods category there are three subcategories. The first subcategory is *staple goods*. They are items that are purchased with little planning. Many food products fit into this category.

The second subcategory is *impulse goods*. The purchase of these goods is generally unplanned and is decided only when the goods are seen. Normally, if the purchase is not made when the goods are seen the sale is lost. The best examples of impulse goods are the pack of gum, candy bar, or magazine purchased while waiting at the checkout line in a store. Another example is souvenirs sold at sporting and entertainment events. Having products displayed at the right place and time is critical to the sale of these items.

The third subcategory is *emergency goods*. The purchase of these products comes at the time of immediate need. This includes snow shovels on the day of the first snowfall, umbrellas on a rainy day, and so forth. Having the product offered for sale at the right time and place is critical to their sale.

The second category of consumer goods is *shopping goods*. These are items that require some thought and comparison as to the selection of product quality, price, style, and so forth. It includes big-ticket items such as major appliances and furniture. The third category of consumer goods is *specialty goods*. These are goods that have a unique characteristic or brand name that

---

The Four Subcategories of Consumer Goods

- Convenience goods—low-cost goods that are purchased frequently with little thought, effort, or comparison shopping.
- Shopping goods—items that require some thought and comparison as to the selection of product quality, price, and style.
- Specialty goods—goods that have a unique characteristic or brand name which consumers seek out.
- Unsought goods—goods that are either unknown to consumers or are not normally sought by most consumers.

causes the consumer to make a special effort to seek them for purchase. This may be a particular brand of clothing or automobile. The fourth category of consumer goods is *unsought goods*. These are goods that are either unknown to consumers (products like microwave ovens and smoke alarms when they first came onto the market) or normally not sought by most consumers (tombstones, encyclopedias, insurance).

Each of these groups of goods has its own appeal to buyers. If a firm can uncover the consumer attitudes, needs, and buying behavior related to a particular category of goods and relate it to the product, it is well on its way to developing a successful marketing mix. This type of understanding of the consumer's product perception is required if the company is to position itself to fill a specific need for some specific target market.

This approach is particularly important for consumer-oriented agribusiness firms since they deal heavily in staple, convenience goods which are often bought out of habit with little thought or planning. A clear product position and heavy use of branding (Hunt's ketchup versus Heinz ketchup, for instance) are often vital to capturing the consumer for these classes of goods. Knowing and understanding consumer buying behavior helps firms to develop a product and a marketing approach that fits these needs.

BRANDING

One of the major decisions surrounding the development of a successful product is the use of branding. Branding is widely used in agribusiness. Even commodities such as chicken now carry brand names such as Perdue, Holly Farms, and Tyson's chicken rather than being sold as plain chicken in the supermarket display case.

By branding a product the firm helps to separate it from its competitors in the minds of consumers. By purchasing a branded product consumers often feel they are getting a special assurance that this product meets their needs better than other similar products. Marketers may gain additional sales and profits because they offer a superior product in the mind of the consumer. These extra profits come about because the firm has established a monopolistically competitive position with a differentiated product the demand for which is more inelastic.

While seeming to be a modern invention, product branding goes back in history to the formation of artists' and craftsmans' guilds in the Middle Ages. By applying his mark to a product the guildsman assured customers that his goods were of known high quality. A *branded product* is any product that employs a name, symbol, design, or any combination of these to distinguish it from all similar products. For example, salt is just salt unless it is Morton's salt, and apples are just apples unless they are marked as Washington State apples. Products without such names are called *unbranded* or *generic products.*

In addition to the possibility of higher profits, branding offers producers a number of advantages including better market segmentation, increased consumer loyalty, more repeat business, easier introduction of new products, and a better corporate image. These are especially important to agribusiness firms that sell staple convenience goods such as food that is bought largely out of habit. If branding is successful, repeat purchasers will automatically buy the familiar, trusted brands, and this can lead to greater sales and profits.

Branding can be done either by the manufacturer or the retailer. A good example of manufacturer branding is Searle's Nutrasweet. When the firm's patent expires and other firms begin to make aspartame, many users will stick with Nutrasweet because of its established brand name. Some manufacturers apply their brand name to a family of items such as H.J. Heinz's 57 Varieties of products. Marketers often try to reinforce this association by including the firm's brand name in the product's name such as Campbell's Tomato Soup or Campbell's Chunky Beef Vegetable Soup. A retailer may also try to establish a family of brands to capture the benefits of branding by using an in-house brand name to cover a variety of products. A&P does this with its A&P Anne Page and Jane Parker brands that are applied to a wide variety of goods from salami to apple pies. The reasons behind this type of behavior were explained as part of the discussion of the dominant core–competitive fringe model that was discussed in an earlier chapter.

Achieving brand recognition among consumers is not an easy task. It requires a good product that consumers feel is different from the "run of the mill," plus a strong promotional effort to reinforce this idea with consumers. Shoppers are willing to buy a branded item without inspection or comparison

---

The Advantages of Branding

- Better market segmentation
- Increased consumer loyalty
- More repeat business
- Easier introduction of new products
- Better corporate image
- Potentially higher sales and profits

shopping when they feel assured of the quality implied by the brand name. "If it's Campbell's, it has to be good!"

Promotion is required so that the brand name becomes identified with the product characteristics desired by the consumer. Otherwise the product might as well be an unbranded, undifferentiated commodity. The purpose of a promotional campaign should be to develop a separate identity for the product that will lead to consumer preference. If the program is successful the shopper should routinely buy Brand XYZ Tomato Sauce each time it is needed without looking at anyone else's tomato sauce.

This process can be facilitated by selecting a good brand name. A good brand name should be easy to read, pronounce, and remember. It should also evoke a pleasant image. For example, Mrs. Butterworth's Syrup may bring to mind an image of a sweet-looking grandmotherly figure making home-made syrup for her grandchildren on her back porch in Vermont. Orville Redenbacher's Gourmet Popping Corn may create the image of homegrown, high-quality popcorn. This somehow helps us feel good about buying it.

It is important to remember that the success of the branding effort still rests heavily on the development of a good product. All promotion does is to get the word out quickly. Good promotion of a bad product may temporarily increase sales but in the longer run it can quicken its demise. A good product poorly promoted is not likely to do well in today's competitive marketplace. Good promotion of a good product is required for success.

PRODUCT LIFE CYCLES

The development of a successful marketing mix depends on the position of the product in its product life cycle. All products pass through a series of distinct stages in market development from introduction to termination. Different marketing mixes of price, place, and promotion are required at each stage of the cycle because of changes in competition, consumer needs, and the market. Failure to adjust the marketing mix to product life cycle stages can lead to lower product sales and profits. The relationship between the stages of the product life cycle and the four Ps of the marketing mix can be seen in Figure 16–1. Each stage has its own characteristics, marketing objectives, and strategies.

The first stage in the product life cycle is *product introduction.* Heavy promotion is needed to tell potential customers about the new product. Sales are low but begin to grow. Profits are nonexistent due to the low sales and high promotion expenses.

Market growth is the second stage where heavy promotional efforts from the product introduction stage begin to pay off. The product becomes

SALES BY STAGE OF THE PRODUCT LIFE CYCLE				
Time →	Introduction	Growth	Maturity	Decline
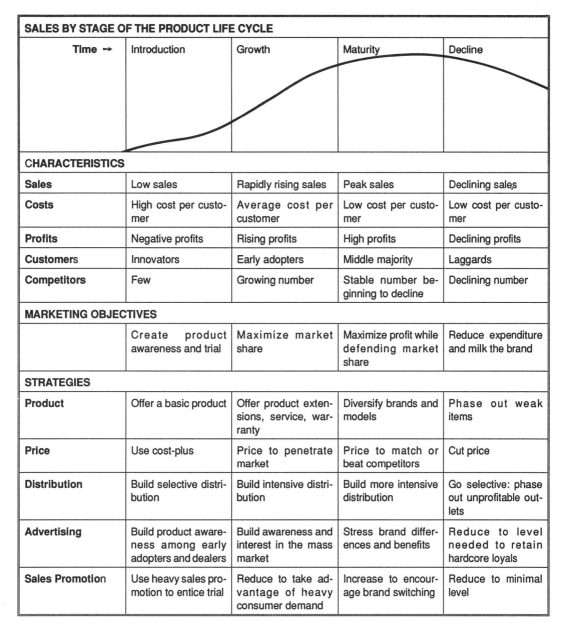				
CHARACTERISTICS				
Sales	Low sales	Rapidly rising sales	Peak sales	Declining sales
Costs	High cost per customer	Average cost per customer	Low cost per customer	Low cost per customer
Profits	Negative profits	Rising profits	High profits	Declining profits
Customers	Innovators	Early adopters	Middle majority	Laggards
Competitors	Few	Growing number	Stable number beginning to decline	Declining number
MARKETING OBJECTIVES				
	Create product awareness and trial	Maximize market share	Maximize profit while defending market share	Reduce expenditure and milk the brand
STRATEGIES				
Product	Offer a basic product	Offer product extensions, service, warranty	Diversify brands and models	Phase out weak items
Price	Use cost-plus	Price to penetrate market	Price to match or beat competitors	Cut price
Distribution	Build selective distribution	Build intensive distribution	Build more intensive distribution	Go selective: phase out unprofitable outlets
Advertising	Build product awareness among early adopters and dealers	Build awareness and interest in the mass market	Stress brand differences and benefits	Reduce to level needed to retain hardcore loyals
Sales Promotion	Use heavy sales promotion to entice trial	Reduce to take advantage of heavy consumer demand	Increase to encourage brand switching	Reduce to minimal level

FIGURE 16–1
The Product Life Cycle and the Four Ps

Source: Philip Kotler, *Marketing Management: Analysis, Planning, Implementation, and Control,* 6th Ed. (Englewood Cliffs, NJ: Prentice Hall, © 1988), p. 367. Kotler lists as his sources: Chester R. Wasson, *Dynamic Competitive Strategy and Product Life Cycles* (Austin, Tex.: Austin Press, 1978); John A. Weber, "Planning Corporate Growth with Inverted Product Life Cycles," *Long Range Planning*, October 1976, pp. 12–29; and Peter Doyle, "The Realities of the Product Life Cycle," *Quarterly Review of Marketing*, Summer 1976, pp. 1–6. Reprinted by permission of Prentice Hall, Inc., Englewood Cliffs, New Jersey.

profitable as revenues from rapidly growing sales overcome promotional costs. The product's success begins to attract competitors, a situation that usually forces price reductions. However, the total market is typically growing fast enough to absorb all the products. Improvements in the product are often made in the form of new features and models in an effort to broaden the customer base.

Market maturity is the third stage of the product life cycle. Sales growth begins to slow down as the market becomes saturated and the competition gets tougher. The product remains profitable but profits begin to level off and there is often little product differentiation. This is the most common stage of the product life cycle for most products. To prolong this stage the firm seeks ways to continue to improve the product and to find new users and uses for it. The fourth stage is *sales decline*. Both the sales and profits fall off as new and better products enter the market. At some point the firm must make the decision to discontinue the product.

The length of the product life cycle varies by type of product but is becoming shorter. While it is true that some products have been around for fifty years or more, for many products the full life cycle may average three years, and it could be even shorter for fad items. Because of the shortness of the product life cycle, profits are often transitory and go mainly to the innovators of new products. The profits of firms that produce "me too" products are often quite small. Thus, firms that are best at product innovation are the ones with the best profit potential. This explains the emphasis on product development and new products by agribusiness firms. However, despite the extensive analysis and screening of potential new products, approximately 40 percent of all new products fail. Those firms that succeed in this area foster an environment where new product ideas that are in tune with the needs of consumers are encouraged.

PRODUCT MIX

Most firms offer a variety of products rather than a single product for sale. Thus, firm managers are faced with the situation of how to manage an assortment of products so the firm can maximize its total profit from the sale of all its products. This type of planning is called the product mix decision. *Product mix* is the set of products included in a firm's product line(s).

There are three dimensions to the product mix (Figure 16–2). First, there is the *width* of the product mix. This refers to the number of product lines or sets of similar types of products the firm offers for sale. For example, a firm may sell corn flakes and wheat flakes. They are both cold breakfast cereals

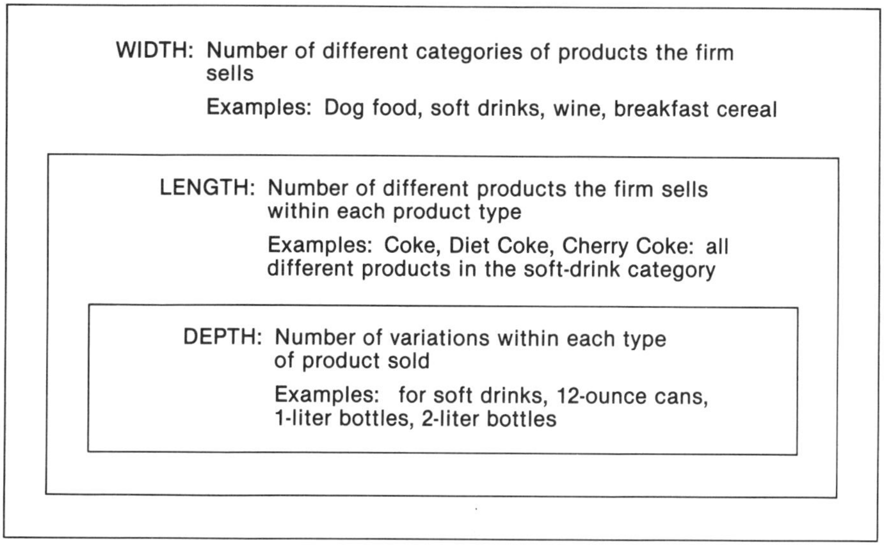

```
┌──────────────────────────────────────────────────────────────────┐
│                                                                    │
│   WIDTH: Number of different categories of products the firm       │
│          sells                                                     │
│                                                                    │
│          Examples: Dog food, soft drinks, wine, breakfast cereal   │
│                                                                    │
│   ┌────────────────────────────────────────────────────────────┐  │
│   │  LENGTH: Number of different products the firm sells         │  │
│   │          within each product type                            │  │
│   │                                                              │  │
│   │          Examples: Coke, Diet Coke, Cherry Coke: all         │  │
│   │          different products in the soft-drink category       │  │
│   │                                                              │  │
│   │   ┌──────────────────────────────────────────────────────┐  │  │
│   │   │  DEPTH: Number of variations within each type         │  │  │
│   │   │         of product sold                               │  │  │
│   │   │                                                       │  │  │
│   │   │         Examples:  for soft drinks, 12-ounce cans,    │  │  │
│   │   │         1-liter bottles, 2-liter bottles              │  │  │
│   │   └──────────────────────────────────────────────────────┘  │  │
│   └────────────────────────────────────────────────────────────┘  │
│                                                                    │
└──────────────────────────────────────────────────────────────────┘
```

FIGURE 16–2
Dimensions of the Product Mix

and would be considered one product line. If the firm offers products such as dog food, soft drinks, wines, cold breakfast cereal, and movies, these are considered different product lines. The more product lines the firm has to offer the greater is the width of its product mix.

The second dimension of the product mix is *length*. This refers to the total number of different products in each of the product lines. For example, for a firm like Coca-Cola the length of the product line in carbonated soft drinks is extensive and would include products such as: Coke, Coca-Cola Classic, Diet Coke, Cherry Coke, Tab, Mr. Pip, Mellow Yellow, and so on.

The third dimension of the product mix is *depth*. This refers to the total number of variations of each product in the product mix. If each of these Coca-Cola products may be packaged in cans, returnable bottles, nonreturnable bottles, plastic two-liter bottles, plastic three-liter bottles, and so on, then the sum of all these product variations is the depth of the product mix for Coca-Cola.

A firm can adjust its product mix by adjusting any of these three dimensions. The firm can widen the product mix by offering new lines of products. It can lengthen the product mix by adding new products within existing product lines. It can deepen the product mix by offering new variations of existing products. The decisions surrounding the makeup of the

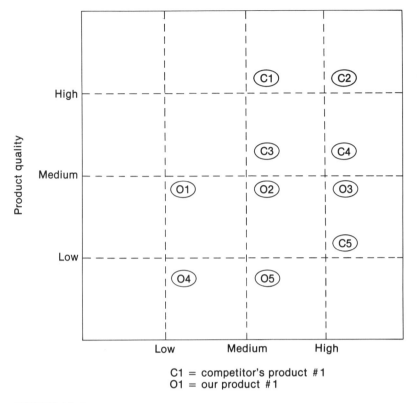

C1 = competitor's product #1
O1 = our product #1

FIGURE 16–3
Product Mapping

product mix are made as part of the firm's strategic plan where the goal is to match the needs of the customers in the target market with the firm's resource base.

Product Mapping

The development of a successful product mix begins with an analysis of the firm's current product mix using *product mapping* (Figure 16–3). Product mapping is often done using two product characteristics that consumers feel are particularly important, such as price and product quality, to see how a firm's products are positioned against those offered by competitors.

Let's assume that product mapping shows that according to a survey of consumers your firm's products (numbered O1 to O5 on the graph) are perceived to be primarily in the medium to low price range and are felt to be of low to medium quality. A similar mapping of a major competitor's products (numbered C1 to C5 on the graph) shows that they are generally perceived as offering higher quality at a higher price. This type of product-mix planning should be part of your firm's strategic planning process since it can identify openings for new products, show where your firm's products compete directly with those of competitors, and point out areas of opportunity where there is little current competition in the market.

The product-mix analysis can also be extended to financial analysis where the percentage of total sales and profits from each product or product line is examined. In Figure 16–4 let's apply some financial analysis to the same five products that are mapped above. The graph indicates that product #1 contributes 20 percent of the firm's total sales and also 20 percent of its profits. Products #2 and #3 are big sellers since they generate 25 percent of total sales, but they account for only 10 and 15 percent of the firm's profits. This may be occurring because each faces intense direct competition from a major competitor so prices are forced to remain low in order to be competitive.

Products #4 and #5 are each responsible for only 15 percent of total sales but contribute 30 and 25 percent of the firm's profits. Both products are lower-priced and lower-quality products in the eyes of the consumers. The firm can make a good profit, however, since there is little competition in this portion of the market and little or nothing is spent on product development and promotion.

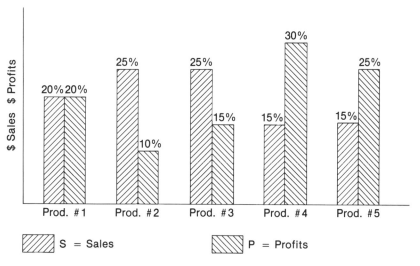

FIGURE 16–4
Product Mix Analysis

After looking at the whole picture the firm must decide whether it makes any sense to stay with products #2 and #3 since they generate so little profit. However, in terms of its overall product mix the firm may need products #2 and #3 to be viewed as a full-line producer; to maintain the channel leadership necessary to get its low-cost and high-profit products (products #4 and #5) into the right retail outlets; and to protect these products from attack by competitors.

In addition, the firm's overall marketing strategy may require this type of product mix in order to be successful, so the firm needs to continue to offer all five products. The firm can anticipate that it will face increased competition from other firms for the markets currently being served very profitably by products #4 and #5. Knowing this it can prepare in advance for such an assault by an aggressive competitor rather than being caught by surprise.

Product-mix analysis of this type can help a firm determine where it is strong and weak, where new products are needed, where it is likely to face increased competition, and so forth. The proper product mix is decided upon as part of the firm's strategic plan, and it can be decided upon for both offensive and defensive reasons. Companies that seek to develop new markets for their products or to go after target markets currently served by competitors need to plan an offensive marketing mix. Product-mix plans can also be developed to protect certain market niches from competitors. Regardless of the plan that is formulated, product-mix mapping and financial analysis can be extremely useful.

For product mapping to be worthwhile the products must be noticeably different from each other in the minds of consumers. The level of product quality should be established according to the needs of the target market. For example, to manufacture a high-quality product which must sell for $50 to return a profit for a target market in which customers are willing to pay only $5 makes little sense. The level of quality must at least meet the expectations of the product's consumers, and should be improved upon over the product's entire life cycle. Other dimensions that help differentiate a product in terms of quality are features and product styles. They help to communicate to consumers the idea that products are in fact different from one another.

Customer Service

An often overlooked part of product planning is the level of customer service that the firm will offer. For many staple convenience goods like food this may mean nothing more than providing a money-back guarantee and a toll-free 800 area code consumer hot line for questions, comments, and complaints. Martilla and James put forth the idea that consumers of a product can tell the producer the types of customer service they most desire and the quality of that service. The way to get maximum consumer satisfaction is to give consumers the maximum chance to complain, and then do what is necessary to alleviate their problems. To illustrate this procedure Martilla and James have developed a four-quadrant diagram where the consumers' responses to the types of service they desire are placed on the vertical axis, while on the horizontal axis how well the firm is doing at each item that is recorded (Figure 16–5).

The items in Quadrant I (upper left) are important to consumers but are being performed very poorly by the firm. They are problems that should be corrected immediately. The items found in Quadrant II (upper right) are also important to consumers but they are being done very well by the firm. The firm must continue to perform these services well. The items in Quadrant III

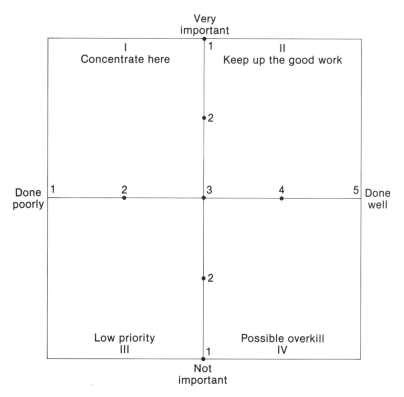

FIGURE 16–5
Mapping Product Performance

Source: Reprinted from John A. Martilla and John C. James, "Importance-Performance Analysis," *Journal of Marketing*, January 1977, pp. 77–79. Published by the American Marketing Association.

(lower left) are not being done very well but they are not very important to consumers. The firm should not ignore them, but they are of lower priority than the items in Quadrants I and II. The level of effort can be reduced for items in Quadrant IV (lower right) since they involve service that consumers care little about. The freed resources can then be used to improve the items listed in Quadrants I and III. In this way the marketer can provide consumers with what they want in terms of service without wasting effort on items that consumers do not care much about.

PACKAGING

Packaging has evolved from a technical matter to a marketing tool. Packaging was originally intended to protect a product from contaminants and in some cases to preserve freshness. The combination of better processing methods and packaging has added greatly to the shelf life of products. This is a worthy contribution, but changes in the marketplace have forced packaging to do a great deal more.

The expanded use of self-service selling, especially in supermarkets, requires that packaging be a marketing tool that helps sell the product. A successful package is now one that attracts attention to the product on the shelf and helps it stand out from the rest. The package carries the sales message to the customer and can be used to highlight the product's desirable features. For example, the label on Paul Newman's Industrial Strength Spaghetti Sauce contains a good amount of blue that matches the actor's famous blue eyes.

The packaging can help reinforce an image by looking classy if the item is supposed to be classy, or looking economical if it is a generic brand. Packaging not only helps a firm project the image it desires to the consumer, but it can also be a way to add functional convenience to the product. Microwavable meals in throw away plastic containers that look like fine dinnerware, frozen vegetables in sealed plastic boilable pouches, and so on are examples of functional packaging that adds to a product's consumer appeal and can lead to greater sales and profits.

SUMMARY

This chapter dealt with the product portion of the marketing mix. A definition of a product was given along with the explanation of why it must be defined in terms of consumer, not producer needs. The role of the product life cycle and the importance of adjusting the product mix to each stage were discussed. Also covered were the role of branding and packaging and how to evaluate product performance as part of an overall marketing mix.

To help marketers understand the product concept, a general classification system of products has been discussed. The first grouping is according to physical characteristics and includes durable goods, nondurable goods, and services. The second grouping is according to product use and includes consumer and industrial goods. Within the consumer goods group are the four subgroups of convenience goods, shopping goods, specialty goods, and unsought goods. Most of the items that are handled by agribusiness firms fall into the convenience goods category since they are purchased frequently but often with little thought, effort, or comparison shopping.

If agribusiness marketers have a better understanding of the motivation of buyers they can help a firm make better decisions surrounding product development and development of profitable product mixes. Buyer motivation also helps to explain why there is increased interest in the use of branding in the food system. Branding permits the firm to capture the greater profits possible from monopolistic competition. Thus, a thorough understanding of the product concept can enhance the marketing efforts of agribusiness firms.

QUESTIONS

1. Using the general classification system presented in this chapter, identify the product class for food. Describe the characteristics of the products in this classification that are of interest to marketing managers.
2. Why is there increased interest in attaching brand names to agricultural commodities such as chicken, oranges, and so on?
3. Describe the four stages in a product's life cycle.
4. Describe the concept of product mix and what the terms width, length, and depth mean in this context.
5. Why must packaging fill a role that extends beyond protecting the product?

17

Managing the Marketing Mix: The Price

Along with the development of a product that satisfies a defined consumer need, the seller must also select a price. Price is an integral part of a firm's marketing mix. All too often decisions regarding price are made entirely separately from the other three Ps of product, promotion, and place. This can lead to serious problems. While each of the four Ps is a separate item, their real strength comes from the synergism possible from the proper mixture of all four.[*]

Establishing the optimal price is important to a firm since it is the only one of the four Ps that deals with revenues; all the rest are expenses. In agribusiness firms that still cling to the production approach to the market, the establishment of the selling price is often an afterthought. This is especially true for firms that feel they have no control over price. This may have been appropriate when demand for most products exceeded supply, but it is generally no longer applicable in today's more competitive marketplace.

Price should be established in the marketing department since it must be part of the firm's overall marketing mix. The pricing procedure should be flexible enough to meet the competition among different, interrelated markets

---

[*]Portions of this chapter are drawn from James G. Beierlein, Kenneth C. Schneeberger, and Donald D. Osburn, *Principles of Agribusiness Management* (Englewood Cliffs, NJ: Prentice Hall, © 1986; a Reston book). Reprinted by permission of Prentice Hall, Inc., Englewood Cliffs, New Jersey.

and adjustable to changing situations within a single market. Proper pricing helps agribusiness firms reach the marketing and financial objectives set in the marketing and business plans by influencing the level of sales, profits, and market share.

The selection of the proper price is made a good deal easier if during the formulation of the strategic plan a firm has developed a clear idea of the target market and how the product is to be positioned. For example, if a firm is part of the dominant core of food manufacturers and during the strategic planning process decides that it is going to sell a very high-quality cookie to high-income households exclusively through gourmet shops, the selection of the proper price becomes a good deal easier since the marketing objectives have already been set.

PRICING TERMINOLOGY

Price means many things to many people. In this section the discussion will focus on identifying some of the more common pricing terms. Pricing, like just about everything else in business, has to be done with a clear objective in mind.

List Price.   List price is the published price for which the product is to sell. It is often provided in print form with a list of products. Premiums and discounts are applied to the list price to fit particular situations. In many instances the list price is the price at which sales actually take place. However, in many other cases it is merely the starting point of negotiations that end in a sale.

Price Discounts.   Discounts from the stated or list price are quite common. They give the seller added flexibility to meet the changing needs of the marketplace.

1. *Quantity Discounts.*   One of the most common types of price discounts is the quantity discount. In exchange for purchases of large quantities of goods the buyer receives either a reduction in the price per unit or some other benefit such as free delivery, free goods, etc. These discounts can be given on individual orders or they can be given for quantities purchased over some specified period of time such as a month or a quarter. For example, after buyers reach a certain level of quantity of purchases during a time period, they qualify for a discount based on those purchases.

2. *Prompt Payment Discounts.*   Another popular form of price discounts is the prompt payment discount. Here purchases are often marked

"2/10, net 30" which means that a 2 percent discount from the value of the invoice (the bill) can be taken if it is paid within ten days of its issuance. If the buyer does not take advantage of the early payment discount, the full amount of the bill must be paid at the end of thirty days. A finance charge is usually added after the thirty days have expired.

3. *Cash Discounts.* Another form of price discount is a cash discount. If payment in cash is given at the time the goods are received by the buyer, this can reduce the seller's cost by eliminating the cost of borrowing money and further collection expenses. In return and as an inducement for cash payment the seller passes some of the cost savings on to the buyer in the form of a discount. The best example is the gasoline stations that give a price discount to those customers who pay cash for their fuel.

4. *Seasonal Discounts.* To even out product demand throughout the year, seasonal discounts can be given. Farmers are often given a price discount if they purchase a bulk tank full of fuel at the end of the harvest season. This reduces the amount of inventory the fuel dealer must carry, gives him some extra sales at the end of the season when his sales might be slow, and improves his cash flow position.

5. *Trade Discounts.* Trade discounts are still another form of price discounts. In this case the seller simply offers the buyer a reduction from the suggested retail selling price. Such discounts are popular for clothing, agricultural equipment, and other types of big-ticket items.

These types of price discounts are often used by sellers to be competitive in the market. But a seller must remember three things about them. First, the seller must know his costs to know how great a discount he can offer without giving away all his profit. Second, these discounts must be given as part of an overall plan that involves all parts of the firm's marketing mix. For example, lowering price with a discount may help the firm to accomplish an overall objective such as increased market share. Third, in order to be legal the discounts must be offered to all buyers of like grade, quantity, and so on. When a firm knows its costs and uses price discounts as a part of its total marketing mix, it can enhance its marketing position.

Price Allowances. Allowances from the stated price can be given in return for certain actions on the part of the buyer. A well-known form of price allowance is the *trade-in allowance*, where a reduction in the selling price of a new item is given for used merchandise that is sold to the seller at the time the new product is purchased. Within the marketing system, *advertising allowances* are given to retailers by manufacturers to encourage them to purchase local advertising featuring the manufacturer's products. Another form of allowance is the *promotional allowance* or "push money" which manufacturers give to retail sales personnel for selling ("pushing") their product. This may be in the form of X dollars per unit sold, trips for those who sell the most, or other gifts.

Loss Leader Pricing.   The practice of widely advertising a below-cost price on a popular item that consumers buy often but generally cannot stockpile (such as eggs, milk, bread, and coffee) is known as loss leader pricing. The intent is to get customers into the store to buy the loss leaders with the hope that they will also buy enough other goods at normal profit margins to more than offset the lost profit.

Special Event Pricing.   Sometimes special prices are set for a limited period of time to coincide with some special event. Thus we see a Superbowl sellathon, an introductory offer, a Washington's Birthday sale, or a grand opening. Because of the "special values" offered during this limited sales period shoppers are encouraged to buy now!

Rebates.   Rebates are a popular form of pricing which came into being in the 1970s when the possibility of wage and price controls existed because of high rates of inflation. The actual selling price stays unchanged, but the buyer can get cash back directly from the manufacturer by sending in a form, and this amounts to a reduction in price. The manufacturer offers the rebate to all, but only those who follow through with the paperwork and are willing to wait actually receive it.

Geographical Pricing.   A popular form of pricing for industrial goods and physically large consumer goods such as automobiles is to quote a price effective at the factory. The cost of transporting the good is borne by the customer. The most common is *F.O.B. pricing*, where the factory will load the item onto a delivery truck or railroad car for free. Once it is loaded, the ownership of the good as well as the risk of loss or damage passes to the buyer. The buyer then must pay the cost of transportation. This is why it is called F.O.B.—Free On Board.

There are several variations of geographical pricing. One is to add a uniform delivery charge to all items, using an average delivery cost. The second is to include transportation in the selling price by incorporating the delivery cost into each item's price. A third variation is a system of shipping charges that is added to the selling price according to the distance from the warehouse. This is often accomplished by establishing shipping zones.

Bait and Switch Pricing. A company advertises a very attractive price for a popular item in order to get customers into the store. Once the customer is at the store, the salesperson explains why the sale item is not really a good buy and suggests a much better item for "just a few dollars more." Customers find it nearly impossible to buy the advertised item. This deceptive pricing scheme known as bait and switch pricing, is illegal.

Odd-Even Pricing. With odd-even pricing prices are set to end in either 5s or 9s. A price of $99.99 or $99.95 is perceived by many consumers to be a good deal less than a price of $100. This system of pricing is also supposed to have been developed as a way to force sales clerks to ring up all sales since they needed to open the cash register in order to give the customers change. There is some question today regarding the effectiveness of this practice.

Psychological Pricing. The rather murky area where prices are set in ranges where consumers perceive "they ought to be" is known as psychological pricing. Only a few years ago paperback books never sold for more than $1.95. There was thought to be great consumer resistance to prices above that level. In time, book publishers were able to change that perception and prices have moved considerably higher. Soft drink firms have encountered this same type of price resistance in vending machine sales. Candy manufacturers overcame it by changing the size of candy bars as their costs changed rather than risk price resistance. In some cases, for certain luxury items such as expensive liquors, cars, and perfumes, a high price may lead to increased sales since to the consumers of these products the high price seems to connote high quality.

PRODUCT LIFE CYCLE PRICING

As was discussed in the previous chapter, products move through distinct stages in a life cycle. Each stage requires a different approach to pricing as part of the marketing mix. The approach taken to pricing depends largely on the type of product involved, the type of market it faces, and the level of competition in the market.

When a new product is introduced, a firm has the option of adopting either *market skimming pricing* or *market penetration pricing. Market skimming pricing* is the concept of setting the initial price very high, then moving it down in steps as consumer demand is satisfied at each level of price. This approach works best in situations where: (1) demand is inelastic and greatly

---

A Firm's Approach to Pricing Depends on:

- The type of product involved
- The type of market it faces
- The level of competition in the market

---

exceeds supply at each price, (2) there is little difference in cost per unit for small volumes versus large volumes of production, (3) a high price will not attract many competitors, (4) the high price gives the firm a high-class image, and (5) repeat sales are not an important part of the market. As competitors begin to enter the market, and as all those who can afford the high price have their needs filled, the firm lowers its price in steps so that other consumers can release their pent-up demand for the product. Lowering the price discourages potential competitors by lowering their profit estimates. This approach permits the firm to gain the maximum revenue and profit from the product demand schedule.

Market penetration pricing is the concept of setting the initial price relatively low in order to: (1) gain maximum market share very quickly, (2) keep competitors out of the market, and (3) gain consumer loyalty for repeat sales. Prices may be cut further as economies of size bring about cost reductions. This approach works best in situations where: (1) demand is elastic and the consumer is price sensitive, (2) the average cost per unit falls very rapidly as volume grows larger, (3) the product can easily be copied by competitors, and (4) repeat sales represent a large part of the market for the product.

A good example of pricing over a product's life cycle is the market for pocket calculators and digital watches. They each began at very high prices ($200–$400) that reflected a price skimming approach. This later evolved into a penetration pricing approach ($3–$8) as the competition became more intense. These changes corresponded to the different stages of the products' life cycle.

PRICE MARKUPS

One of the areas of greatest confusion in pricing is markups, or the setting of a selling price when the seller's cost is known. Markups can be done in a variety of ways. Small retailers who have many different items to sell often find it useful to use a standard markup amount or percentage. The markup is added to their cost to give the selling price.

$$\text{cost} + \text{markup} = \text{selling price}$$

The point that causes the greatest confusion is that *the markup is given as a percentage of the selling price*. For example, if an item costs the seller $1.00 and the firm has a goal of a 20 percent gross profit, it will need to sell the item for $1.25 to accomplish this objective.

Selling price	$1.25	100%
Less: cost	−1.00	−80%
Gross margin	$ .25	20%

Many people are inclined to apply the markup margin to the cost of the item rather than to the selling price. This gives the retailer less than a 20 percent gross profit. If 20 percent is added to cost this will give a selling price of $1.20 but a gross margin of only 16 2/3 percent ($.20/$1.20).

Selling price	$1.20	100.00%
Less: cost	−1.00	−83.33%
Gross margin	$ .20	16.67%

Markups are calculated based on the selling price for several reasons. First, it assures the seller of achieving a target gross profit. Second, this method corresponds to the gross margin figures widely used in accounting and financial planning. Third, it matches the way many allowances and discounts are calculated using the suggested retail price.

THE RELATIONSHIP OF SELLING PRICE TO PROFITS AND RETURN ON ASSETS

Another misconception related to markups is the idea that the secret to higher profits is a higher markup. Except for unusual situations, nothing could be further from the truth. The goal is to maximize *total profits* from sales and not profit per unit of sales. Remember, total profit is calculated from profit per unit multiplied by the number of units sold. One method to increase total profits is to lower the price of the item. By charging a lower price and taking a lower profit per item, the firm hopes to increase the number of units that can be sold. If the demand for the item is elastic, this will lead to greater total revenue and profits.

A widely used measure of the effectiveness of management in using a firm's assets is return on assets (ROA). ROA is calculated by dividing profits by the value of the assets used to earn them. The value of the assets is found on the firm's balance sheet.

$$\frac{\text{return on}}{\text{assets}} = \frac{\text{profits}}{\text{assets}}$$

ROA can also be calculated by multiplying profits as a percentage of sales times the ratio of sales to total assets, or:

$$\frac{\text{return on}}{\text{assets}} = \frac{\text{profits}}{\text{sales}} \times \frac{\text{sales}}{\text{assets}}$$

ROA gives the level of profits relative to the level of assets invested. It can be measured against the rate of interest that can be earned on money invested in a savings account or other similar investment. It is one of the things that investors and banks look at to see how profitable the firm is, and how effective the firm's management is in employing the assets it has at its disposal. More importantly, it shows how the setting of price can affect the firm's accomplishment of its marketing and financial goals as set in its overall business plan. Thus, there is a great incentive for managers to seek the highest possible levels of return on the assets used in a business.

A manager can raise the level of return on assets by doing the following: (1) raising the amount of profit per dollar of sales, assuming the level of sales and assets do not change; (2) increasing the level of dollar sales, assuming the profits per dollar of sales and assets remain the same; (3) decreasing the level of assets while keeping sales and profits the same; or (4) some combination of these.

By looking at the ROA equation it is obvious that if the firm can increase sales by decreasing the selling price and profit per unit when demand is elastic, it can obtain higher total revenues, total profits, and a higher ROA. A less obvious way to increase ROA is to reduce the level of assets. One way to do this is through better inventory management. By increasing inventory turnover ratio (sales divided by average inventory), a firm can decrease the level of assets and obtain a higher ROA.

For example, if the ratio of sales to inventory is 2 to 1 (that is, sales are twice the average level of inventory), a firm with sales of $1,200,000 should need an average inventory of $600,000. But if through better management a firm can raise its inventory turnover ratio to 3 to 1, this same level of sales can be supported with an inventory of only $400,000. This releases $200,000 of assets to the firm for other uses. It may mean the firm needs to borrow less to finance its inventory and can now support the same level of sales with fewer assets. Therefore, the level of return on assets will rise.

Supermarkets are particularly adept at this type of asset management. They accept a low profit per dollar of sales (usually around 1 percent), but they maintain an attractive ROA (often 10 to 15 percent) by having a high level of sales per dollar of assets. They accomplish this by having very efficient, low-cost operations that have high inventory turnover ratios (often averaging around 24 times per year) made possible by maintaining very low levels of inventory. A look at the back room of most supermarkets shows little area devoted to inventory. Supermarkets increasingly rely on direct store delivery from suppliers as a means to limit inventory levels. Thus, the ability of supermarkets to pursue a marketing mix strategy that includes low prices and margins while retaining an acceptable ROA is made possible only because of their ability to turn over inventory very quickly and efficiently. Understanding the relationship between profit per dollar of sales and return on assets can greatly assist a firm in establishing the prices of its products.

Some food retailers have refined this concept still further by employing a system of variable markups that is sometimes referred to as variable price merchandising. Fast-moving items are often given low markups, since by pulling more shoppers into a store they can increase a store's sales volume. There is also some evidence that low markups on these items may make some economic sense since they are often less costly for the store to stock. Some food retailers have extended their cost control systems to include the measurement of the expenses associated with the handling of specific products within the store to determine the actual profit or loss from selling a product.

The increased reliance on the marketing approach has also led to a number of changes in the way products are designed. Firms are more likely to start with a detailed consumer preference analysis when establishing the parameters of their products. This often includes a consumer response as to what a product "ought to sell for." The production people and all the others involved in product development should incorporate these price preferences in their product development plans. This means not developing a product that must sell for at least $50 when consumers indicate they would not be willing to pay more than $12 for such an item.

The final issue to be addressed in this section deals with *product line pricing*. This refers to establishing the prices for a number of items sold by the same firm in such a way as to maximize the firm's overall profits. If a firm offers a full line of products from low quality to high quality, the differences in price between the products should reflect different levels of quality to consumers. The jump in price from a product of one quality to the next higher one should indicate the level of quality or some other characteristic that is discernible to the consumer. The price difference should not be so large as to discourage the buyer from "trading up," but it should always exceed the difference in cost to the firm between the two items if it is to improve the firm's profit picture.

PRICING STRATEGIES

At the beginning of this chapter it was stated that all pricing decisions should be made with a clear objective in mind. Worthy objectives could be to obtain a certain level of profits, or sales, or market share. This section is devoted to explaining how this is accomplished. The development of a good pricing policy is critical to the long-run success of a business. The development of such a policy requires that the firm know (1) its costs for each product so that price can be set at a level that will generate a profit, (2) the responsiveness of product sales to changes in price (elasticity), (3) the current prices and probable costs of operation of major competitors, and (4) the probable response of major competitors to anything the firm might make. Knowing these things in advance can greatly assist a marketing manager in developing the pricing part of the marketing mix. It should also reduce the chances of being caught by surprise by actions on the part of the firm's customers or competitors.

There are almost as many pricing strategies as there are marketing managers, but there are several strategies that are widely used. These are discussed below.

To Develop Effective Pricing Policy a Firm Needs to Know:

- Its costs for each product
- The responsiveness of sales levels to changes in price
- The current prices and probable costs of operation of major competitors
- The probable responses of major competitors to anything a firm might make

---

Cost-Plus Pricing

Cost-plus pricing is a simple procedure to apply and merely involves adding a constant markup (amount or percentage) to the seller's cost per unit. As a general rule cost-plus pricing has the advantage of being fast and simple to apply, especially where there are many different products; but it should be applied with caution since it does not take into account elasticity of demand or the competitive situation.

Pricing at the Market

The simplest policy is to price at the market. All it requires is setting the price equal to that of other sellers. This can be a reasonable thing to do if the local market is dominated by a large competitor. However, the establishment of this price represents the competitor's costs, perception of the market, and view of how customers will respond, not yours. A better approach is to examine these same items from the point of view of your own firm.

Pricing Using Contribution Analysis

The determination of the most profitable level of output can be done on a per unit basis. To do this requires building a formula that covers the fixed costs of production, the variable costs of production, plus some provision for profit.

$$\frac{\text{selling price}}{\text{per unit}} = \frac{\text{total cost}}{\text{per unit}} + \frac{\text{profit}}{\text{per unit}}$$

This can also be written as:

$$\frac{\text{selling price}}{\text{per unit}} = \left[\frac{\text{fixed costs}}{\text{per unit}} + \frac{\text{variable costs}}{\text{per unit}}\right] + \left[\frac{\text{profit}}{\text{per unit}}\right]$$

Let's make a simplifying assumption and change fixed costs per unit to overhead costs per unit, since that is the most common name that business uses for these costs. Next let's rearrange some of the terms in this equation to get the formula for profits into a more usable form by moving the variable cost per unit to the other side of the equal sign.

$$
\begin{bmatrix} \text{selling price} & \text{variable costs} \\ \text{per} & - & \text{per} \\ \text{unit} & & \text{unit} \end{bmatrix} = \begin{bmatrix} \text{overhead} & \text{profit} \\ \text{per} & + & \text{per} \\ \text{unit} & & \text{unit} \end{bmatrix}
$$

Now the difference between the selling price and variable costs per unit must equal to the overhead costs and profit per unit. Let's suppose that an agribusiness firm did this for one of its products and found that its variable costs of production are $75 per unit. If each unit sold for $125 there would be $50 per unit left over for overhead costs and profits.

Selling price	$125 per unit
Less: Variable costs	− 75 per unit
Left to pay overhead and profit	$ 50 per unit

This $50 per unit would be available to contribute to paying overhead and profit, and it is possible to call the difference between the selling price per unit and variable costs per unit *contribution.*

$$
\begin{bmatrix} \text{selling} & \text{variable} \\ \text{price} & \text{costs} \\ \text{per} & - & \text{per} \\ \text{unit} & \text{unit} \end{bmatrix} = contribution = \begin{bmatrix} \text{overhead} & \text{profit} \\ \text{per} & + & \text{per} \\ \text{unit} & & \text{unit} \end{bmatrix}
$$

Contribution can be used to establish a selling price. Continuing the example above, it is possible to calculate a *contribution margin percentage* which is the percent of the selling price that is left after paying the variable costs per unit. In this case the contribution margin percentage is 40 percent and is calculated as follows:

Selling price	$125 per unit	100%
Less: Variable costs	− 75 per unit	− 60%
Contribution	$ 50 per unit	40%

If this contribution margin percentage (40 percent) is typical of all the items that are sold by this firm, the selling price of any other item can be quickly determined once the variable costs per unit are known by using the following formula:

$$
\text{selling price per unit} = \frac{\text{variable costs per unit}}{(1 - \text{contribution margin percentage})}
$$

For example, if the firm sold another product that had a variable cost per unit of $120, its selling price would be:

$$\text{selling price per unit} = \frac{\$120}{(1 - 0.40)}$$
$$= \$200$$

Thus by knowing and applying the concept of contribution, marketing managers can greatly simplify pricing procedures for firms with many products. The real value of contribution analysis becomes more apparent when it is used in break-even analysis.

Pricing Using Break-Even Analysis

The contribution concept (selling price per unit – variable costs per unit = contribution to overhead and profits per unit) can also be applied to break-even analysis. Break-even analysis is perhaps the marketing manager's most valuable tool. It can be used to answer a number of important questions in making marketing decisions. In its simplest form break-even analysis seeks to determine the level of sales that will yield the firm neither a profit nor a loss but merely leave it even (that is, profits = 0).

The *break-even point* is calculated from the profit equation where profit is equal to zero.

$$\text{profit} = 0 = \text{total revenue} - \text{total cost}$$
$$= P{\cdot}Q - (VC{\cdot}Q - FC)$$

where P = selling price per unit
$\quad Q$ = quantity sold
$\quad VC$ = variable costs per unit
$\quad FC$ = fixed costs

Rearranging the terms of the equation to solve for the quantity (Q) that must be sold to reach the break-even point (*BEP*) where profit is equal to zero gives:

$$0 = P{\cdot}Q - VC{\cdot}Q - FC$$
$$= (P - VC)Q - FC$$
$$Q = \frac{FC}{(P - VC)}$$

where Q = number of units that must be sold to break even

The result is that the break-even point is determined by dividing the fixed costs by the *contribution per unit* $(P - VC)$.

To illustrate the use of break-even analysis, let's draw upon an earlier example. Market research indicates that sales in a particular market should be 20,000 units in the coming year if an item is priced at $125 per unit. Variable costs per unit are $75. If the firm's overhead (fixed cost) is $750,000, how many units must the firm sell to break even? This is the same as asking how many units, each contributing $50 to overhead and profit, must be sold to pay off the fixed cost of $750,000. Using the formula given above, the number of units that must be sold to break even is:

$$Q = \frac{FC}{(P - VC)}$$
$$= \frac{\$750,000}{(\$125 - \$75)}$$
$$= \frac{\$750,000}{\$50}$$
$$= 15,000 \text{ units}$$

To see whether this worked, let's apply the profit equation.

$$\begin{aligned}
\text{profit} &= P{\cdot}Q - VC{\cdot}Q - FC \\
&= (\$125)(15,000) - (\$75)(15,000) - \$750,000 \\
&= \$1,875,000 - \$1,125,000 - \$750,000 \\
&= 0
\end{aligned}$$

The level of profits is exactly equal to zero, and 15,000 units is the break-even quantity.

If the firm sells the 20,000 units its market research indicates it will sell at this price, how much profit will it make?

$$\begin{aligned}
\text{profit} &= P{\cdot}Q - VC{\cdot}Q - FC \\
&= (\$125)(20,000) - (\$75)(20,000) - \$750,000 \\
&= \$2,500,000 - \$1,500,000 - \$750,000 \\
&= \$250,000
\end{aligned}$$

The predicted sale of 20,000 units will give the firm a profit of $250,000. Thus, sales can be as much as 25 percent below the sales forecast before the firm starts losing money. This is valuable information for managers trying to assess the chances for success. It is also important to note that profit with the expected sales of 20,000 units is also equal to the contribution per unit times the number of units sold above the break-even quantity ($50 × 5,000 units = $250,000). Drawing a graph can provide a way to visualize this situation (Figure 17-1).

As can be seen from the graph, once sales expand beyond 15,000 units, all the fixed costs are paid. Any additional contribution goes directly to profit. This is why the profit at 20,000 units is equal to the contribution per unit ($50) multiplied by the number of units over the break-even quantity (5,000 = 20,000 – 15,000 units) or $250,000.

The break-even point can also be calculated in terms of dollar sales. This is done using the contribution margin percentage and the following equation:

$$\frac{\text{break–even point}}{\text{in dollar sales}} = \frac{\text{fixed costs}}{\text{contribution margin percentage}}$$

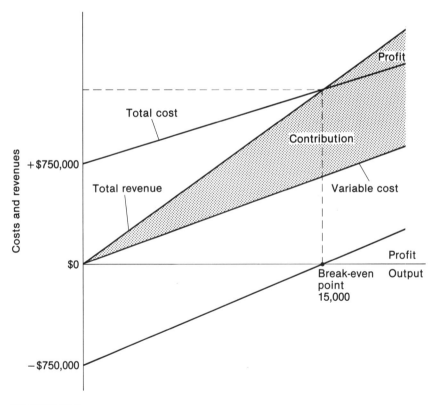

FIGURE 17-1
Break-Even Chart Showing Contribution to Profit

Using the same example as above, the break-even point in dollar sales is:

$$\frac{\text{break--even point}}{\text{in dollar sales}} = \frac{\$750,000}{0.40}$$

This equation answers the question of what level of sales is required so that 40 percent of it is equal to $750,000 (the fixed costs). In this instance the answer is:

$$\frac{\text{break--even point}}{\text{in dollar sales}} = \$1,875,000$$

This can be translated into units by dividing sales by the price per unit ($1,875,000 divided by $125), which gives:

$$\frac{\text{break--even point}}{\text{in units}} = \frac{\$1,875,000}{\$125}$$
$$= 15,000 \text{ units}$$

Break-even analysis can be used to establish a selling price by rearranging the contribution equation from:

$$\frac{\text{selling price}}{\text{per unit}} - \frac{\text{variable costs}}{\text{per unit}} = \text{contribution}$$

back to:

$$\frac{\text{selling price}}{\text{per unit}} = \frac{\text{variable costs}}{\text{per unit}} + \text{contribution}$$

The level of contribution can be determined from the break-even equation by rearranging it from:

$$Q = \frac{\text{fixed costs}}{\text{contribution}}$$

to:

$$\text{contribution} = \frac{\text{fixed costs}}{Q}$$

Using the values from the previous example where fixed costs are $750,000, variable costs are $75 per unit, and the estimated sales are 15,000 units, it is possible to determine a break-even selling price consistent with these figures. The first task is to determine the level of contribution from each unit of sales.

$$\text{contribution} = \frac{\$750,000}{15,000 \text{ units}}$$
$$= \$50 \text{ per unit}$$

The next task is to calculate selling price.

$$\text{selling price} = \text{contribution} + \frac{\text{variable costs}}{\text{per unit}}$$
$$= \$50 + \$75$$
$$= \$125$$

Thus, a selling price of $125 is consistent with the firm's costs and projected sales figures. If the sales estimate is revised to 20,000 units with costs held the same, a break-even selling price consistent with this data would be calculated as follows:

$$\text{contribution} = \frac{\text{fixed costs}}{Q}$$
$$= \frac{\$750,000}{20,000}$$
$$= \$37.50$$

$$\text{selling price} = \text{contribution} + \text{variable costs}$$
$$= \$37.50 + \$75.00$$
$$= \$112.50$$

If the firm wished only to sell 10,000 units and use a price-skimming approach, it would have to have a price of at least $150 per unit to break even, calculated as follows:

$$\text{contribution} = \frac{\text{fixed costs}}{Q}$$
$$= \frac{\$750,000}{10,000}$$
$$= \$75$$
$$\text{selling price} = \text{contribution} + \text{variable costs}$$
$$= \$75 + \$75$$
$$= \$150$$

On the other hand, suppose the firm has decided to adopt a penetration pricing approach. Market research has estimated the firm can sell 100,000 units but only if the selling price is no more than $75 per unit. This strategy can be evaluated using break-even analysis. If the current plant has the capacity to produce this volume and fixed costs remain the same, the contribution per unit becomes:

$$\text{contribution} = \frac{\$750,000}{100,000}$$
$$= \$7.50$$

To reach the goal of a $75 price, the firm must seek ways to lower the variable costs per unit, since the current configuration of costs and sales volume will require a selling price of $82.50 just to break even at 100,000 units (selling price = $82.50 = $7.50 + $75). Armed with this information, the production people can seek ways to reduce the fixed and variable costs. Let's assume that because of price discounts received through high-volume purchasing, the firm is able to reduce variable costs per unit to $60. Now the break-even selling price would be $67.50 (selling price = $67.50 = $7.50 + $60) at 100,000 units. Therefore, at a selling price of $75, the sale of the 100,000 units should net the firm a profit of:

$$
\begin{aligned}
\text{profit} &= P{\cdot}Q - VC{\cdot}Q - FC \\
&= (\$75)(100,000) - (\$60)(100,000) - \$750,000 \\
&= \$7,500,000 - \$6,000,000 - \$750,000 \\
&= \$750,000
\end{aligned}
$$

Thus, by using break-even analysis a marketing manager can examine a variety of price and quantity relationships that will allow the firm to meet its objectives. By knowing the variable costs per unit, estimated sales, and the level of fixed costs, it is possible to determine a selling price that is consistent with these values. By using break-even analysis, managers can know *beforehand* the level of profits (if any) possible from each combination of values.

Break-Even Analysis and Target Return Pricing

Break-even analysis can also be used to determine the minimum level of sales needed to meet a profit objective set as either a percentage of sales or as a fixed dollar amount.

Meeting a Profit-per-Dollar-of-Sales Objective. When the objective is to reach a profit objective set as a percentage of sales objective, the most appropriate formula is the one giving the break-even point in dollars, or:

$$\text{break–even point} = \frac{\text{fixed costs}}{CMP}$$

where CMP = contribution margin percentage

For example, if a profit equal to 10 percent of dollar sales is necessary before a firm will enter a business, the minimum level of sales required to meet that objective can be calculated by modifying the break-even formula to:

$$\text{break–even point} = \frac{\text{fixed costs}}{(CMP - RPP)}$$

where RPP = required profit percentage

Using the values from the earlier example where

fixed costs contribution	= $750,000
margin percentage	= 0.40
required profit percentage	= 0.10
selling price	= $125/unit

the minimum level of sales needed to make profits equal 10 percent of sales will be:

$$
\begin{aligned}
\text{break–even point} &= \frac{\$750,000}{(0.40 - 0.10)} \\
&= \frac{\$750,000}{0.30} \\
&= \$2,500,000 \ (20,000 \text{ units at } \$125/\text{unit})
\end{aligned}
$$

Let's use the profit formula to see if this works.

$$
\begin{aligned}
\text{profit} &= P{\cdot}Q - VC{\cdot}Q - FC \\
&= (\$125)(20,000) - (\$75)(20,000) - \$750,000 \\
&= \$2,500,000 - \$1,500,000 - \$750,000 \\
&= \$250,000
\end{aligned}
$$

The profit of $250,000 is 10 percent of total sales, and the profit objective is met. Thus, annual sales must be at least $2,500,000 for the firm to achieve its profit objective. The firm must assess its chances of reaching this level of sales given its product, market area, and marketing mix.

Meeting a Specific Dollar Objective.   It is also possible to determine the minimum level of sales needed to reach a specific profit objective using break-even analysis. If the profit objective is set as a fixed dollar amount it can be treated as an addition to fixed costs. All that is needed is to modify the break-even formula to yield:

$$\text{break--even point} = \frac{FC + PO}{CMP}$$

where PO = profit objective

Using the values from the example above and adding that the firm will not enter a market if the annual level of profits is not at least $100,000, what is the minimum level of sales needed to accomplish this? The solution becomes:

$$\text{break--even point} = \frac{\$750,000 + \$100,000}{0.40}$$
$$= \$2,125,000 \ (17,000 \text{ units at } \$125/\text{unit})$$

Testing this in the profit equation gives:

$$\begin{aligned}
\text{profit} &= P{\cdot}Q - VC{\cdot}Q - FC \\
&= (\$125)(17,000) - (\$75)(17,000) - \$750,000 \\
&= \$2,125,000 - \$1,275,000 - \$750,000 \\
&= \$100,000
\end{aligned}$$

To meet the fixed profit objective of $100,000 per year requires sales of at least $2,125,000. Hence, break-even analysis provides a quick and objective means to evaluate the influence of price, profit objectives, and level of sales on the firm.

Contribution and break-even analysis are powerful concepts that can greatly assist a firm in establishing and analyzing the price portion of its marketing mix. However, it is important to remember the limitations of these tools so that they can be used wisely. The chief limits are found in the assumptions behind them and include: (1) all products are produced and sold in the same period (that is, there are no inventories), (2) all sales and purchases are for cash, (3) only one time period is considered, and (4) all prices, products, and production processes are fixed.

Despite these shortcomings, the value of break-even analyses comes from their use as "first cut procedures" or "ballpark techniques" to determine whether an idea has any merit on the surface. If an idea passes these tests, it should be given greater scrutiny. Given their ease of use, contribution and break-even analysis can be of great value in showing the relationship among sales, production, costs, and profits. They are also valuable tools in increasing the effectiveness of management decision making.

SUMMARY

This chapter explored the price portion of the firm's marketing mix. Pricing must be given careful attention since it is the only part of the marketing mix that deals with revenues. This is the reason that pricing should be established in the marketing department rather than in the accounting department. Proper pricing helps agribusinesses reach the financial and marketing objectives set in their marketing and business plan by influencing the level of sales, profits, and market share. The selection of a proper price is made easier if the firm has a clear idea of who its target market is and how it wishes its products to be positioned.

Since price means many things to many people, it is important that marketing managers understand pricing terminology. This includes knowing the difference between list price and F.O.B. price, for example. Failure to understand the difference can seriously jeopardize the accomplishment of the business's objective. For this reason a major portion of the chapter was devoted to explaining some of the most commonly used pricing terms.

The pricing of a product is also affected by its position in the product life cycle. A price that is appropriate at one part of the cycle may lead to disaster if applied at another. New products can employ either a market skimming or a market penetration pricing scheme, depending on the marketing objective.

Several technical subjects related to pricing were also addressed in the chapter. The confusion surrounding the proper way to calculate a price markup was discussed first. The best way to calculate markups was shown to be as a percentage of the selling price of the product. This approach is the one that is most consistent with other pricing and accounting procedures. The impact of pricing decisions on the firm's profits and return on assets was also illustrated, to remind managers that pricing decisions have far-reaching implications across the firm. Break-even analysis helps managers establish good pricing policies and illustrates the relationship that exists between prices, quantities sold, and costs. It is important that managers appreciate how these three different items are related, can affect profits, and can form the basis of a firm's pricing strategy.

It is vital that managers understand the impact that pricing has on the success of a firm and the pricing alternatives that are available. The ability to properly manage this aspect of the business can allow managers to more easily accomplish the financial and marketing objectives established in the business plan.

QUESTIONS

1. Why must price be set in the marketing department and as a part of the firm's overall marketing mix?
2. What is the difference between a price discount and a price allowance?
3. What are market skimming pricing and market penetration pricing, and in what situations are each appropriate?
4. What is a price markup, how is it calculated, and why does it correspond to the gross margin used in accounting?
5. Explain how supermarkets can increase their profits by lowering prices?

18

Managing the Marketing Mix: The Place

A critical but often overlooked part of a successful marketing mix is place. Place deals with the movement of products from producers to consumers. Place involves all the people, firms, and activities that insure that the right product, carrying the right price, is in the right place so that the consumers in the target market can conveniently purchase it.

Success of the place portion of the marketing mix requires the development of two separate market channel systems. The first one involves the selection and organization of a system of market channel middlemen who will efficiently and effectively move the firm's products to the consumers in the target market. The second one involves the establishment of a physical distribution system that will actually move the products through the system of market channel middlemen to consumers.

Both market channel systems can take many years to develop, and once in place can be hard to change. This is why development of the place portion of the marketing mix must be done with great care. However, despite its importance, place is the portion of the marketing mix that the firm can least control. The members of the market channel system are not normally under the direct control of the producer of the product; they are independent businesses who have their own marketing mixes and objectives.

THE ROLE OF MARKETING CHANNEL INTERMEDIARIES

Marketing channel intermediaries include all those people and firms that facilitate movement of products from the producer to the final consumer. This group includes wholesalers, retailers, brokers, manufacturers' representatives, sales agents, and other middlemen that move the products through the marketing channel. It also includes the transportation, warehousing, and other firms that are involved in the physical movement and storage of products.

These firms exist in the marketing system because they perform a number of valuable marketing functions that are desired by consumers but are usually beyond the ability of producers to perform efficiently. These functions normally add time, place, and possession utility to products.

One of the major marketing problems solved by market channel intermediaries is the quantity-assortment problem. The *quantity-assortment problem* is that product manufacturers are generally organized to turn out large quantities of a few products, while consumers seek to purchase small quantities of a relatively large assortment of products. Marketing channel intermediaries solve the quantity-assortment problem by purchasing large quantities of individual products from many firms, and then offering this wide assortment of goods in smaller unit sizes to their customers.

For example, a wholesale grocer may buy a railroad carload of each of the fifty-seven varieties of products offered by H.J. Heinz, a tractor-trailer load of each kind of canned good that Del Monte sells, and so on. The wholesaler breaks this assortment of larger unit-sized orders (carloads, trailer loads) into a wider assortment of smaller-sized units (pallets and cases) that are desired by individual retail grocery stores. The retailer may buy from several wholesalers in order to offer an even wider assortment of products to consumers who purchase the smallest size units available (individual cans, boxes, and bottles).

The middlemen exist because they carry out necessary marketing functions, and they survive because they perform these functions more efficiently than producers. For example, Heinz and Del Monte would not find it practical to sell their own products directly to consumers. They would have to acquire transportation equipment, build and staff distribution centers and retail outlets, and solve a host of other problems to accomplish this. Even if they did all this it is doubtful that consumers would be willing to go from store to store if each store carried only the products of a single producer.

All of the market channel or place functions must be performed if the marketing system is to function efficiently. However, there is no certainty about who must perform each marketing function. In agribusiness many of these activities are performed by channel intermediaries, but they can and are increasingly being carried out by product manufacturers and retailers. Who performs each function for a specific product depends upon custom, the type of product, and the marketing objectives of individual firms involved.

The length of the marketing channel can also vary. The shortest marketing channel is found with *direct marketing* where the producer sells directly to the consumer. Roadside marketing, farmers' markets, and pick-your-own operations are common examples of the direct marketing approach. Producers of custom-made products and providers of services often market directly to purchasers. This type of marketing is often done by sellers of steel buildings, food processing equipment, aerial spray applications, and tax preparation services.

Most agribusiness products move through traditional, longer marketing channels that include some or all of the following participants:

Producers→Processors→Manufacturers→Wholesalers → Retailers→Consumers

This longer channel does not normally include any direct contact between manufacturer and consumer, and is referred to as *indirect marketing*. The remainder of this chapter is devoted to a discussion of indirect marketing since it is the most common form of marketing.

DEVELOPING INDIRECT MARKETING CHANNELS

As was stated earlier, one of the objectives of the place part of the marketing mix is the development of a strong system of middlemen who will give the firm's product a high level of attention. Since the middlemen also stand to profit from product sales, they should be viewed as market channel partners. In fact, one way for manufacturers to gain the cooperation of market channel participants is to point out the benefits of working together in an informal marketing partnership.

When the marketing plan is developed it should include a determination of which marketing channels will help the firm best accomplish its marketing objectives. Again, knowing *who* the customers are, *where* they are located, and *what* their shopping habits are can help a firm decide where to make their products available for sale, what types of marketing channels to use, and what types of middlemen to employ in the development of the marketing channels.

In general, the ideal level of market exposure is to have the product sufficiently available to be conveniently located for the members of the target market, but not more than that. Flooding the market with the product can lead to excessive distribution costs, high levels of unsold and returned merchandise, and low profits. On the other hand, if the product is hard to find it can lead to lower sales and profits. The best solution is to find the most efficient level of market exposure that is consistent with the firm's marketing objectives.

Depending upon the type of product and level of service required in the market channel, the firm can select from three approaches when deciding where to sell its products. A firm can employ *intensive distribution*. With an intensive distribution approach, the firm sells its product through any outlet that is willing to take it. This approach is very popular for most staple convenience products such as food, chewing gum, and candy. This is one reason that consumers can generally find these items in places like airports, gas stations, and factories as well as in food stores. Intensive distribution gives these goods maximum place utility, which is important for high sales of this class of product.

A second approach is the use of *exclusive distribution*. In this approach the firm selects just a few intermediaries to handle its products in specified territories. In return for this exclusive selling right the manufacturer expects to get a strong sales and service effort from the market channel intermediary. This approach is used more with shopping goods where consumers spend considerable time looking for particular brand names, require technical help, and make product comparisons as a common part of the purchasing decision.

The third approach, *selective distribution*, falls between the other two approaches. In this case the producer sells only through those intermediaries that the firm selects, but the middlemen are not given an exclusive right to sell the product. The intermediaries selected are the ones that are willing to give the product special attention, put forth a strong selling effort, pay their

---

Three Approaches to Distribution

- *Intensive Distribution*—the firm sells the product through any outlet that is willing to take it
- *Exclusive Distribution*—the firm selects just a few intermediaries to handle its products in specified territories
- *Selective Distribution*—the producer sells only through those intermediaries that the firm selects, but the middlemen are not given an exclusive right to sell the product

bills on time, and show concern about maintaining profit margins on the products they sell. This approach is more popular for shopping and specialty goods. Agribusinesses use all three of these approaches. However, selective distribution is most common in the input industries, while most consumer food products companies utilize an intensive distribution approach.

Manufacturers can foster sales growth in distribution channels by utilizing either push or pull marketing (that is, pushing or pulling their products through the distribution system). *Push marketing* is accomplished by having product manufacturers initiate a strong personal selling or sales promotional effort directed at market channel intermediaries.

For example, an agricultural chemical company might implement an early order promotional campaign. Because of this push a field representative employed by the chemical company might call on a wholesale distributor and offer a price discount and a wholesale sales incentive program (such as a trip to the Superbowl for the wholesaler with the highest sales) if the wholesaler orders a certain amount of product before some specific date. The agricultural chemical company's reasoning is that the wholesaler will actively sell the product once it is in inventory and the incentive program will encourage the wholesaler's sales force to push the product on through to retailers.

Pull marketing attempts to raise the level of sales by using a strong mass selling effort directed at the users or final consumers. The objective is to put pressure on retailers to stock the product by having consumers demand it. Pull marketing is often used by food manufacturers to promote new products. Since shelf space is limited, a new product must displace an old one in order to gain its spot on the supermarket's shelf. If large numbers of customers ask for a new product, supermarket managers are more likely to stock it. Both of these approaches are most effective when coordinated with other parts of the marketing mix.

DEVELOPING THE PHYSICAL DISTRIBUTION SYSTEM

The second system in the place portion of product mix deals with the development of a physical distribution system that can efficiently and effectively move products to the consumer. For these efforts to be successful physical distribution should be viewed from a marketing perspective, not thought of as an extension of the production process. The marketing functions performed in the market channel are an integral part of the product because they can influence its level of sales. This means that physical distribution is an indispensable part of the marketing process.

Although the stated objective of many firms is to minimize physical distribution costs, it is important to keep in mind that the proper objective for the firm with respect to place is to determine the most convenient placement of the product for the consumer and thereby maximize the profits of the firm. Physical distribution involves control of inventory levels, selection of transportation modes (for instance, rail versus truck versus ship), and location of plants, warehouses, and retail outlets. All three areas play a part in the overall physical and technical efficiency of the firm and its ability to satisfy the needs of consumers. They affect the quality of customer service by influencing the length of delivery times, the number of customer order mistakes, and the number of stock outs. Such matters must be addressed as part of the firm's marketing plan. Minimizing physical distribution costs is not the best objective if it fails to lead to greater consumer satisfaction and higher overall profits for the firm.

The physical distribution planning process begins with an examination of the tasks affecting consumer satisfaction that are related to place utility. According to Kotler[*] these are: order processing, warehousing, inventory, and transportation.

Order Processing

A computer-assisted order processing system can speed up the process so that consumers can receive their goods more quickly. The use of computers can also reduce errors in order transmittal. This can only lead to greater consumer satisfaction and service, and enhance the firm's competitive edge in the market. The system can be designed to produce shipping documents, update inventory, bill customers, confirm orders to customers, and so on, all at one time.

Warehousing

The location and design of warehouses can greatly affect a firm's ability to meet consumers' needs efficiently. One food distribution firm made a great improvement in warehousing efficiency by having order forms printed with the products listed in the order in which they are stored on the shelves. For example, the first item on the first page of the form is found in the first aisle, in the first bin on the top shelf. The last item on the form is found in the last

---

[*]Philip Kotler, *Marketing Management, Analysis, Planning, Implementation, and Control*, 6th ed. (Englewood Cliffs, N.J.: Prentice-Hall, 1988, p.579.

aisle, in the last bin on the bottom shelf. This allows the warehouse personnel to pick orders quickly without backtracking. The same firm makes sure delivery trucks are loaded so that the first stop's order is the last one loaded, while the last stop's order is the first one loaded. These are details, but they can make a significant difference in costs and can lead to increases in customer satisfaction.

Inventory

The maintenance of inventory is expensive, but so are stock outs (not having a product in inventory). Carrying large inventories guards against stock outs, but it is also very expensive in terms of warehouse space and interest and insurance costs. But not having an item in inventory can lead to lost sales. The objective is to have the right amounts of the right products on hand at all times. That is not an easy task. However, computerized inventory systems have proven to be a very effective way to accomplish this, and have led to greater efficiencies in this area.

Transportation

The selection of the best mode of transportation should be based on carrier costs and the level of customer satisfaction desired (on-time delivery performance of carrier, condition of the goods when they arrive, and so on). The deregulation of the transportation industry has made these decisions more complex, but also provides marketers with opportunities to negotiate more favorable rates and conditions.

SUMMARY

Place plays an important role in the makeup of a successful marketing mix. Place decisions insure that the right product, at the right price is put into the right location so that it is convenient for the consumer to purchase it. The place portion of the marketing mix requires the development of a system of middlemen who will make a strong effort to market the firm's products. Place also includes the development of an efficient physical distribution system. The place portion of the marketing mix will be more effective if it is approached as part of the firm's overall marketing effort rather than as an extension of the manufacturing process.

QUESTIONS

1. What are the two systems that must function effectively for the place portion of the marketing mix to function properly? Briefly explain how each operates and why it is important to the success of this portion of the marketing mix?

2. What are marketing channel intermediaries and what is their role in the marketing system?

3. What is the difference between direct marketing and indirect marketing?

4. What is the difference between pushing and pulling a product through the marketing system?

5. How can the use of computers increase the efficiency with which an agribusiness firm fills the place portion of its marketing mix?

19

Managing the Marketing Mix: The Promotion

Promotion is the fourth part of the firm's marketing mix. With promotion the firm attempts to communicate to members of the target market that the product that will completely satisfy their special unmet needs is available at the right price and in the right locations. Promotion involves all forms of communication between the seller and potential buyers; it is designed to influence attitudes and buyer behavior. More specifically, the objective of promotion is to convince members of the target market to buy the seller's product.

This objective can be realized through the application of the following three promotional methods: *mass selling*, *personal selling*, and *sales promotion*. Most agribusiness firms use a combination of the three. The selection of the proper mixture is largely dependent upon the firm's objectives as defined in the marketing plan. However, for this communication process to be effective, the message and how it is communicated should be defined largely in terms of the needs and perceptions of the consumers in the target market. After all, successful communication requires not only an exchange of information but also mutual understanding.

Mass selling is selling to a large number of potential consumers at one time. There are two forms of mass selling. The first is *advertising*, which includes all forms of paid mass selling. The second is *publicity*, which includes all types of unpaid mass selling.

Personal selling is one-on-one selling by a salesperson. It is generally felt to be the most effective method of communicating with individual members of a target market, because a good salesperson can adjust his or her marketing mix on the spot to fit the unique needs of each customer. Unfortunately, because of the high level of attention that is devoted to each customer, it is generally the most expensive promotional method. It is sufficiently different from mass selling and sales promotion to warrant discussion separately in the following chapter.

Sales promotion includes all activities that complement personal and mass selling. Contests, coupons, in-store signs and banners, and give-aways are all part of promotion. Sales promotion is sometimes hard to separate from mass selling and personal selling because it is usually most effective when done in concert with other forms of promotion. For example, in-store signs and banners might be used to announce a contest that is also being promoted in the firm's advertising program.

Like every other element of marketing, promotion can be effective only if the other parts of the marketing mix are carefully chosen. This means that there must be a good product that fills a consumer need. It must be priced right and available in the right locations. The function of promotion is to make sure that the previously identified target market is made aware of all this. After all, consumers cannot buy what they do not know about. Remember too that if the product is lousy, overpriced, and not readily available, the best promotion program in the world will not convince customers to buy it.

MASS SELLING THROUGH ADVERTISING AND PUBLICITY

Mass selling, like all the other parts of promotion, is a form of communication. This means it is concerned with the exchange of ideas. The whole process will work only if the firm has a clear and simple promotional message to send to the members of the target market. This in turn means that the firm must have a well-defined market objective in mind.

The marketing objective should be as specific and measurable as possible so the firm can evaluate the results. For example, the marketing objective might be to increase the sales volume of a product by 10 percent in the next ninety days. Or it could be to introduce a new product or service. Or it could be to help a previous buyer to reconfirm a prior buying decision. These marketing objectives should be developed from the firm's marketing plan.

Once the marketing objective has been decided, the marketing manager must decide what the goal of the promotional message is to be. If the

---

The Promotional Goals

- To Inform
- To Persuade
- To Remind

---

marketing objective is to introduce a new product, an appropriate promotional goal might be *to inform* the target market. If it is to increase sales 10 percent in the next ninety days, an appropriate promotional goal might be *to persuade* the target market to buy this product now. If the marketing objective is to help a buyer reconfirm a previous buying decision, an appropriate promotional goal might be *to remind* the members of the target market that this is really a good product that will give them the benefits they seek. In each case the goal of the promotional campaign is different depending on what the firm has as its marketing objective. If this planning process is followed, the final step of developing the actual clear and simple message becomes considerably easier because the marketing manager already knows who the target market is, what their needs are, how the product fills these needs, what the firm's marketing objectives are, and what the promotional goals are.

Once the marketing objectives and promotional goals have been agreed upon, the manager must select the medium (television, radio, newspapers, direct mail, billboards, and so on) that will most effectively communicate this clear and simple message to the target market. Having developed the business and marketing plan, the marketing manager already knows who the target market is and where it is located. All that is needed is to select the medium

---

Developing the Promotional Message Is Easier When the Marketing Manager Already Knows:

- Who the Target Market Is
- What Its Needs Are
- How This Product Fills These Needs
- What the Marketing Objectives Are
- What the Promotional Goals Are

---

that can most effectively reach the target market. Part of this decision is determining whether to use paid mass selling (advertising) or nonpaid mass selling (publicity). Most firms use as much advertising as they can afford since they gain greater control over where their message is sent.

Representatives of each newspaper, radio station, and so forth should be able to tell a marketing manager about the demographics (that is, age, sex, income, location, and the like) of its readers, listeners, or viewers. The goal is to find a good fit between the firm's target market and the audience served by a particular medium. The next concern is the cost to reach each member of the target market. The best medium is the one that delivers the largest coverage of the producer's target market at the lowest cost per member.

Experience shows that there is rarely one best medium to use in accomplishing promotional goals. Most firms find they must use a mixture of media in order to be successful. Remember, there are many examples of radio stations that advertise themselves on television and in newspapers, and vice versa.

The selection of the best media mix is still an art, but several guidelines exist. In many small towns there is only a single newspaper or radio station. It can be used effectively since it probably reaches the vast majority of the people in the community.

A marketing manager should not overlook the use of direct mail. One lawn-care firm located in a small town that had two distinct residential areas used two versions of direct mail ads quite successfully. In the older section of town the houses were thirty to forty years old. Their owners were typically older, higher-income people whose children were grown and who could afford to hire others to do their yardwork. In this section of town the firm advertised its snow-shoveling, grass-cutting, and old-tree-and-shrub-removal services. In the newer section of town the houses were either new or recently built. The owners of these homes were usually young families with lower incomes and great interest in do-it-yourself projects. In this section of town the firm advertised its trees and shrubs for sale, as well as low-priced lawn mowers, rakes, grass seeds, and fertilizers. The firm also advertised its free advice on lawn and garden care.

The firm was able to mount this dual promotional campaign on a limited budget by hiring a local youth group to put its advertisements on doorknobs. Different ads were used for the two sections of town. In this way the firm kept its promotional costs low, reaching only the people it wanted with messages tailored to fit their special needs; and the youth group got a nice contribution to its treasury. This is an example of an efficient and very effective advertising campaign.

Classification of Advertising

Advertising is classified by objective. Those ads that develop good will for a firm or a general product category are referred to as *institutional ads*. This type of ad is widely used in agriculture to support various commodities such as milk, potatoes, beef, or raisins. Those ads that develop good will for a specific product are referred to as *product ads*.

Within the product ad category there are three subgroups. The first is called *pioneering advertising*. Its objective is to develop the demand for a general category of products rather than for a specific brand. It is normally done at the introduction stage of the product life cycle and is especially needed for innovative products such as freeze-dried foods, irradiated foods, microwave ovens, implements and chemicals used in no-till farming, and so on. The promotional objective in this situation is to inform consumers of the availability and value of the product, not to persuade them.

The second subgroup is *competitive advertising*. It is a very common form of advertising and its objective is to develop the demand for a specific product. It can accomplish this by taking a *direct approach* and aiming for immediate buying action on the part of the consumer. For example, such an ad may proclaim "Larry's, America's favorite red hot chili, is on sale just this week. Hurry on down today before it's too late!"

Competitive advertising can also take an *indirect approach* that merely identifies a product's many advantages and could lead to a sale sometime in the future. For example, such an ad might say "Larry's Chili uses only the finest grade of fresh ingredients, nothing artificial. This is why Larry's Chili is America's favorite chili!"

A third subgroup of competitive advertising is *comparative advertising*, where specific brand comparisons using actual brand names are made. Taste tests between different brands of cola soft drinks and fast-food hamburgers are examples of this form of advertising. The direct and indirect types of

---

The Three Classifications of Advertising

Institutional—develops good will for a firm or a general product category
Pioneering—develops the demand for a general category of products rather than a specific brand
Competitive—develops demand for a specific product

advertising are often used during the growth and maturity stages of the product's life cycle. Comparative advertising is used more often in the maturity stage.

A third category of product advertisements is *reminder advertising*. The goal here is to reinforce an earlier promotion. The promotional goal is to keep the firm's name before the public. An example of this type of ad would be "Ronald's Hot Breakfast Cereals—the Family Favorites for Nearly 80 Years." No particular products are being advertised. All the ad does is to remind and reinforce the idea in the minds of consumers that Ronald's products are long time family favorites.

The frequency of advertising depends on the type of advertising being done. Institutional or reminder advertising should be done on a regular but not necessarily frequent basis so consumers do not forget about the firm and its products. Product ads should be run to accomplish a specific short-run goal or to support specific sales events (a spring clearance sale, a Labor Day sell-a-thon). Here frequency pays off. A firm will schedule a series of advertisements to run in a short period of time for maximum impact.

Measuring the Effectiveness of Advertising

While the actual composition of the advertisement should be left to professionals, it is possible to evaluate the effectiveness of an advertisement by using the AIDA Model. An ad is effective if it:

1. Gets the consumers' **A**ttention
2. Holds their **I**nterest long enough so they can receive the promotional message
3. Arouses their **D**esire for the product
4. Leads to consumers taking **A**ction to acquire the product

Thus, an effective ad is one that passes the AIDA test of **A**ttention, **I**nterest, **D**esire, and **A**ction. This last part is the most critical because unless the ad brings the desired action on the part of the consumer (buying the product), it is a failure.

If the marketing objective has been clearly defined and is stated in some measurable way (increase sales 10 percent in the next ninety days, increase market share in this territory 5 percent this year), it is possible to measure the success of an advertising program. However, even with clear-cut criteria such as these, success is often hard to measure since it requires the full power of all four parts of the marketing mix pulling together to make sales happen.

Developing Effective Advertising

The first secret of effective marketing is to give customers what they want, when they want it. The same holds true for advertising. A firm should ask its customers to buy when *they* are ready to buy. To do otherwise is likely to limit the chances for success.

Many food products have a seasonal consumption pattern. Hot breakfast cereals normally are consumed in greater amounts during the winter months. Iced tea consumption is greatest in the summer. Apple cider demand peaks in the fall, while egg consumption rises in the spring around Easter. Successful firms recognize differences in consumption patterns for products and allocate advertising expenditures to match seasonal consumption patterns. A useful first step is to plot the percentage of the product's annual sales that takes place in each month (Figure 19–1). This will show when people buy the product. Doing this for several products will show that monthly sales patterns can vary widely.

The annual advertising budget for each product should be allocated to match its monthly pattern of consumption. By following the normal con-

FIGURE 19–1
Matching Advertising Expenditures with Sales

sumption pattern a firm can lower the advertising cost per unit sold because the firm is offering the consumers what they want, *when* they want it.

Sometimes sellers use advertising in an attempt to increase sales of a product during the off-season. For example, the maker of a hot breakfast cereal may highlight the use of the cereal to make cookies or other goodies such as cool summertime snacks. If successful, this can boost overall yearly sales of a product and smooth out production to better utilize manufacturing plants and people. The seller has to realize that advertising during the off-season may not be very successful since it is going against normal consumption patterns.

Separate advertising campaigns for different geographic regions of the country may be used to take advantage of differences in rates and patterns of consumption. Communities only a few hundred miles from each other may have totally different consumption patterns for the same products. While it is important to know why these patterns differ, the vital concern is that the seller know they exist in order to get the maximum sales boost from advertising expenditures.

The second secret of effective advertising is to plan the ad around a single idea, making it easy for the consumer to understand the message. In the space of the few seconds that the typical consumer spends looking at an ad, he or she is not able to absorb more than one or two simple messages.

The third secret of effective advertising is to identify the name of the product clearly and mention it as often as possible in the ad. An advertisement for a retail store should clearly give the name, location, hours, and services offered.

The fourth secret is that an advertisement should emphasize the benefits of products, not just the features. For example, an advertisement for a new food product may emphasize the easy-opening, reusable container. This is a feature which may appeal to consumers, but the important benefit of using

---

Five Secrets of Effective Advertising

1. Ask customers to buy when *they* are ready to buy.
2. Plan the ad around a single idea.
3. Clearly identify the name of the product and mention it as often as possible.
4. Emphasize the benefits of the product as well as the features.
5. Develop an ad format that forms a company identity in the consumer's mind.

the product is that it helps busy people save time. As another example, a new meat product may be advertised as low in calories. However, the benefit that consumers are seeking is the reduced risk of heart disease because the product is low in fat and contains no cholesterol. The benefits of a product that consumers are seeking should be emphasized. In yet another example, a new herbicide may have the convenient feature of versatile application: pre-emergence or post-emergence. The benefit a farmer is looking for, however, is clean fields to boost yields and income. The advertisement could mention versatile application but should emphasize the important benefit of more money in the farmer's pocket.

The fifth secret of effective advertising is that all of a firm's ads should have a similar format so the consumer can quickly distinguish this firm's ads from all the rest. The red and white checkerboard of Ralston-Purina, Titus Moody and his Pepperidge Farm products, and Charlie the Tuna for Star-Kist are all classics in this area.

Establishing an Advertising Budget

Whenever agribusiness people discuss advertising, one of the first questions that comes up is, How much money should be spent? There are a number of ways this can be determined. Four of the most traditional ways of budgeting for advertising are (1) as a percentage of sales, (2) on a per unit of sales basis, (3) as a residual (that is, what money is left over after everything else is taken care of), and (4) using the objective and task method.

Establishing an advertising budget as a percentage of sales is a widely used method, and since this is the way budgets are established for many other business expenses, it is easy to calculate. All that is necessary is to multiply a percentage by product sales to arrive at the advertising budget. The most common question with this approach is what percentage of sales to use. The answer varies from zero to over 50 percent of sales depending on the product and industry. Typically, the answer is around 2 percent, with a range of 1 to 7 percent. The best approach may be to look at industry averages and adjust the percentage to fit the firm's advertising objectives. The next question is what level of sales to use. Should it be current sales, future sales, or average sales? One approach is to use a realistic assessment of future sales.

A second way to establish an advertising budget is to allocate a predetermined dollar amount per unit sold, for example, 7 cents per case of product sold. The decision about the proper amount to spend on advertising per unit can be based on industry averages and the firm's past experience. The proper level of sales to use is a realistic projection of future unit sales.

The third approach is to make advertising expenditures a residual expense. This means that after all other expenses are taken care of, what is left is spent on advertising. This approach is obviously easy to adopt since it does not require setting any goals or doing any planning. The residual expense approach also does not recognize that sales are dependent upon advertising.

The objective and task method of establishing an advertising approach is the most sophisticated approach. It can be summarized as the "what it takes to do the job" approach. It uses the market planning that has been discussed in this text. Marketing objectives and promotional goals must be clearly defined beforehand. A budget is developed from the tasks that must be done to accomplish these goals, and the desired results determine how much is spent. The major difference from the other approaches is that the advertising budget is decided upon according to the firm's marketing objectives or promotional goals. If this approach results in a budget that exceeds what the firm can afford, the goals must be adjusted or the advertising plans scaled back. This can be done by ranking the advertising goals and doing the most important ones first.

SALES PROMOTION

Sales promotion is designed to complement mass and personal selling. It can be very effective in raising the short-run level of demand by speeding up the time of purchase. However, there is some uncertainty surrounding its long-run effectiveness, especially if increased sales in this period lead to reduced sales in the next period. In fact, since sales promotions are generally employed along with other promotional activities, their effects are hard to single out.

In general there are three approaches to sales promotion. The first targets the consumer of the product. These efforts are the familiar in-store point-of-purchase (POP) items such as banners, free samples, aisle displays, coupons, and contests. The second approach targets the people in the marketing channel (wholesalers, jobbers, retailers). These efforts are generally price related and include price deals, promotional allowances, sales contests, and gifts. The third approach targets the firm's own sales force. It includes selling aids, bonuses, contests, etc. Each of these approaches is designed to increase the sales of the firm and to complement mass and personal selling methods.

Developing a successful sales promotional campaign requires the same careful planning that is required for mass selling. First, the marketing objectives and promotional goals must be clearly defined. Second, a clear and simple message defined in terms of consumer needs and perceptions regarding the product must be developed. The use of sales promotional campaigns has grown in popularity in recent years. If done with some thought and planning and used as part of the firm's marketing mix, sales promotion will lead to greater sales and profits.

SUMMARY

The promotion part of the marketing mix can insure that the availability of the right product, at the right price, at the right locations is communicated to the members of the target market. Promotional efforts involve the use of mass selling, personal selling, and sales promotion. Most firms use a combination of the three in order to accomplish their marketing objectives.

To successfully manage the promotion portion of the marketing mix, a manager must understand its three basic parts: mass selling, personal selling, and sales promotion. Mass selling is the best known, and includes advertising and publicity. Advertising is paid mass selling; publicity is unpaid mass selling. Personal selling (the subject of the next chapter) is one-on-one selling done by a salesperson. It is typically the most effective way to sell but it is also the most expensive. Sales promotion includes all the selling activities that complement both personal and mass selling.

Regardless of which is used, each promotional effort should have a well-defined goal that can be measured in objective terms. When promotion is combined with the other parts of the firm's marketing mix it can be effective in accomplishing the firm's overall objectives.

QUESTIONS

1. What is the objective of promotion? Explain why it is heavily involved with communication.
2. What is the difference between mass selling, personal selling, and sales promotion?
3. Why is it easier to plan an effective promotional campaign if there is a detailed marketing plan?
4. What is the AIDA model and how can it be used to evaluate the effectiveness of advertising?
5. What are some steps to developing an effective advertising campaign?

20

Personal Selling and Merchandising

Personal selling is one of the most challenging and rewarding careers a person can enter, yet many people do not think of selling as part of marketing, much less as a viable career choice. This chapter is designed to change this thinking by showing how personal selling and merchandising make a vital contribution to the success of an agribusiness firm's marketing efforts.

This mission will be accomplished in two parts. First, we will examine the role that personal selling plays in agribusiness marketing. We will discuss a variety of different sales situations to see what motivates people to buy and what the salesperson can do to encourage the buyer. The selling process will be looked at closely to demonstrate that selling is a series of steps that nearly everyone can successfully master if given proper training.

Second, we will examine the subject of commodity merchandising. Commodity merchandising is a subject that is nearly unique to agribusiness. Merchandising is considered an entry level position for aspiring agribusiness commodity marketing managers and, in many commodity oriented companies, a necessary experience for anyone striving for a top management position. At the completion of this chapter the reader should be able to fully appreciate the roles commodity merchandising and personal selling play in the successful marketing of agricultural inputs, agricultural commodities, and food products.

THE ROLE OF PERSONAL SELLING IN MARKETING

Personal selling is an important component of the promotion portion of the marketing mix of product, price, place, and promotion. Within the promotion part of the marketing mix personal selling is one of three major promotional methods, the other two being mass selling and sales promotion. Personal selling, simply put, is direct face-to-face contact with potential buyers by a person representing the firm. The company representative can be the president of the firm or a sales clerk. For example, the president of the selling firm can meet with the president of a firm that is interested in a large purchase of the first company's products. Usually much smaller quantities are involved and sales representatives from the company call on wholesalers, retailers, and consumers to convince them to place an order for the company's products. In most cases the sales representative is hired, trained, and supported for the express purpose of selling the company's products. It is not unusual for an agribusiness firm to spend more on personal selling than the combined amount spent on mass selling and sales promotion. It is also not uncommon for the company's top salespeople to earn more than the company's president.

The reason why firms are willing to spend this much on personal selling is that a terrible thing happens if no one sells...nothing! If buyers do not buy the company's products, inventories will build up and production workers will be laid off. Because of the decline in revenue, the staff lawyers, the financial staff, and the secretaries may also be laid off. If the company president cannot turn things around, the board of directors will fire him or her too. So everyone is heavily dependent on the company's salespeople for the success of the firm.

The people in sales are at the cutting edge of the corporation. This is called the *boundary role* of the salesperson. The salesperson is the final link between the company and the customers. All the firm's efforts to develop the right product, determine the right price, decide the right locations for its sale, and develop the right mass selling and sales promotional programs will be wasted if the salesperson does not provide every potential customer with the necessary information about the firm and its product in a persuasive manner. If potential buyers can be made to understand how the benefits of using this company's product can satisfy their needs, chances are they will buy the product.

Accordingly, the definition of *selling* is *the performance of all those activities that help prospective customers fulfill their needs and wants with the firm's products*. Selling involves helping potential buyers *determine* their needs. Only after this is done can the salesperson determine which products best fit the needs. The key to successful personal selling is in providing the information necessary for the customer to decide what need this firm's products best satisfy.

Selling is not fast-talking the buyer into a signature on the order form. It is not pulling the wool over the buyer's eyes. It is not pushing unwanted products into the hands of easily manipulated buyers. The purchasers of agribusiness products are for the most part knowledgeable, sophisticated buyers. If they find out they have been fooled by a salesperson, they will never buy from him and his firm again. Given the competitiveness of most markets, agribusiness firms cannot afford that kind of buyer behavior. Customers buy products because the value to them in consumption or use exceeds price. The job of the salesperson is to establish in the mind of the buyer the value of the products he sells. After all, the sale takes place in the mind.

Today, selling is a profession, and salespeople, agribusiness salespeople included, are professionals. The dictionary definition of a profession is an occupation requiring advanced training usually involving mental rather than physical work in which a person strives to maintain certain standards worthy of the calling. Personal selling, as it is practiced in agribusiness, fits this definition. Most firms require salespeople to have college degrees, and they continue to educate them throughout their careers. Salespeople receive training in technical product knowledge, selling skills, customer behavior, and marketing. Those who are serious about selling as a career develop a personal code of ethics, usually reinforced by company policy, that allows them to develop long-term relationships with their clients based on mutual trust.

Selling also offers other benefits that are associated with professional careers such as independence. In most cases a salesperson is responsible for all company activities in her sales territory. The salesperson essentially manages her own business with little supervision. Personal satisfaction is another attribute of professionals. Salespeople can set and achieve high personal goals such as a high income and at the same time help others. Salespeople usually have the highest starting salaries among new college graduates, and the earning potential for a good salesperson can be virtually unlimited.

Salespeople usually have many opportunities for advancement up the management ladder. Ironically, for some top salespeople this means taking a cut in income, at least temporarily. More than half of the top executives in industry started in marketing, usually in sales. Salespeople make ideal candidates for promotion to the top ranks because they are exposed to all aspects of a company's business from research to billing and credit. Good salespeople develop management skills including leadership, the ability to teach, and sound judgment. Perhaps more importantly they learn to deal effectively with people. It is not surprising that many salespeople eventually start their own businesses.

TYPES OF PERSONAL SELLING

There are four general types of selling situations, each requiring its own approach to personal selling in order to be successful. These situations are defined by the type of customer being served; they include: (1) wholesalers and retailers who resell the product, (2) purchasing agents, (3) product users, and (4) consumers.

Wholesalers and Retailers Who Resell the Product

The buying behavior of wholesalers and retailers is so similar that they can be discussed together. These buyers are interested only in the profits that can be made when the products are resold. Wholesalers and retailers normally require some service along with the products they buy, such as financing, inventory protection, and promotional plans. They may also want help in training their own employees to be better salespersons.

Salespeople that call on wholesalers and retailers spend a large portion of their time servicing their accounts. They provide a high level of service because the wholesalers and retailers require it and will look elsewhere if they fail to receive it. Ordinarily a salesperson spends very little time giving formal sales presentations where the objective is to get a signed order. A large portion of the salesperson's time is spent discussing financing plans and promotional plans with wholesalers and retailers. The salesperson may even hold meetings to train client employees on how to sell, or keep them up to date on technical information. Planning local promotional campaigns and working with the media can also occupy a portion of the salesperson's time.

Salespeople develop very close working relationships with wholesalers and retailers in their territories. It can best be described as an informal partnership. If the salesperson can help a wholesaler or retailer increase sales, they are both better off. The wholesaler or retailer makes more profit and the salesperson benefits from the monetary rewards that greater sales in the territory bring. Wholesalers and retailers are most receptive to company sales representatives that give them the best products and service. The service will improve sales and profits from that particular company's products and because of spillover effects this helps increase sales and profits from other products the wholesaler or retailer might sell. It is truly a partnership relationship where both parties can benefit.

Purchasing Agents

The second category of buyers is purchasing agents. Purchasing agents buy goods and services for their company as inputs for a manufacturing process. The inputs are used to produce other products that the company sells to its clients. For example, a food manufacturer needs a wide variety of ingredients, packaging materials, etc. to make the products it sells, and it is up to the purchasing agent to acquire all these inputs in a timely and efficient manner.

The purchasing agent is a professional, knowledgeable buyer. The salesperson may be able to offer technical advice, but what the purchasing agent is really looking for is value and service. Where quality is important, the purchasing agent may not buy the product with the lowest price. However, uniform quality along with timely delivery, rapid repair, or other service factors will weigh heavily in the purchasing agent's decision to buy. In most cases the purchasing agent is not totally responsible for making the purchasing decision. The agent represents others who make the purchasing decision in consultation with the purchasing agent. The agent acts as a coordinator of buying, receiving, service calls, and so forth.

Product Users

Product users are included here as a separate category although they behave much like purchasing agents in making buying decisions. Product users are those customers who use the product in a production process rather than consume them, but are usually too small to have a designated purchasing agent. The principal owner(s) may make the buying decisions. Farmers, ranchers, and other small agribusiness firms fall into this category.

Product users are usually knowledgeable buyers but rely more on the salesperson for technical information than the purchasing agent does. Product users are interested in increasing their profits and look for products and services which help them increase revenues or lower costs. Occasionally emotion may enter the purchasing decision. For example, the salesperson may appeal to pride of ownership in selling new tractors painted a certain color. Most product users are rational decision makers, however.

A group of customers closely related to product users is consulting professionals. Bankers, veterinarians, extension agents, fieldmen, and the like all influence buying decisions of agribusiness product users. A salesperson will call on these professionals to influence their opinions about a company's products so they will recommend the products to the users. The salesperson does this by providing technical information about products, giving the professionals free product samples, or describing the benefits that users who are influenced by these professionals can gain, thereby making the professional look good in the eyes of the users.

Consumers

Consumers make up the mass market and actually consume the product. Their consumption takes place to satisfy human needs. The needs that products fill range from basic physical needs including food, shelter, and clothing to needs of the mind such as status and the need to develop fully as an individual. These needs can be fulfilled by the benefits generated from consuming products.

Salespeople rarely call directly on consumers except in attempts to sell very expensive items such as houses and cars. Even in those cases the prospective buyer is likely to seek out the salesperson. There are simply too many potential buyers for the salesperson to personally visit them all. Instead, the salesperson will call on retailers to make sure that they are doing everything possible to sell the salesperson's product.

The salesperson may train the retailer's salespeople to increase their product knowledge and selling skills so they can be more successful in selling to consumers. Often the salesperson will become involved in a retailer's promotion and merchandising program in order to help him or her do a more effective job of influencing the buying decisions of consumers. The effective use of local advertising, contests, point-of-purchase displays, and product placement on shelves or racks can all significantly boost sales of products to consumers.

THE SELLING PROCESS: THE SIX STEPS

The salesperson's job is to help prospective buyers determine their needs and then help them locate products (hopefully made by the salesperson's firm) that will completely fill these needs. When this is done, selling is easy.

Nearly anyone with the proper training can be a good salesperson. Success begins with having a good product that fills a well-defined consumer need. It also helps to represent a company that is well-thought-of by its customers. When salespeople can see that the products they sell make their customers' lives better or help them make more money in their business, they become enthusiastic about selling and take great pride in their ability to match consumer needs with product benefits. The result is a successful salesperson and increased sales for the company.

Some salespeople seem to be naturals. That is, they do not seem to work hard at selling. They just strike up a conversation with a prospective customer and in a short time end up with a signed order. This apparent ease is deceptive. Through trial and error these salespeople have developed a sales approach that works for them. But a closer analysis of what they do would show that they had progressed through the six steps of the selling process. These steps must be completed in just about every sale regardless of what is being sold.

A systematic approach to selling is the key to success for beginning as well as experienced salespeople. All salespeople must go through the steps of the selling process in one way or another. Selling success rates can be improved by carefully planning and implementing each step of the selling process. The six steps of the selling process are:

1. Prospecting
2. The approach
3. The presentation
4. Handling objections
5. Closing the sale
6. The follow-up

Prospecting

Thousands, even millions, of people may live in a salesperson's territory. The purpose of prospecting is to reduce that large number to a reasonable number of prospective buyers to which there is a high probability of making a sale. Prospecting, the information-gathering stage of selling, helps a salesperson accomplish this. Using a variety of sources, the salesperson puts together a prospect profile for each potential buyer. Potential buyers might include wholesalers, retailers, end users, or a combination of these. At the very least the profile should include each prospect's name and location, telephone number, and an estimate of the needs or problems he or she is likely to have. A prospect who has no needs or problems is not a prospect.

Prospecting information can come from a variety of sources. Publications such as telephone directories, trade magazines, and organizational newsletters can yield names. They can also provide more detailed information about sales prospects such as size of the firm, number of employees, and so forth, that can help the salesperson better define them and their needs before the first sales call is made. Referrals from current customers and other business contacts can be rewarding sources of this type of information. Other sources include company records, purchased name lists, and trade shows.

After gathering information about prospects, the salesperson is ready to qualify them. This means ranking prospects according to the probability of making a sale. Qualifying factors might include demonstrated need for the product, size of potential purchases, cooperativeness, financial strength, and potential for growth in sales. By qualifying prospects the salesperson can use his or her time more efficiently and effectively by concentrating primarily on those potential customers who are most likely to purchase.

The Approach

The next step in the selling process is the approach. Successful salespeople accomplish the following four tasks: (1) gain access to the prospect, (2) get the prospect's attention, (3) sell themselves, and (4) shift the prospect's attention to the product.

1. Gaining Access to the Prospect.   Just getting in to see a prospect may not be an easy matter. Some people are so busy that they are nearly impossible to catch. In their busy season prospects may not want to take time to talk to salespeople. Some prospects use a secretary or other office staff as a screening device, letting only those salespeople through whom they want to see or who are persistent or clever enough to slip through the screen.

The salesperson should use the information gathered in the prospecting stage to determine the best time of day to call. Some prospects are more receptive early in the morning before they get busy with the day's activities. Other people prefer to talk with a salesperson later in the day after they have the day's activities under control. In other cases the prospect may set aside certain time periods to meet with salespeople. The key to success is to know the prospect's preferences and schedule the sales call for that time. The salesperson may have to convince a secretary or office manager of the importance of talking with the prospect. The sales call on the boss may be a much easier task than convincing the keeper of the gate to grant access. In most cases the salesperson should make an appointment to see the prospect. It is a professional way to conduct business and gives the prospect a chance to be ready for the sales call rather than being surprised. It may be a good idea to invite the prospect out for coffee or lunch to get away from the distractions of the office.

2. Getting the Prospect's Attention. The best way to get the prospect's attention is to immediately describe a benefit that will come from using the company's product. For example, opening statements such as "This new product can increase your overall profit by five percent" or "How would you like to save $500 on expenses next month?" can help the prospect immediately understand the value of your product and why it should be purchased instead of someone else's.

While such claims may get the prospect's attention, they must never go beyond what is actually possible, since one of the salesperson's objectives is to develop a long-run relationship with clients. Such relationships are built on honesty, trust, and performance. This is why it is imperative that the salesperson make good on every claim about the product and the service that comes with it (for instance, delivery by 8 A.M. each Wednesday or lowest price per case in the region). Each and every one of these promises must be fully met on each order even if it means the seller takes a loss on the sale. The history of selling is full of heroic stories of salespeople who have filled their own cars with an order and driven all night through blinding snowstorms or other adverse conditions in order get an important order to a customer on time. Customers remember those who best take care of them and reward this level of service with continued business. It is nothing more than treating customers the way you would like to be treated if you were the buyer.

3 and 4. Selling Yourself and Shifting Attention to the Product. Selling yourself to the prospect and shifting the prospect's attention to the product go hand in hand because they must occur almost simultaneously. The idea is to gain the prospect's trust so he or she will allow you to continue with the sales presentation and seriously consider purchasing the product. Salespeople can gain trust by conducting themselves in a businesslike manner; demonstrating self-confidence and confidence in the product; living up to all product claims and benefits; and sincerely trying to help the prospect realize the benefits from the product. They must shift the attention of the prospect

---

How the Salesperson Can Gain Trust:

- Conduct himself or herself in a businesslike manner
- Demonstrate self-confidence and confidence in the product
- Live up to all product claims and benefits
- Help the customer realize the benefits from the product

to the product as quickly as possible to avoid turning the sales call into a gab session.

The Presentation

Only after gaining access, getting the prospect's attention, selling himself or herself, and shifting the prospect's attention to the product is the salesperson ready to make the presentation. The approach stage may take only sixty seconds. The presentation may last from a few minutes to more than an hour depending upon the complexity of the presentation and the prospect's involvement in it.

Part of the approach stage in the selling process is planning the presentation. Many salespersons do not plan their sales presentations. They feel that their product knowledge and experience will get them by. They ad lib their way to the order...sometimes. More often than not, they become sidetracked or they forget an important point which they realize they should have covered as they drive away from the sales call without the order. It is best to plan the presentation ahead of time. There are two ways to do this: the canned presentation and the structured presentation.

The *canned presentation* is a memorized script which the salesman recites to each prospect. The canned presentation is designed by the marketing staff in the home office to generate interest in the product by stressing the product's features, advantages, and benefits. *A product feature is a characteristic of the product.* For example, a product feature for a herbicide may be that it controls broadleaf weeds, while for a livestock feed the product feature may be that it offers balanced nutrition.

A product advantage is how the product improves the situation. For example, an advantage for a particular brand of herbicide is that it may improve crop yields by 10 bushels per acre; for a livestock feed it may be that it improves the rate of gain by 15 percent. *A product benefit is what the use of the product means to the prospect.* For the herbicide and feed in these examples, the salesperson would point out the dollar value benefit of increased returns or decreased costs.

In the canned presentation the salesperson would link the product's benefits with the prospect's needs, which in this example would be the need for improved profits. Then the salesperson would get the prospect to agree, following the canned script, that the benefits received are greater than the price of the product. The canned presentation may even anticipate objections on the part of the prospect and lead the salesperson to the close of the sale.

Canned presentations work very well for inexperienced salespeople. If well written, they cover all the important points, include pleasing words and phrases, and will be successful most of the time. But it is hard for salespeople to sound fresh each time they give it. The tendency is to rattle through the set presentation with little regard for the involvement of the prospect. The canned presentation obviously cannot be used twice on the same person. Also, the salesperson has to memorize a canned presentation for each product.

The *structured presentation* may be better. It is planned in detail and may cover all the points of the canned presentation, but it is not memorized. The salesperson knows the outline of the presentation but will alter the order of the parts depending upon the interest and questions of the prospect. The structured presentation also encourages more participation by the prospect. It is not uncommon for the prospect to state his or her needs and criteria for adopting a product early in the presentation.

For example, a prospect may say "We have experienced unevenness in our cookie dough because lumps in the flour cause the measuring device to malfunction. We need a flour that is free-flowing under all conditions." The flour salesperson would then go over that portion of the sales presentation covering flour flow properties and quickly move to close the sale. The structured sales presentation, when carefully planned in advance, can be an extremely efficient and effective selling procedure.

Meeting Objections

Every salesperson, no matter how experienced or skillful, will encounter resistance in the form of objections. These are reasons given by the prospect for not buying the product. Objections can range from "Sorry, not interested" to "It's too expensive" to "I can't afford it."

A salesperson may be inclined to turn and walk away, but she owes it to herself and her employer to make an attempt to overcome the objections. This is easier if she understands that most objections are really questions raised by the prospect. "Sorry, not interested" may really mean "I do not understand what you are saying about your product" or "Tell me why I should be interested in your product." The price objection is the most common. Some people always feel obligated to negotiate a lower price. In other cases a prospect may not see that the value of the product outweighs the price he has to pay. If the salesperson is patient and skillful in discovering the true objection, a little more work in explaining the product's benefits may enable her to make the sale. However, a good salesperson will quickly recognize when the answer no really means no, and will move on to another prospect.

Closing the Sale

Closing the sale means getting a signature on the order form. The prospect becomes a customer. Ironically, the close seems to be the hardest step in the selling process for many salespeople. They do just fine in moving the prospect through all the other steps. However, when it comes time to ask for the sale they handle it clumsily, or worse, fail to ask for the order at all.

Salespeople may be afraid of offending the prospect by asking for the order or may be afraid of being turned down. But people like to buy things, especially when they feel they are making a good buying decision. Even when prospects have made a decision to buy a product, they will seldom make the verbal commitment without being asked. The key is for the salesperson to ask for the order.

Closing the sale can be done very easily, and the salesperson need not wait until the end of the presentation to ask for the order. The salesperson should use a number of *trial closes* during the presentation. After the presentation of an important benefit, the prospect may smile and nod in agreement. This is an important buying signal. The salesperson should respond with a trial close, perhaps asking, "Which model of our product would suit your needs best?" If the prospect names a model, the sale is made and the salesperson writes up the order. The prospect may say "Wait, what about maintenance?" The salesperson continues the sales presentation with a section on maintenance and then tries to close again.

If the trial closes do not work after a lengthy sales presentation, the salesperson may summarize the product's benefits and close by saying "This additional profit can be yours if you will just OK this for me," handing the prospect a pen. There are many other techniques for closing a sale. Each salesperson finds those that work best. The point is, in order to be successful the salesperson must ask for the order after moving through the steps in the selling process.

The Follow-Up

A critical but often overlooked part of the sales process is what occurs after the sale has been made. All too often once the ink dries on the order form the salesperson vanishes. But that is just the time to forge a long-term relationship with the customer. A telephone call or visit after the product has been delivered to make sure that the customer is getting the promised benefits shows that the trust and concern the salesperson spent all that time developing was in fact sincere and not just a technique to get the customer's money.

Salespeople who care that the product fulfills the customer's needs will be interested in seeing that the resources of their company are available to insure customer satisfaction. This not only helps establish that long-run relationship with a customer which leads to repeat sales, but it also sets the stage to ask for referrals to others who might also be interested in the product. Satisfied customers can be valuable allies in the search for new customers, and the process begins again. The salesperson who does a good job of prospecting, planning the approach, making the presentation, handling objections, asking for the order, and following up after the sale will be the one who succeeds and is rewarded.

AGRIBUSINESS MERCHANDISING

A dictionary definition of merchandising is buying and selling, but in practice merchandising includes many more activities. In agribusiness there are two distinct types of merchandising: (1) product merchandising and (2) commodity merchandising.

Product Merchandising

Product merchandising takes place in agribusiness in input supply stores and food retailing. Input supply stores sell seed, feed, fertilizer, agricultural chemicals, tools, gloves, boots, pet food, and so on. Retail food stores sell food but also many other products such as household cleaners, health and beauty aids, and so forth.

Merchandising in the most narrow sense *means purchasing the most appealing variety and assortment of products and offering them to consumers in the most pleasing way possible. Variety* means the mix of products a store carries. *Assortment* means the range of choice within each variety. Choices can include ranges of brands, models, colors, sizes, and price levels.

In a broader sense merchandising also includes all promotional activities intended to stimulate consumer demand for products. In-store displays can have a significant impact on sales. For example, merchandise displayed at eye level or in special end-of-the-aisle displays will sell much better than the same merchandise displayed above or below eye level. Sales promotion materials such as shelf talkers and point-of-purchase (POP) displays draw the customers' attention to a product and promote sales. Contests and free items draw customers into a store.

Personal selling can also be part of merchandising. Some retailers train personnel in personal selling techniques so they are better able to offer product information to customers and gently encourage them to buy.

Commodity Merchants

The position of commodity merchant is pretty much unique to agribusiness. In many other commodity industries such as coal, cement, and steel, most of the transactions involve long-term contracts. In the agribusiness commodity markets most business is done in the short run using the spot (cash) markets.

The term *commodity merchandising* in agribusiness is usually reserved for situations in which firms purchase raw agricultural commodities and either resell them or process and then sell the commodity-like products. For example, a soybean merchant working for a soybean processor buys soybeans. If the price of soybeans rises, they may be sold raw. But more than likely they will be shipped to the firm's processing plant to be processed into soybean meal and soybean oil. The soybean merchant then sells the commodity-like soybean meal and soybean oil to make a profit.

Firms that hire commodity merchants include grain traders and exporters; commodity processors such as feed millers, flour millers, and corn wet millers; and food manufacturers who use commodities such as grains and oilseeds. Other agricultural commodities are also traded and include items such as sugar, frozen orange juice, tallow, boxed beef, frozen pork bellies, alcohol, dried citrus pulp, and molasses. Nontypical products handled by agribusiness traders include fertilizer, salt, and barge freight.

The commodity merchant's job is to make buying and selling decisions and make a profit. It sounds easy—just buy low and sell high. But frequent and hard to predict price fluctuations complicate the job. Fortunately, futures market contracts are available for many commodities which gives merchants the option of hedging away most of the risk of price fluctuations. But then the merchants must keep track of futures market prices as well as cash market prices. (See the following chapter for a full discussion of how to manage this type of market risk.)

Another complicating factor is that commodity merchants often have opportunities to sell commodities before they have acquired them. This puts them in the ticklish position of selling commodities they do not own. They will not hesitate to make such a trade if they expect to be able to buy the commodity at a favorable price before having to deliver on the contract. It is commonly said in the industry that commodity merchants who know their business can make money buying then selling in a rising market, and selling and then buying in a falling market.

Individual commodity merchants are usually set up as profit centers within an agribusiness firm. This means each merchant is responsible for all aspects of his or her own trading business, from writing up contracts to arranging transportation to collecting the money. At the end of each accounting period such merchants receive a profit and loss statement showing the results of their trading activity. They are usually paid a salary plus a bonus based on profits earned.

Commodity merchants rarely meet face to face with the people with whom they deal because most commodity merchandising is done by telephone. Verbal contracts made on the telephone are considered binding although most are followed by written contracts just to keep memories honest.

The commodity merchant's job is much broader than the job of an agribusiness salesperson. Both are considered to be entry-level positions. (Commodity-oriented firms often view commodity merchants as a pool of future managerial talent.) Although salespeople manage a territory, they tend to think of themselves primarily as salespeople, not as managers. Because of the broad range of activities and responsibilities, commodity merchants think of themselves as managers.

The three activities discussed in this chapter—personal selling, product merchandising, and commodity merchandising—form the foundation of most agribusiness firms. Those firms that are able to place well-trained, hardworking people in these positions tend to be successful. Entry-level positions in personal selling, product merchandising, and commodity merchandising offer young people challenging and rewarding career opportunities.

SUMMARY

This chapter discussed the role that personal selling and merchandising can play in the successful marketing of agribusiness commodities and products. Selling is shown to be a critical activity often overlooked by many people. Those who sell are given a unique opportunity to operate across a wide spectrum of the firm's activities and in the process gain vast and varied experience. But success at selling is not just reserved for those that are considered to be natural-born salespeople. Selling is a skill that can be taught, and as with most other business skills, proper training and planning can improve anyone's ability. Critical to success in selling is consciously moving through the six steps in the selling process.

An equally important area is merchandising. Those retail agribusinesses that sell directly to final consumers are involved with product merchandising. Product merchandising means offering products in the most appealing ways possible to consumers. A second form of merchandising, one that is unique to agribusiness, is commodity merchandising. It deals with the buying and selling of raw agricultural commodities and commodity-like products.

The proper use of personal selling and merchandising can go a long way toward helping an agribusiness firm meet its marketing objectives. These activities are like many others in the marketing system that must function effectively if the agribusiness firm is to be successful.

QUESTIONS

1. Briefly describe the role that personal selling plays in developing a successful marketing mix for a product in an agribusiness firm.
2. Why are people that are involved in personal selling referred to as professionals?
3. What are the four general types of selling situations and why do they require different approaches to selling to be successful?
4. Why is selling a good product for a good company an easy job?
5. What is merchandising? What is the difference between product merchandising and commodity merchandising?

21
Managing the Market Risk

Anyone who operates a business encounters risk. Risk is just one of the many challenges that business managers must confront, and like everything else that goes with managing a business, it must be managed *successfully*. Part of the salaries paid to managers is for successful risk management.

All business firms face many forms of risk. Agribusiness firms have to deal with an inordinate amount and variety of risks. In fact, the risks inherent in running an agribusiness firm are one of the things that sets it apart from most other types of businesses. A drought, a rapidly spreading livestock disease, a grain elevator explosion, a piece of glass found in a food container, a burned-out compressor in a supermarket frozen food case, or a failed new product after a multimillion dollar promotional campaign are just a small sample of the many risks which agribusiness firms may face. This chapter will identify a number of the more common forms of risk. It will also show how marketing managers can reduce their exposure to many of them and will concentrate on how to manage *market risk*—the risk of adverse movements in the prices of inputs and products.

FINANCIAL RISK AND BUSINESS RISK

There are two general types of risk that are faced by any business: financial risk and business risk. *Financial risk is the possibility that the firm will be unable to meet its financial obligations.* As the amount of debt in a firm's capital structure increases relative to equity (net worth), so does the level of financial risk. Lenders insist that interest be paid on debt. They also expect the full amount of the debt to be repaid according to the loan agreement. If a firm cannot pay its debt because of low or negative income, the lender will take steps to recover the borrowed capital. This could mean either taking the assets pledged against the loan or foreclosure. Either one could mean disaster for an agribusiness firm.

A firm can reduce its financial risk by keeping the amount of debt in its capital structure within acceptable limits. The proportion of debt to equity that is acceptable varies with economic conditions and from business to business. It also depends upon the abilities of management. Lenders will warn the firm's managers when debt is getting out of hand. Eventually lenders will raise the interest rate to a borrower and may refuse to lend further funds when they feel the financial risk is too high.

The second form of risk is business risk. *Business risk is the variation in net income that arises from normal fluctuations in business activity.* The level of business risk varies from industry to industry. In industries where there is little unexpected variation in product demand and prices over long periods of time, such as the electric utility industry, the level of business risk may be low. In industries such as agribusiness where the amount of capital invested can be large, the products are perishable, production cannot be quickly adjusted to meet changes in the level of demand, and prices can vary greatly, the level of business risk can be very high. Despite the high levels of business risk, agribusiness marketing managers have a number of methods, some unique to agribusiness, to reduce the level of risk they must face.

Types of Business Risk

Some of the more common types of risks faced by agribusiness firms include:

1. *Production Risk*—The biological nature of production processes for agricultural producers, commodity processors, and food manufacturers creates production risk which adds uncertainty to the expected level of output. Weather, disease, and pest infestations are the most common sources of production risk.
2. *Casualty Risk*—Casualty risk originally meant the loss of life due to unforeseen occurrences but has come to mean loss of property as well. Some of the unforeseen occurrences include fire, flood, theft, and vandalism.

3. *Technological Risk*—The adoption or nonadoption of new technology, obsolescence, and equipment breakdowns all create technological risk.

4. *Personnel Risk*—The illness, injury, or death of one of the principals in a firm can severely affect the business. There is also the risk that a key employee will quit and go to work for a competitor.

5. *Risk Due to the Actions of Others*—Most people in business are reliable and responsible. But there are always a few, both in your firm and in the firms you deal with, that can cause problems and risk of loss.

6. *Market Risk*—There are a variety of things that can happen in the market (change in consumer tastes and preferences, embargoes, and so on) that can cause adverse price movement and negatively impact a firm's profit picture. This would mean a price decline for someone intending to sell a commodity or a product, or a price increase for someone needing to buy commodities.

Ways To Reduce Business Risk

Most agribusiness firm managers and owners are averse to risk. This means they avoid taking risks if they can. They just want to run their firms as efficiently as possible and make what profit they can without the danger of losing everything. There are ways to reduce business risk.

Although it does nothing to reduce risk, one way to guard against the possible consequences of business risk is to maintain a financial cushion. A cash reserve, a large balance in a checking or savings account, can help the manager of a risky agribusiness firm sleep better at night. Another way to have a financial cushion is to maintain a reserve of borrowing capacity. A manager might borrow only a portion of the approved amount of a line of credit, for example. In times of difficulty, the manager can use the rest of the line of credit.

Maintaining a financial cushion doesn't reduce or shift the risk in an agribusiness, but it can insure that the business will survive the adverse consequences of risk. However, not all firms can afford to maintain a large enough financial cushion to take care of all contingencies. It may be very costly in terms of lost investment opportunities. There are other ways to guard against business risk.

Some risks can be insured. Casualty risk (fire insurance), personnel risk (life insurance), and even some production risks (hail insurance) can be reduced or shifted entirely by purchasing insurance. Insurance companies have calculated the probability of losses and the expected amounts of losses from various risks. An insurance company will assume the risk of loss and charge each of the insured a premium. If and when a loss occurs, the company uses the proceeds from the premiums to pay off the loss. By purchasing insurance against these types of losses agribusiness firms trade the known probability of annual small losses (the premiums) for the unknown probability of potentially large losses.

One large agribusiness firm found it very expensive to pay the annual premiums on all its commodity inventories, people, buildings, and vehicles. The executive management team decided that they could withstand losses of $1 million per year if necessary, but they needed protection from truly catastrophic losses. They negotiated a policy with their major insurer to cover all insurable losses over $1 million with one insurance policy.

Three business strategies that an agribusiness can use to reduce business risk are diversification, vertical integration, and rapid adoption of new technology. *Diversification* is doing business in more than one industry. In this era of specialization, firms tend to concentrate efforts on one or just a few commodities or products. If the market for a firm's only product runs into hard times it could find itself with sharply reduced revenues and profits. By diversifying into different products, even different businesses, a firm can reduce the risk that a downturn for one product or business will put the firm's future in jeopardy. It is unlikely that the seed business and the feed business, for example, would both hit a down cycle at the same time.

Vertical integration can also reduce risk. *Vertical integration* occurs when one firm enters a business at two or more levels in a marketing channel by either acquiring a firm or through contractual agreement. For example, a large farmer purchases a local elevator to handle his or her grain, or a vegetable canner arranges with farmers in the area to grow vegetables under contract. Firms integrate vertically to assure themselves of a supply of a raw material, to guarantee an outlet for products, to protect themselves from the actions of others in the marketing channel, to reduce the cost of buying or selling raw materials or products, or to gain more market power. Whatever the motivations, vertical integration reduces risk for the integrating firms.

Rapid adoption of new technology can by itself be risky. The risk is that it will not work. The adopting firm will have incurred costs with no accompanying increase in revenue. Perhaps this explains why some firm managers or owners are hesitant to adopt new technology until they have seen it work. However, if everything works properly, new technology can reduce risk. A drought-resistant variety of seed can reduce production risk for a farmer. A fully automated, computerized food processing plant can reduce the firm's reliance on key personnel. If the new technology reduces unit production costs for a firm, it can also reduce the risk from a decline in the price of the commodity or product.

Reasons Why Firms Use Vertical Integration to Reduce Risk

- To assure themselves of a supply of raw material
- To guarantee an outlet for products
- To protect themselves from the actions of others in the marketing channel
- To reduce the cost of buying or selling raw materials or products
- To gain more market power

There are several government programs which reduce risk for agribusiness firms. General disaster relief programs allow agribusiness firms along with others in an area to obtain low-interest loans when struck by a natural disaster such as a flood or earthquake. From time to time there are industry-specific programs to ease the impacts of changes in laws or regulations such as the banning of pesticides, more stringent emission controls regulations, or changes in food inspection practices.

One of the major objectives of the farm program is to reduce risk for agricultural producers. The disaster payment program in effect reimburses farmers for production costs if by some act of nature they are prevented from planting or harvesting a crop. Many features of the program are aimed at reducing the risk of low commodity prices. Examples include the nonrecourse loan program, the deficiency payment program, and the commodity purchase program, discussed in Chapter 10.

WAYS TO MANAGE THE MARKET RISK

Agribusiness firms have a number of unique ways to reduce the amount of market risk they experience because of adverse price movements. As was discussed in Chapter 8, the inelastic nature of demand and supply for raw agricultural commodities means that small shifts in supply can lead to large changes in market prices. Because agribusiness managers want to avoid risk as much as possible, market instruments were developed to reduce the amount of market risk caused by price fluctuations.

Forward Contracting

For agribusiness firms one of the most important ways to reduce market risk is to use forward pricing. *Forward pricing* is the establishment of the exchange price of a commodity or product before the physical transfer to the new owner. Just about everyone has used forward contracting at one time or another. For example, you may make a deal to buy a new car at a set price, but the dealer does not have the car in stock. You sign a purchase agreement and the dealer orders the car from the manufacturer. When the car arrives in a few weeks you take delivery.

When you signed the purchase agreement you were forward pricing the new car. If the automobile manufacturer raised prices after you signed the agreement you would not care since the price of your car has already been determined in the purchase agreement. But on the other hand, if the manufacturer started to offer rebates the day after you signed the agreement, you would not be eligible for them either.

Locking in the price is the most important feature of forward contracting. Forward contracting nearly eliminates market risk, the risk that an adverse price movement will cause a loss. It works for both sellers and buyers. The seller is assured of a selling price before physical delivery is made. The buyer knows in advance the price of a raw commodity or product purchased for use in processing or for resale.

Cash Forward Contracting. Forward contracts made in the cash market are called cash forward contracts. In a cash market the price of a commodity or product is normally the subject of negotiation, and physical delivery of the item in the contract is expected. It is not uncommon for farmers to sell at least part of their grain far ahead of harvest using cash forward contracting. For example, in July when a farmer has some idea of the size of the corn crop he will produce, he or she will go to the manager of the local grain elevator to negotiate a price on the corn to be delivered at harvest in November.

After the contract is signed the farmer does not have to worry about a drop in the price of corn wiping out the year's profit. The elevator manager also benefits by knowing that a certain quantity of grain will be coming in November at a given price. In turn, he or she is likely to negotiate another cash forward contract with a buyer before November to lock in profit and eliminate market risk on the selling side.

Futures Market Forward Contracting. Agribusiness firms can also forward price by using the futures markets. The futures markets are separate and distinct from the cash markets for commodities. The two are related only because (1) prices in the two markets respond in a similar fashion to the same factors, and (2) physical commodities can be delivered to fulfill futures market contracts.

In the futures market for any commodity only the price of the contract is left open for negotiation. All the other factors are standardized and are already written into the contract. They include specification of quantity, quality, date of delivery, as well as the place of delivery. Price for a contract, by law, is discovered through public auction in a specified trading area of federally licensed exchanges.

The seller of a futures contract promises to deliver the commodity as specified in the contract at the time set in the contract. The buyer of that contract agrees to take delivery of the commodity and pay the seller the price agreed upon. What is unusual about all this is that neither the buyer nor the seller generally intends to fulfill the promises made in the agreement. This is because the contract's major purpose is to temporarily shift the risk of adverse price movements to someone else. The promise of the seller to deliver the commodity can be cancelled by buying back the contract. Likewise, the buyer of a futures contract can cancel his or her obligation by selling another contract. Thus, by making equal but opposite transactions in the futures market anytime before the due date of the contract, traders can cancel their contractual obligation to deliver or receive the commodity specified while still getting the price protection offered by the futures contract.

Hedging.   The process of shifting price risk by forward contracting using the futures market is called hedging. *Hedging is the simultaneous taking of equal but opposite positions in both the cash and futures markets.* There are two basic types of hedges: the selling hedge and the buying hedge.

The selling hedge is used by persons who own a commodity and want to shift the risk of a downward movement in price to someone else. In a selling hedge the owner of the commodity sells futures contracts to protect a cash market ownership position. Farmers, marketing middlemen, processors, and food manufacturers routinely use selling hedges to protect themselves from very real losses due to price declines on the commodities they own.

The buying hedge is similar in concept to the selling hedge, but the motivation and implementation are just the opposite. In a buying hedge the person wishing to purchase the commodity buys futures contracts to protect a cash market ownership position against an upward movement in price. An unexpected price increase for a commodity purchased as a raw ingredient or for resale can wipe out any profit and may put the firm in a loss position. Consistent users of buying hedges include commodity merchants, processors, and food manufacturers. These firms routinely make commitments to sell commodities or products at a negotiated price, often before they have purchased the commodities needed to fulfill the commitments. They live in fear of unexpected price increases and use the buying hedge to shift the risk of price increases to someone else.

Let's look first at an example of a selling hedge to see how the risk of adverse price movements can be shifted. Assume that Farmer Smith would like to protect his profit from growing an estimated 50,000 bushels of corn from a decline in price. He has set a selling price target of $3.00 per bushel as part of his marketing plan before the growing season began. In early July he notes that the futures market price for December delivery of corn in Chicago has reached $3.40 per bushel, which he knows translates into a local elevator price of $3.00 per bushel. Since this meets his target price goal, Farmer Smith would like to lock in this price and the profit it guarantees him even though it is still many months before he can harvest his grain.

Smith can lock in his profit and the $3.00 per bushel price in early July by forward contracting in the futures market. He does this by selling 10 corn futures contracts for December delivery (Table 21–1). Each of the 10 contracts is for 5,000 bushels of corn which in total is equal to the 50,000 bushels he expects to harvest in December. Once Smith sells the futures contracts he is hedged. He has taken equal but opposite positions in the cash

TABLE 21–1   An Example of a Selling Hedge

Cash Market	Futures Market
July	
Expected local elevator price for corn in December is $3.00/bushel	Farmer sell 10 corn futures contracts for December delivery @ $3.40/bushel
November	
Farmer sells corn to the local elevator @ $2.00/bushel	Farmer buys 10 corn futures contracts for December delivery @ $2.40/bushel
Result	
Cash market = loss $1.00 per bushel	Futures market = gain $1.00 per bushel

The Final Outcome	
Price received per bushel in cash market in November	$2.00 per bushel
Plus gain on futures market trading	$1.00 per bushel
Total price received per bushel	$3.00 per bushel

and futures markets and no longer has to worry about a decline in the price of corn.

Let's say that his worst fears come to pass. The price of corn falls by $1.00 per bushel during the fall and the farmer is able to get only $2.00 per bushel from the local elevator at harvest time. If he had not hedged he would have missed his price target and would have received $50,000 less for his crop than he had planned on in July.

To complete his hedging activity he lifts his hedge immediately after harvest by buying ten corn futures contracts for December delivery. Since the price of cash corn and the price of corn futures are affected by the same market forces, the price of the December corn futures contract has also fallen $1.00 per bushel. But this decline in price is in the farmer's favor. He was able to buy back in November for $2.40 per bushel what he had sold in July for $3.40 per bushel which gives him a profit of $1.00 per bushel. He will receive a check for $50,000 from his commodities broker. This will replace the $50,000 he "lost" in the cash market between July and November.

Combining the $1.00 per bushel profit he made on the futures market with the $2.00 per bushel that he receives for his grain from the local elevator, the farmer is still able to obtain the $3.00 per bushel he saw in July. He successfully locked in his target price in July by using a selling hedge to forward price his crop.

Now let's look at the mechanism of the buying hedge. In this case the procedures are basically the same but the objective is quite different. Assume that it is early March and a feed manufacturer, ABC Feeds, receives a large order for livestock feed to be delivered in mid-April for a fixed price. ABC agrees to sell the feed at this price based on the current price of its major ingredient, soybean meal which is $140 per ton. If the price of soybean meal rises before ABC can purchase it, the slim profit margin on the sale will vanish.

To protect itself, ABC undertakes a buying hedge by purchasing five soybean meal contracts (at 100 tons each) (Table 21–2). In early April it buys 500 tons of soybean meal in the cash market but must pay $145 per ton to get it. The increase of $5 per ton may be enough to completely wipe out the profit from the feed sale. However, since ABC employed a buying hedge, it is protected. It lifts the hedge in mid-April by selling five soybean meal contracts. The profit on the futures market ($5.00 per ton) just offsets the higher price it has to pay for meal in the cash market, and its ingredient costs remain unchanged ($140 per ton). This preserves the original profit margin in the feed contract for the manufacturer.

TABLE 21–2   An Example of the Buying Hedge

Cash Market	Futures Market
March	
Feed manufacturer enters contract with assumed soybean meal @ $140/ton	Feed manufacturer buys 5 soybean meal futures contracts for May delivery @ $150/ton
April	
Feed manufacturer buys 500 tons of soybean meal @ $145/ton	Feed manufacturer sells 5 soybean meal futures contracts for May delivery @ $155/ton
Result	
Cash market = loss $5 per ton	Futures market = gain $5 per ton

The Final Outcome

Soybean meal ingredient cost per ton (cash market)	$145
Less profit from futures market buying hedge	–$ 5
Net cost of soybean meal per ton	$140

The Remaining Market Risk.   The two example hedges just used are referred to as *perfect hedges* since all the price risk was assumed to be eliminated. The losses in the cash markets caused by adverse price movements were exactly offset by gains in the futures markets. In practice, this almost never happens. Most of the price risk can be eliminated, but not all of it. One reason why all the price risk cannot be eliminated is that it is difficult to have equal and opposite positions in the cash and futures markets. A perfect hedge can be attained only if the hedger can use the futures markets to hedge a cash market commodity position bushel for bushel or pound for pound.

Another problem is *production risk*. The farmer in the example projected his production of corn at 50,000 bushels. Unusually favorable weather or a drought might cause him to produce more or less than 50,000 bushels. For the amount of corn produced over the 50,000 bushel hedge, the farmer would be subject to the full amount of downward price risk in the cash market because that corn is not hedged. If the farmer produces less than the amount estimated, those bushels of corn would be subject to the price risk in the futures market. For that quantity of corn he would be speculating not hedging in the futures market.

Another difficulty in taking equal and opposite positions in the cash and futures markets is that futures market contracts are written for specific amounts of a commodity. For example, grain contracts are for 5,000 bushels, sugar contracts for 112,000 pounds, and livestock contracts for 40,000 pounds. It is rare that a hedger will deal in cash market commodities in the exact amounts called for in the futures contract. Over- or underhedging will leave the farmer or firm open to a small amount of price risk.

Basis Risk. The accomplishment of the perfect hedge is nearly impossible because of another form of price risk called basis risk. *Basis* is the difference between the futures market price and the cash price. In the selling hedge example done above it was stated that the futures market price in Chicago of $3.40 per bushel translated into a local elevator price of $3.00 per bushel. In this example the basis is 40 cents per bushel ($3.40 – $3.00). This difference represents the sum of the transportation costs from the local area to the nearest delivery point allowed by the futures market, the cost of storage between now and the expiration date of the futures contract, and other conditions that might affect local cash prices.

The normal situation is for the futures price to be greater than the cash price. When this occurs the basis is said to be positive. The difference between the futures price and the cash price usually narrows during the life of the contract since less and less time is needed for storage, and this lowered cost is reflected in the price difference.

Because of the threat of delivery on the day the futures contract matures, the price of the commodity in the futures contract should be exactly equal to the cash price at that location. Thus, the cash price of corn in Chicago should be equal to the Chicago Board of Trade futures market price of corn on the day the futures contract expires. If the farmer in the selling hedge example is located in Iowa, the only price difference on futures contract expiration day should be the cost of transporting the corn from his farm to Chicago. In this example it was assumed to be 40 cents per bushel.

Now that the concept of basis has been established, it is possible to examine what is meant by basis risk. To do this let's use a selling hedge put in place by a wheat grower, Bauer, who seeks to protect his stored crop from a price decline (Table 21–3). After consulting the marketing plan that he devised before the planting season, Bauer finds that the current price of $4.00 per bushel meets his marketing goals, but he does not wish to sell until November. Rather than risk a price decline between July and November he

TABLE 21–3 A Example of Positive Basis Risk

Cash Market			Futures Market

July 20

Cash Market			Futures Market
Producer has his wheat placed in storage with the current cash price @ $4.00/bushel			Producer sells futures contracts for wheat for December delivery @ $4.50/bushel

	Futures Price	–	Cash Price	=	Basis
	$4.50	–	$4.00	=	+50 cents

November 20

Cash Market			Futures Market
Producer sells his wheat in cash market @ $3.80/bushel			Producer buys futures contract on wheat for December delivery @ $3.85/bushel

	Futures Price	–	Cash Price	=	Basis
	$3.85	–	$3.80	=	+5 cents

Result

Cash Market	Futures Market
Cash Market loss on market price decline of 20 cents/bu.	Futures market gain on futures market trade 65 cents/bu.

The Final Outcome

Loss in cash market from not selling in July	–20 cents/bu.
Cost of storage for 4 months @ 10 cents/bu.	–40 cents/bu.
Gain on futures market trading	+65 cents/bu.
Net position over a perfect hedge	+ 5 cents/bu.

places a selling hedge on July 20th by selling a December futures contract with an expiration date of December 20th. The basis at this time is +50 cents per bushel (that is, the market is giving those who are willing to store wheat from July 20 to December 20 10 cents per bushel per month to cover their storage costs over this period). Let's assume that this is equal to the producer's storage cost.

On November 20 Bauer sells his cash wheat and lifts his hedge by buying a December futures contract. If this had been a perfect hedge the difference between the futures market price and the cash price would have been 10 cents per bushel, which is the cost of one more month's storage. The $4.00 per bushel price for the wheat would have been exactly preserved. However in this example the basis has narrowed by more than one would have expected, to 5 cents per bushel rather than 10 cents per bushel. (With one month's storage cost left, the expected basis should have been 10 cents per bushel, not 5 cents.) Because of this "extra narrowing" of the basis Bauer makes an extra 5 cents per bushel because of hedging. The extra nickel comes from advantageous movements in the basis. This is an example of favorable basis movement. It is entirely possible that Bauer could have suffered a loss due to adverse movement of the basis.

Not only did Bauer protect himself from cash market price declines, but he also made money on movement in the basis. This is often the case for selling hedges that are held for a period of time. Buying hedgers normally lose money on basis movement, but since basis is fairly predictable they can factor it into their decision making process. Buying hedgers tend not to hold their hedges very long because of the nature of their business.

The calculation of basis and the presence of basis risk are important considerations when using futures markets. When agricultural economists study price movements of commodities that are traded in the futures markets, they normally find that while prices vary greatly from year to year, the basis is fairly steady. For that reason there are some traders that make all their trading decisions by correctly forecasting changes in basis rather than on the movement of the underlying cash and futures market prices.

While nearly all the price risk can be shifted away by hedging a commodity, it is impossible to completely eliminate the remaining basis risk. Basis risk is relatively small compared to price risk, however, and therefore most agribusinesses hedge the commodities they handle whenever possible.

Options Markets

Once hedged, agribusiness managers no longer have to worry about adverse price movements. On the other hand, they eliminate the opportunity to profit from advantageous price movements. There are several ways to capture the profits possible from favorable price movements, including: (1) not using hedging until the price begins to move in an unfavorable direction, (2) placing a hedge but being ready to lift it to take advantage of a favorable price movement, and (3) using options. The first two can be risky and costly if not done just right. The use of options offers the user a new way to overcome these problems and reduce exposure to price risk.

Options on futures contracts are fairly new. However, they have been used before and were quite popular in the late nineteenth and early twentieth centuries until they were banned because of trader misuse. An option gives the buyer the right, but not the obligation, to buy or sell an agricultural futures contract at some specified time in the future for a price set at the time the option is purchased. The option contract for the right to buy a futures contract is called a *call*. The option contract for the right to sell a futures contract is referred to as a *put*.

The buyer of an option contract can choose not to exercise the option to buy the underlying futures contract at a set price (the *exercise* or *striking price*) if price movement of the commodity would produce a loss. However, if the cash price moves favorably, then the option buyer can use the option as protection from the adverse price movement. Thus, through the use of options the hedger gains the flexibility to take full advantage of favorable movements of prices while still being able to gain the protection from adverse price movements offered through hedging. To gain this protection the buyer must pay a *premium*. The premium which must be paid at the time the option contract is purchased can be looked upon as a price risk insurance premium payment.

The Speculator.   Agricultural producers, commodity processors, exporters, food manufacturers, and others use the futures market to shift market risk (the risk of adverse price movements) to someone else. The one who assumes this risk is the speculator.

A commodity speculator is a rational businessperson who is willing to take on price risk in hopes of making a profit. Such speculation is not just gambling such as that found in Las Vegas. The difference is in the nature of the risk. In a casino the risk is deliberately created. For example, in the games blackjack or roulette the risk of loss is created. People are willing to take the risk in the name of entertainment. They are hoping to profit even though they know the odds are against them. When people assume this artificially created but real risk of loss there is no positive benefit to society.

The commodity speculator, on the other hand, assumes a risk that occurs naturally. In agribusiness, price risk is a natural part of holding inventories of agricultural commodities. If agribusiness firms were not able to shift price risk to speculators, their costs would increase because of the losses incurred from adverse price movements. Eventually the increased costs would show up as higher prices for food and fiber products. Because the commodity speculator assumes price risk, agribusiness firms can produce products at lower cost, and society benefits.

Some people are concerned that commodity speculators exert undue influence on futures market commodity prices. At times in the distant past this may have been true, but it is unlikely to occur today. First of all, competition in the marketplace quickly punishes those who try to raise or depress prices. Second, there are two layers of supervision that would soon detect the efforts of a large-scale buyer or seller trying to corner the market or a group of speculators conspiring to manipulate prices.

Futures Market Regulation.   The Commodity Futures Trading Commission (CFTC) is the independent regulatory agency established by Congress to oversee the trading of futures contracts in the United States. The CFTC has been granted rather broad powers ranging from licensing futures market exchanges to levying fines against violators of laws and rules regulating trading. The CFTC can require certain futures traders to stop activities which may be injuring others in the marketplace and submit trading records for examination. It has the power to take emergency action when actual or suspected market manipulation takes place.

The CFTC actually represents a second level of regulation of futures market activities. The first level is the commodity exchanges themselves. Besides providing a facility for trading, the ten or more futures exchanges in the United States are required to develop rules for trading and then supervise trading. The exchanges enforce the rules vigorously. If they did not, the CFTC would take action against the exchanges as well as the traders involved. In addition, the bad publicity resulting from a price manipulation incident would cause hedgers and other traders to take their business to another futures market exchange. It is for these reasons that it is highly unlikely that anyone would be able to successfully manipulate commodity prices and remain undetected.

SUMMARY

Agribusiness marketing managers face a wide variety of risks in the operation of their businesses. The two major categories of risk are financial and business risk. This chapter focused on ways to manage business risk. Many forms of business risk, such as losses due to fire, death of a key employee, and so on can be handled through insurance policies. Market risk in the form of adverse movements of commodity prices can also cause great variation in the net income of an agribusiness firm. Because of the price risk inherent in agribusiness, several market instruments have been developed to decrease risk such as cash forward contracting, futures markets, and options markets. Each offers users a way to reduce the level of price risk the firm has to face.

QUESTIONS

1. What are the two basic types of risk an agribusiness faces?
2. What is market risk? Describe some of the ways it can affect the prices paid or received by an agribusiness firm.
3. Describe three strategies an agribusiness firm can use to reduce its business risk.
4. Briefly describe how a selling hedge and a buying hedge work and explain how they differ.
5. What is an option and how does it differ from a futures contract?

PART FIVE

Organizing and Evaluating the Marketing Function

This final section puts all the previously discussed material into perspective. Chapter 22 will help the reader to integrate all this knowledge into a workable approach to agribusiness marketing management, and to see how marketing relates to the other areas of business management. The final chapter attempts to outline the role that marketing will play in the future success of agribusiness. A good understanding of the material in these two final chapters means the reader has grasped the major points of this text and the authors have accomplished their mission.

22

Organizing and Evaluating the Marketing Function

The way a business is structured has a great deal to do with how it perceives its work, makes decisions, and performs. This is why it takes more than a decision by the president of the company to transform a firm with a production approach to one that subscribes to the marketing approach. What is required to bring this transformation about is strong leadership from the firm's top management. Managers, along with all of the firm's employees, must possess a shared idea of what the firm's purpose and objectives are. The satisfaction of consumer needs must be at the center of their plans, and they must pursue this goal relentlessly and enthusiastically, making it well known both within the company and publicly. The result will be that employees and consumers know the firm's philosophy and accept management's motives as genuine and worthwhile.[*]

The transformation process begins with the development of the firm's business plan where it defines its purpose and objectives. The firm's purpose (that is, what consumer needs it is going to fill) and objectives (that is, how

---

[*]Portions of this chapter are drawn from James G. Beierlein, Kenneth C. Schneeberger, and Donald D. Osburn, *Principles of Agribusiness Management* (Englewood Cliffs, NJ: Prentice Hall, © 1986; a Reston book). Reprinted by permission of Prentice Hall, Inc., Englewood Cliffs, New Jersey.

it is going to fill these needs) must clearly establish the concept that the profitable satisfaction of consumer needs is the driving force behind the firm. How this concept is to be realized should be clearly defined within the marketing plan, and made operational as part of the firm's overall marketing mix of product, price, place, and promotion.

Once the planning is done it is up to top management to develop an organizational structure that will permit the firm to efficiently reach the goals that have been set. This is a critical step in the adoption of the marketing approach. It is necessary to carefully plan both the structure of the agribusiness and how the work will be done so that the organization does *what* was intended, *how* it was intended, and *when* it was intended.

Without continuous and vigorous leadership directed at satisfying consumer needs, firms often find themselves focusing more on satisfying the needs of their employees and owners than on the needs on their customers. This often leads to the production of products that are either easy to make or technically interesting to the firm rather than those that will profitably fill a consumer need. Successful agribusinesses resist this tendency. They have a strong and continuing external focus to their business that helps keep them constantly on the lookout for changes in customer needs and more profitable ways to meet them.

From the definition of the firm's purpose and objectives, managers should be able to identify the *critical tasks*. Critical tasks are those that must be performed well in order to accomplish the corporate purpose or that if done poorly will cause the firm to fail. Once these have been identified, an organizational structure should be designed to see that they are performed correctly and that other less important tasks do not take priority. Critical tasks must be given first priority since they are the ones that give the firm its competitive edge.

For example, if a firm is in the business of repairing and servicing food processing equipment and feels its competitive edge comes from its ability to provide faster and better quality service than its competitors, its critical tasks might be to insure that: (1) a proper inventory of repair parts is *always* on hand so that fast service can be given, and (2) a highly trained, efficient crew of mechanics is *always* available that can provide high-quality service. The firm may also have a program to monitor repair and operating expenses to keep the business profitable to the owners. But the cost control program takes a lower priority than these two critical tasks, since the failure to perform well on the critical tasks will cause the business to lose its competitive edge in the marketplace.

In the above example, these two critical tasks must never be subordinated to any other activity of the business. For example, if the purchasing department can save money by placing large orders for certain repair parts every three months, but there is a high probability of being out of some key parts at the end of the quarter, the firm must pass up the cost savings because of its commitment to *always* having the right parts on hand so it can give quick service. The commitment to customer service is given higher priority than the commitment to reducing inventory costs because service is the source of the firm's competitive edge and leads to greater overall long-run profits and sales. By strictly, consistently, and publicly pursuing this objective, the firm builds its image with its target market.

MARKETING AND THE CORPORATE STRUCTURE

The evolution of marketing can be seen through the changes that have occurred in corporate structure. Many early corporations were organized along functional lines, with separate departments for production, accounting, sales, finance, and so on. In many cases the head of the production department was first among equals and wielded the most power. Production was at the center of the firm's focus and to a great extent determined its profitability. The head of sales ran the firm's sales force and dabbled a bit in advertising and other marketing functions. As time went on and firms grew, it was not unusual to appoint a director of marketing who worked under the head of sales and who handled all the department's nonselling marketing activities.

Later, these nonselling marketing activities (market research, customer service, advertising, and so on) grew in size and importance to the point where separate marketing departments were established. At this time the sales and marketing departments were often given equal status in the firm's organizational structure. Later, firms began to realize that selling was really part of the firm's marketing mix, and the sales department was absorbed into the marketing department. A marketing department at this point included advertising, market research, customer relations, and physical distribution, as well as sales.

The final step in this evolutionary process comes when this organizational structure is replaced by one that includes a common vision of corporate purpose that puts all parts of the firm into the business of profitably satisfying consumer needs. This modern approach requires that the territorial disputes and the "us versus them" arguments of the past be banished from the corporate scene. At this point top management must exert strong, consistent leadership or the firm will fall back to its old ways where the production department, for example, could take the attitude that "Our job is just to produce this stuff; its up to those guys in marketing to get rid of it!" Only when *all* employees in *all* areas of the firm see themselves as being in the business of profitably satisfying consumer needs is this evolution complete.

In order to keep the firm on target, top management must develop a consistent approach to consumer need satisfaction. This means that the marketing department must assume a central role within the organization. Marketing's function is to determine and evaluate the needs of the target market that the firm will try to satisfy. It is then up to the other departments to carry out their mission in light of the consumer needs that have been defined by the marketing department.

APPROACHES TO MARKETING DEPARTMENT STRUCTURE

With the firm's organizational structure set, it is now possible to focus on developing the operating organizational structure in the marketing department. As with other areas of business, there are several principles that can be applied. First, develop a system that is as simple as possible, with as few layers of management and interrelationships as are needed to get the job done. This simplicity will help insure that all members of the department have a clear view of what they and their unit are supposed to do, and how they contribute to the accomplishment of the overall corporate purpose and goal.

Second, make sure that critical tasks are given prominence so that employees know the importance of correct and timely accomplishment of them. Third, keep the work units within the department as small as possible. The small size will permit each member to feel a part of the group's work effort. The unit should be just large enough to meet the challenges of the work assignment. Fourth, keep support staff (personnel, legal, engineering, and so on) to a minimum. They are important, but most of the time they do not

---

Principles for Developing Organizational Structure

1. Develop a system that is as simple as possible with as few layers of management and interrelationships as needed to get the job done.
2. Make sure employees know the importance of critical tasks so that efficient and timely accomplishment of them becomes a top priority.
3. Keep work units within the departments as small as possible so that each member will feel a part of the group's work.
4. Keep support staff to a minimum.

perform critical tasks. Strict adherence to these four principles should keep the management ranks lean, and keep everyone in a department close to the action and focused on the job of profitably satisfying consumer needs.

There are several approaches that can be applied to the structuring of the marketing department. One method is to *organize by function*. Under this approach each section in the marketing department is assigned a different function such as sales, market research, physical distribution, customer service, and so on. This approach allows grouping of similar activities in the department. If a problem arises with any one of the functions it is easy to identify those people concerned with it. This centralized approach can, however, result in a loss of flexibility for products that face unique or rapidly changing market conditions.

A second approach is to *organize according to product*. Under this approach each product is assigned a *product manager* who handles all the marketing activities related to a particular product. This makes one person responsible for managing the proper marketing mix for each product. This approach has proven to be very effective. However, some of the efficiencies of the functional approach are lost.

A third approach is to *organize by type of market served*. Here all the products sold to particular classes of customers such as retail customers or government agencies or industrial firms or institutions are each handled by a different section in the marketing department. This approach works best when these different classes of customers have needs or problems that require special handling. The difficulty of this approach is that no one has responsibility for specific products and some products tend to get neglected.

A fourth approach is to *organize along geographic lines*. In this approach each department handles all the firm's activities and products in a specific geographic area. This puts the manager who is geographically closest to the customer in charge of operations. It works best in situations where marketing in a specific geographic region requires a unique marketing mix.

Each of these approaches has advantages and disadvantages. The firm must weigh these against the type and level of customer service it desires to provide in a particular market, and the impact of each approach on the accomplishment of its long run objectives. Regardless of the structural approach taken, it is important that the marketing department work well with all other departments within the firm. This type of teamwork is essential if the business is to accomplish its purpose. It is marketing's job to identify and evaluate consumer needs, but it takes the efforts of all functional areas of the firm to fill those needs efficiently and profitably. Marketing certainly cannot do it alone. But the job gets easier if all departments share a common vision regarding the importance of profitably satisfying consumer needs. Again, strong leadership by top management that does not waver from this objective is essential.

EVALUATING THE MARKETING PROGRAM

Agribusinesses exist because they efficiently and profitably meet the needs of their target markets. This section will review some of the key performance factors that agribusiness marketing managers must monitor if they expect to operate healthy, competitive, and profitable businesses. This will be done by examining the business from three viewpoints: revenues, costs, and financial planning. Each is part of the overall picture of the firm. Each dollar of revenue and cost can be attributed to relevant factors. For example, revenues are determined by price and volume of sales. They, in turn, are affected by the level of consumer demand, which is influenced by still other factors. The secret for success is for managers to isolate those key factors that influence revenues, costs, and financial planning, and to monitor them in order to effectively evaluate the performance of business.

Revenue

Revenue is the income received from selling products or providing services. The level of revenue depends on the price charged per unit and the number of units sold. This means a successful agribusiness manager must be able to determine: (1) what products to sell, (2) what prices to charge, and (3) how many will be sold. Although each of these topics was covered in detail earlier in this text, it is wise to review those factors that affect the firm's revenues.

1. Consumer Demand.   Demand is the quantity of product that consumers are willing and able to buy at various prices. Effective marketing managers will know the shape of the demand schedule facing their products because they intimately know the customers in their target market, what their needs are, and how this product satisfies them. Marketing managers are always on the lookout for anything that could affect the level of consumer demand since a leading cause of business failure is not staying abreast of changes in consumer needs.

2. Market Area.   Once consumer demand has been defined, the next set of questions is how many people are in the target market, where are they located, and how many of them the firm can realistically count on to buy the product. It is generally true that agribusinesses must serve increasingly larger market areas in order to remain profitable. In times past it was often enough for a retail business to draw customers from a radius of fifteen to thirty miles. Today's agribusiness firms find that their trading areas must be larger than that and may extend over state and even national borders.

3. Pricing Policy.   Having the "right price" is critical to the firm's success. It must be set in conjunction with the product, place, and promotion parts of the firm's marketing mix. The price should be set to accomplish specific objectives as defined in the firm's marketing plan. Price must be established in light of the type of consumer demand being faced, the degree of competition in the market, and other factors that affect consumer buying behavior.

4. Degree of Competition.   Agribusinesses face a variety of competitive situations. It is important for the manager to know the degree and type of competition faced by each product within each market. Greater control over marketing decisions and profits is possible by uncovering untapped market niches and developing differentiated products which will permit the firm to operate in a less competitive environment.

5. Customer Awareness.   Making customers aware that the right product at the right price is now available at the right locations is the purpose of the promotion part of the firm's marketing mix. The marketing manager who has planned correctly will know the target market, where potential customers are located, how the product satisfies their needs, and how the product is perceived by them. This will make it much easier to decide the type, the frequency, and the budget for promotional efforts. It will also aid in establishing the proper mix of mass selling (advertising), personal selling, and sales promotion to use in reaching marketing objectives.

6. Sales Policy.   Ninety percent of agribusiness sales are on credit. The effectiveness with which an agribusiness manager extends credit and handles the collection of accounts receivable can also affect sales revenues. This may be primarily a financial concern, but when it affects the level of sales it also becomes a marketing concern. Trade credit is extended on a sale based on trust. Customers expect it. The major objective in granting credit is to expand sales by keeping existing customers happy and to attract new customers who will increase sales volume with the regularity of their purchases. The key is to collect on credit sales and to get an appropriate carrying charge from the extension of credit.

7. Customer Service. Customers expect to receive some level of service along with the products they buy. For many agribusiness products such as retail food items it may be very little. In other parts of the agribusiness system the level of service may greatly affect sales. Repeat business is often a function of the level of service offered. Customers expect sellers to be knowledgeable and truthful about their products and to stand behind them. If the firm gives the impression that it is not interested in making sure a product completely satisfies the consumer's needs, customers will buy elsewhere.

Costs

Each item that generates revenue normally leads to a corresponding entry on the cost side of the business. If the firm is to make money, the costs must be less than the revenues. Although each of these topics was covered in detail in earlier chapters, lets briefly review those items most likely to affect the firm's costs.

1. Efficiency. Efficiency is measured by the amount of output produced per unit of input. Although it is most often associated with production, it is applicable to marketing management. It can be used to evaluate the efficiency of resource use in marketing by measuring such things as selling costs per dollar of sales, cost per 1,000 customers reached in an advertising campaign, the increase in sales per square foot of retail floor space from a sales promotional program, and so on. An agribusiness that fails to constantly monitor its efficiency may find its costs out of control and its profits dwindling.

2. Break-Even Point. Once the level of efficiency in the business has been dealt with, the level of sales needed to achieve the break-even point (i.e. zero profits) should be determined. A break-even point should be calculated for each major product. This will enable the marketing manager to identify the critical cost items, assess the profit potential, and develop a means to control revenues and costs. Knowing these can help determine each product's chance for success.

Financial Planning: Records and Analysis

The third side of the business that requires a marketing manager's attention is financial planning. Everything that happens in marketing management has some financial impact. The marketing objectives are often linked with the firm's financial objectives. Experience shows that those agribusinesses that are most likely to succeed are those in control of their financial affairs.

In spite of the obvious importance of keeping good financial records, many firms still do not maintain adequate ones. Poor records are often cited as a major factor contributing to business failure. Marketing managers need records to measure the effectiveness of their efforts. Examples of information obtained from records applicable to marketing management include: market share, the ratio of marketing expenses to sales, customer attitudes toward specific products and the firm, sales and marketing expenses relative to budgeted amounts, and so forth. Good records provide management with a basis for effective decision making and allow for informed control over marketing operations. Through proper feedback and evaluation of marketing performance, the firm can increase its odds for success.

SUMMARY

This chapter brings together a variety of the topics that were covered in this text. It should help the reader see how these topics relate to each other and how they can be combined to design a successful marketing program in an agribusiness. This chapter also shows how marketing managers can utilize many general management procedures in planning, organizing, controlling, and directing the marketing department within an agribusiness firm. The successful transformation to a market-oriented firm requires careful planning and a strong commitment from top management. Employees and customers must both see and accept the commitment as genuine and long-lasting before they will follow. This is why it is vital that they see signs every day that the firm remains honestly committed to these ideals.

The commitment is not present in just business planning. It should also show up in business organization. The way the flow of work proceeds through the firm should reflect the preference for meeting customer needs over employee needs. Both are important, but the customer comes first. Nothing should inhibit the performance of those critical tasks that give the business its competitive edge in the market. This is also why the marketing department and the other departments in the firm should be kept small, with as few levels of management as possible between the top and bottom.

The evaluation of the marketing program is a critical task for management. It insures that the firm is efficiently, effectively, and profitably meeting the makers of the target market. This type of analysis requires examining the business from three points of view: revenues, costs, and financial planning.

Each provides a different perspective of the firm that is important to its overall success. Each requires careful planning on the part of managers, close attention to detail, and good record-keeping. How successful the manager is at integrating all these diverse activities is often a good measure of his or her value.

QUESTIONS

1. What steps are necessary for an agribusiness firm to successfully adopt the marketing approach to the markets in which it operates?
2. What are the critical tasks in the firm and why must they be performed smoothly for the firm to succeed?
3. What is the proper place for marketing in the corporate organizational structure?
4. What are some of the approaches a firm can take to organizing its marketing department?
5. Briefly describe the steps that need to be taken to effectively evaluate the marketing program for an agribusiness firm.

23

The Future of Agribusiness Marketing

Throughout this book a number of concepts and procedures have been presented that agribusiness marketing managers must understand and follow if they wish to prosper. This chapter reviews some of these key concepts and attempts to integrate them into a workable approach to marketing management.

This task will be accomplished by briefly reviewing the evolution of agribusiness marketing and the development of the marketing concept. Ongoing changes are examined in an attempt to determine their effects on agribusiness marketing in the near future. The impacts of these changes are examined at the firm level to see how they may change the role of the marketing manager in agribusiness. The chapter concludes with a look at some of the opportunities these changes offer agribusiness firms and individuals building careers in agribusiness marketing.

THE EVOLUTION OF AGRIBUSINESS MARKETING

In order to understand the dynamic changes occurring in agribusiness marketing it is necessary to look briefly to the past. About 10,000 years ago people started giving up the nomadic life to take up farming. The Agricultural Revolution caused fundamental changes in the way people lived their lives and led to the first attempts at marketing.

Because people had to stay in one place to make farming work, they built villages. The more successful farmers produced more than their own families could consume. They traded surplus agricultural commodities for other products produced by craftspeople in the villages. This trading or bartering constituted the first agribusiness marketing.

Agribusiness marketing didn't change much for thousands of years. While the invention of money and advances in transportation and communication did facilitate the exchange of goods, farmers, who made up a majority of the population, continued to exchange their scant supply of surplus commodities with townspeople for goods, services, or money they needed.

The Industrial Revolution of the nineteenth century was the next major step in the evolution of agricultural production and marketing. The underlying force in the Industrial Revolution was the substitution of machine power for human and animal power. Machine power was used because it was less expensive than human and animal power, and it also reduced some of the risk associated with agricultural production.

Firms and industries sprang up to market newly invented machines to farmers. Farmers became more productive and could count on regularly producing more commodities than their families consumed. The growing population centers of factory workers made up a hungry market for food. New firms and industries developed to process raw agricultural commodities into food products.

Throughout this period there are two facts that stand out with respect to agribusiness marketing. First, except for unusual periods of time, most input products, agricultural commodities, and food products were in short supply. Second, agribusiness firms tended to sell products and commodities rather than market them. Because of the relative shortages of these goods there was little incentive to devote much attention to marketing. An agribusiness firm could sell all that it could produce at the prevailing market price.

The next step in the evolution of agribusiness marketing began in 1960 with the advent of the information revolution. This is not an arbitrary date. In 1960, for the first time, slightly more than half of the people in the United States were employed in information related jobs. The information revolution is, of course, based on the use of computer technology to make people more productive.

The electronic brains of computers are replacing or augmenting relatively higher cost human brains. This revolution is occurring because: (1) information has become the key to success in just about every human activity, including marketing, and (2) people who use knowledge are very expensive. As an example, a high income commodity merchant's livelihood depends upon the availability, timeliness, and accuracy of market-related information. In another example, a well-paid product manager working for a food manufacturer makes marketing mix decisions based upon information that can be gathered from a variety of sources. Computers are needed to collect and process the data in the time needed to make the decision. In jobs where humans would normally calculate, monitor, or control an activity, computers can usually perform the same tasks more accurately, quicker, and at a lower cost.

Another major development that paralleled the beginning of the information revolution and brought about a fundamental change in agribusiness marketing was that farmers were able to produce more agricultural commodities than the market could absorb. Except during World War II, a few years in the 1970s, and periodic drought years, there have been persistent surpluses of most agricultural commodities. Even many developing nations that were commodity importers a few years ago are now attempting to export agricultural commodities. Experts say that even with population growth it is now possible to eliminate world hunger; what remains to be done is to solve a few but rather difficult political and distributional problems.

The surplus production situation extends to input suppliers and the food processing-manufacturing sector. Input suppliers face declining markets much of the time when the government attempts to reduce costly surpluses by reducing crop acreages. Food manufacturers are finding that there is a limit to the capacity of the human stomach. In fact, per capita consumption of many food products has declined in the United States in the past few years. The same situation exists in other parts of the industrial world.

THE MARKETING CONCEPT

Faced with large supplies and slow-growing demand for agricultural commodities and food products, many agribusiness firms are utilizing computer technology to help them apply the marketing concept. The marketing concept as discussed earlier in this book consists of two steps: (1) identifying a need of users or consumers, and (2) organizing the activities of the firm to profitably fill that need.

Adopting the marketing concept leads an agribusiness firm to cease being a seller and start being a marketer. Why even produce a commodity or a food product that will not sell or will sell at a price so low that it is difficult to realize a profit? In such a case the message from the market is that the need is not as great as the supply of that product or commodity. The need is the starting point of the marketing and production process.

Accordingly, agricultural producers are giving more attention to marketing. With the present level of technology, there may be greater potential for producers to increase profits through improved marketing than through better production. Many producers have found unmet needs in the marketplace and have filled the gaps. Farm-produced products with different quality-price characteristics or different physical characteristics have done well in some areas of the country. Other farmers are offering special services along with their products.

Here are some examples of farmers who have successfully adopted the marketing concept:

1. A Texas family recently built a small slaughtering facility next to their feedlot. They are producing chemical-free beef. They use no pesticides on the feed they raise, and their cattle receive no medicine or feed additives. They market the beef directly to people with a high degree of concern for health.
2. A Kansas farm family switched all of their acreage to the production of alfalfa. They bought transportation equipment and a sales route from a retiring hay hauler. They are supporting four families by selling high-quality alfalfa hay to dairies in the Kansas City area.
3. An Ohio farmer is selling vegetables to urbanites through his roadside stand. To further increase his income he has started a pick-your-own operation that includes apples, strawberries, green beans, cucumbers and other fresh produce.

Adopting the marketing concept commits a firm to continual change. This can be unsettling to people who are used to taking a "set and forget" approach to conducting business. The needs of consumers or users drive the marketing–production system. Needs change continuously. Therefore, the marketing-concept firm must continuously reorganize its activities to fill changing needs if it hopes to remain profitable. This is the challenge to present day agribusiness marketing managers.

THE CHANGING ENVIRONMENT

The environment includes all the economic, political, social, and technological factors that affect the markets for agribusiness products and commodities. In many cases it is difficult to separate these factors by category. For example, the current farm program contains acreage reduction provisions meant to reduce the production of commodities in surplus and to protect fragile soils. Acreage reductions certainly have economic impacts, but they also influence local politics, affect the sociology of rural communities, and have an impact on the use of technological inputs by farmers.

A major economic factor facing agribusiness marketing managers is the changing competitive structure of markets at the international level. The newspapers are full of articles pointing to industries where foreign producers are able to underprice American firms because either their production costs are lower or their governments subsidize them. Because of this, America has lost its dominant position in the market for several commodities.

Similar changes are also influencing the agricultural input industries. For example, in the next few years the United States is likely to become a net importer of nitrogen fertilizers. Few if any new nitrogen plants have been built in this country since the petroleum price increases of the mid-1970s. The new nitrogen plants in the world have been constructed in countries with cheap, abundant supplies of natural gas, the major raw ingredient for the production of nitrogen. In most cases the natural gas was being flared or burned just to get rid of it. Now these countries have harnessed this fuel and are turning out large quantities of nitrogen fertilizer which they can put on the world market at very low prices.

Domestic competition has become fierce. Many agribusiness industries have become more concentrated in the last few years as a result of acquisition and merger activity. Many economists, relying on economic theory, would say that the concentration (that is, fewer firms in an industry) should lead to less competition. The fact is, competition is more heated than ever before as firms battle for market share. In the input industries, periods of declining overall crop acreages mean firms have to work harder to maintain their market shares. In commodity processing, the fewer but larger firms have been able to take advantage of cost-reducing technology and use marketing innovations to stay on top.

A great deal of well-publicized merger activity has occurred in the food manufacturing area as firms strive to obtain products and geographic coverage that will allow them to be successful in increasingly fragmented markets. Even food distributors have joined the fight. For example, McDonald's is no longer the largest fast-food company in terms of number of outlets. Pepsico is now the largest, with ownership of Pizza Hut, Taco Bell, and Kentucky Fried Chicken. Why has Pepsico gotten into the fast-food business? Besides being very profitable if well run, fast-food restaurants sell lots of beverages. Just try to order the major competitor's beverage in a Pepsico-owned fast-food restaurant.

Influencing Political Decisions

Agribusiness has become politicized. This means firms are affected, sometimes severely, by political decisions. In turn, the firms have become very active in trying to influence political decisions. This means lobbying.

Lobbying is not a dirty word. We live in a pluralistic democratic system. This means we all have natural affiliations to one or more groups. For example, wheat farmers, fertilizer manufacturers, cookie manufacturers, retail grocery store owners, and so on all have economic interests in common with others in their respective industries. A change in the farm program, for example, that would reduce wheat acreage and cause the price of wheat to rise could affect all these groups. The groups may band together to influence the political decision to change the wheat acreage restrictions. On other issues these same groups may oppose one another. The point is, in our system of government individuals have the right to band together into groups to try to influence political decisions. It is in their economic best interest to do so.

Agribusiness firms have become more active in trying to influence political decisions in the past few years and can be expected to become even more active in the future. Large firms usually assign this activity, often called public affairs, to a high-level officer of the company. This executive may be called to testify before congressional committees, talk directly with legislators, and work with industry groups. Professional lobbyists may even be hired to represent the company on special issues. Small agribusiness firms engage in similar activities, although they tend to rely more on industry groups to represent them.

Market Fragmentation and the Food Market

The social factor which is having the greatest effect on agribusiness marketing and which will continue to affect it into the foreseeable future is market fragmentation. Market fragmentation is the result of changing demographics and the changing lifestyles of the American public.

A mass market for food products used to exist in this country. The mass market was driven by the needs of the typical family consisting of a working father, a mother who did not work outside the home, and two school-aged children. The mother did the food shopping for the family in a predictable manner. In other words, she looked for quality as well as value, and responded to price incentives such as coupons.

This mass market consisting of consumers with like needs and predictable buying behavior made life relatively easy for food marketers. They developed products, promoted an image of quality and value, ran the same advertisement in all media and geographic markets, and occasionally offered price incentives.

This mass market has all but disappeared. The last census showed that fewer than 13 percent of all households exhibit the characteristics of the "typical" American family of a few years ago. Many households consist of families where both husband and wife work, and often there are no children. Other households consist of single parents with children. There has been a sharp increase in single-person households and households made up of retired couples.

Shopping patterns have changed. The household food buyer is more likely to be a male, a teenager, or a single person than a housewife. Food buyers do not necessarily look in retail grocery stores for food. About half of the at-home meals consist of food that has been partially to totally prepared elsewhere and then taken home to be eaten.

The products and promotional activities that worked well in a homogeneous mass market work less well in a fragmented market. Working mothers do not have the time to clip coupons and go from store to store looking for specials. Male food buyers tend not to comparison shop. They move down the grocery store aisles flipping products into the cart and checking things off the list so they can get home to watch the football game or go play golf. No one has really determined how teenagers shop or how to advertise to them effectively. The point is, the emerging fragmented markets for food products represent tremendous challenges for food marketers.

Market Fragmentation and the Input Supply Market

Market fragmentation also extends to the input supply market. Farmer buyers, at least on a geographic basis, used to be rather homogeneous. We now see three rather distinct groups of farmers. The first group consists of the large commercial farmers who take advantage of economies of size in their operations. They are very knowledgeable about production technology, so they require little service along with the input products they buy. They are willing to assume some of the marketing functions formerly performed by input suppliers such as storage, transportation, risk of ownership, and financing. They want to buy inputs in large volume at low prices.

The second group consists of farmers whose operations tend to be smaller in size but who still realize most of their income from agricultural production. They may require some help in adopting new technology, especially with new input products. Because of their smaller size they cannot take full advantage of volume purchasing and tend to expect input suppliers to provide the full range of marketing services.

The third group consists of small or part-time farmers. Although large in number they really do not contribute much to total agricultural production because of their small size. A high proportion of this group's total income comes from off-farm sources. Some of the people in this group are small farmers who live on the farm but also hold full-time jobs in nearby towns and cities. Many people are former urbanites who have purchased a small parcel of land to enjoy country living.

Although this third group is not very important on a volume basis, some input suppliers have found selling to these "farmers" to be very profitable. They tend to buy in small lots and require a lot of service along with the products, but they are willing to pay premium prices for a special horse feed or a spray for prized apple trees or animal health products for their children's 4-H project lambs.

In the near future, the large commercial farmer category and the small, part-time farmer category are expected to grow in number, while the middle-sized farmers will be forced either to get larger to be able to take advantage of economies of size or to supplement their farm incomes with off-farm jobs (Table 23–1).

Technological Change

Agribusiness has always been affected by technological change. Many of the industries included in agribusiness today owe their birth and existence to the development of technology. There has been a bias toward rapid technological adoption in agribusiness to lower costs and risks. This has contributed to the trend toward larger firms.

TABLE 23–1   Distribution of Farms by Sales Class, 1986 and Projected to 2000

Classification (Sales in dollars)	1986		2000	
	Percent	No.	Percent	No.
Part-time (Less than $20,000/yr.)	61	1,400,000	70	1,750,000
Small ($20,000 - $99,999/yr.)	26	600,000	10	250,000
Medium ($100,000 - $499,999/yr.)	12	275,000	16	400,000
Large ($500,000 - over)	1	25,000	4	100,000
Total	100	2,300,000	100	2,500,000

Source: Office of Technology Assessment and USDA.

There are significant technological advances yet to come for agribusiness. The benefits of computerized information technology, for example, are just beginning to be realized. The adoption of small computers at all levels of agribusiness is well underway. A new managerial style is evolving where a single manager at a computerized work station can handle a broad scope of activities and can make a large number of informed decisions. This is leading to broad, flat organizational structures where each individual can be highly productive and less time can be spent on paper shuffling.

Another area of technological development that will have significant impacts on agribusiness is biotechnology. Biotechnology has the potential to increase production, lower costs, and perhaps give us entirely new food and fiber production systems. In the input industries there will be new products, new firms, and possibly new industries. The first new biotechnology products are just starting to affect agricultural production. Improved seed, new plant varieties, animal growth hormones, and other new products to come will boost production while deceasing costs. Food processing industries are already feeling the effects of new biotechnology. Light beer and high fructose corn syrup are among the first products of the new biotechnology processes.

Many people are predicting that biotechnology will have revolutionary effects on all three sectors of agribusiness. As one industry executive put it, "We'd better get ready for the biotechnology freight train that is bearing down on us all."

AGRIBUSINESS MARKETING CAREERS

Marketing in agribusiness provides and will continue to provide a wide array of career opportunities for young people. Table 23–2 lists a sampling of marketing-related positions in agribusiness. A study completed by the U.S. Department of Agriculture showed that agribusiness marketing is one of the areas of employment that offers the greatest number of opportunities for college graduates with expertise in agriculture and agribusiness.

Preparation for a person seeking to take advantage of agribusiness marketing career opportunities should include a range of courses from the agricultural sciences or even specialization in one of the agricultural sciences such as agronomy or animal science. In addition, at least one course from each of the functional areas of marketing, management, and finance would be looked upon as minimal preparation. Several courses in agribusiness marketing would be better.

Management courses will prove to be valuable as a person moves up in an organization and is given responsibility for managing people, money, and

TABLE 23–2 Agribusiness Marketing Positions

Sales representative	Grain merchandiser	Landscape contractor
Food buyer	Food merchandiser	Food broker
Commodity broker	Livestock buyer	Livestock broker
Purchasing agent	Tobacco buyer	Field representative
Territory manager	Producer merchandiser	Meat products salesperson
Farm real estate agent	Dairy products salesperson	Nursery stock salesperson
Food manufacturer representative	Agricultural pharmaceutical salesperson	Commodity futures account executive
Public relations specialist	Food brand manager	Market analyst
Product manager	Insurance agent	Technical service representative
Advertising account executive	District sales manager	Market planner
Market researcher		

Source: Jane K. Coulter, Marge Stanton, and Allen D. Goecker, "Employment Opportunities for College Graduates in the Food and AGricultural Sciences," USDA Higher Education Programs, July 1986.

time. The value of finance courses will become apparent as soon as a person has to develop and submit a first budget or capital investment proposal. Even entry-level marketing people get involved in financial analysis.

A working knowledge of computers is essential. One does not have to become a computer programmer, but at the very least a person entering an agribusiness marketing position should be able to use a spreadsheet program, a word processing program, and perhaps a data base management program.

Agribusiness recruiters rank communication skills very high when evaluating potential marketing candidates on college campuses. They look for both oral and written communication skills, because much of what marketers do relies on communication.

The most usual entry into agribusiness marketing is through sales. For commodity-oriented firms it is commodity merchandising, but the career paths are similar. The new employee is trained to become successful in the position for which he or she was hired, but always with an eye on future advancement. In a sense an agribusiness marketer is always in training for the next position of greater responsibility.

From a sales position a person can move into one of the functional areas of marketing: marketing planning, product development, market research, or advertising and promotion. Eventually, a person takes on managerial responsibilities in marketing. Then he or she moves on into general management and on to the top of the corporate hierarchy. Perhaps not so surprisingly, a large number of top agribusiness corporate officers had their start in marketing.

For a person interested in a career in marketing, it is difficult to think of an industry that offers more opportunities than agribusiness. Agribusiness is a technology-based, dynamic group of industries. Marketers face an endless stream of challenges in domestic as well as international markets. In the near future, as in the past, emerging technology will serve as the basis for new products and new industries. The well-prepared person entering agribusiness marketing as a career will be in a position to reap substantial rewards.

SUMMARY

The agribusiness system is rapidly changing. This means that in order for agribusiness firms to be profitable they will have to devote the same level of attention to marketing that they have devoted to production. Agribusiness firms will be required to become marketers and not sellers of commodities and food products. The critical step in this process will be the adoption of the marketing concept where profitably meeting the needs of a well-defined group of consumers becomes the focal point of all the firm does.

Target marketing must replace the mass marketing approach that has been used in the past. This change is vital for success in agribusiness since the mass markets once reached by a broad marketing approach no longer exist. In fact there is evidence of increasing fragmentation of markets and even more diversity of the consumers within them. In addition, agribusiness firms face opportunities for new products and new industries that are likely to arise from developments in biotechnology.

All in all, there is a bright and challenging future in agribusiness for those willing to learn and apply the marketing approach. This is truly an exciting time to be a part of agribusiness. The authors hope the material in this text has helped to open a window to the future as students prepare themselves for careers in agribusiness. For most, knowledge of marketing will play a large role in achieving success.

QUESTIONS

1. Briefly describe the evolution of marketing in agribusiness.
2. Define the marketing concept and explain why it should lead to greater long-run profits for an agribusiness firm.

3. What is meant by market fragmentation, and what are its implications for the future of agribusiness marketing?
4. What is expected to happen to the middle-sized farms in the future? Explain why this is likely to happen.
5. What types of impacts is biotechnology expected to have on agribusiness in the future?

Glossary

Advertising. Paid mass selling.

Agribusiness System. All the firms that are involved in supplying inputs or services to production agriculture or that handle, process, or manufacture farm outputs and that distribute, wholesale, or retail these products to the final consumer.

Agricultural Input Sector. The group of firms that constitute one of three major parts of the agribusiness system and that supply approximately 75 percent of all the inputs used in production agriculture.

Arbitrage. The process of capturing extra profits by buying in one market and selling in another market.

Assembly. The physical collection and movement of commodities by an individual or firm into larger lots normally used by processors, wholesalers, and other similar firms.

Asset. An item the firm either owns or controls and uses in its business.

Balance Sheet. A document that summarizes a firm's financial position at a given point in time and lists the firm's assets, liabilities, and net worth.

Basis. The difference between the cash price of a commodity and the futures price at some point in time.

Battle of the Brands. The marketing competition between private labels and manufacturers' brands of products.

Brand Name. A word or group of letters or words that can be recognized and pronounced and that customers will readily associate with a product.

Break-Even Analysis. The process of determining the level of sales necessary to cover all costs at given prices.

Break-Even Point (BEP). The level of sales where total costs equal total revenue (i.e., profit equals zero) at given prices.

Budget. A formal, written plan detailing how the firm will use its resources, what amount of sales are expected, and so on, during some future time period.

Business Plan. A description of the firm's overall approach to its business which tells how it is going to gain a successful competitive edge in the market. The plan also includes a clear and concise statement of the firm's purpose and objectives.

Buying Function. One of the nine required marketing functions that deals with how to obtain ownership of products desired by others. The buying function overcomes the ownership barrier to greater consumer satisfaction by making it possible for others to buy what is for sale.

Call. An options contract that gives the right to buy a futures contract.

Capital. Economic assets invested in one period that will bring benefits for many periods in the future.

Capital Structure. The firm's mix of long-term liabilities and equity.

Capper-Volstead Act. A 1922 federal law exempting bona fide cooperatives from federal antitrust statutes.

Cash Cow. A product which gives the firm a dominant position in a market but where the potential for market growth is low. Products in this category normally generate consistent and large profits with little variation from year to year.

Change in Quantity Demanded. Movement along a demand schedule in response to a change in a good's own price.

Channel Leader. The firm in the marketing channel that is recognized as the leader, or the innovator, whom everyone else follows.

Clayton Act. A federal law that prohibits combinations of firms that would lessen competition.

Commodity. An undifferentiated product such as wheat, milk, and pork. The location of production or the identity of its producer is normally not important to the buyer. Industry grades and standards normally fully describe a commodity.

Competitive Fringe. The small firms in an industry that provide competition for the dominant core firms.

Complementary Good. A good or service used in conjunction with another good or service that enhances the satisfaction of that item (e.g., sugar in coffee).

Concentration Ratio. The proportion of total sales in a market accounted for by the sales of the largest four to ten firms.

Conduct, Market. One of the elements in the evaluation of how markets operate as part of the structure-conduct-performance model. The structure of a market (i.e., the number of firms) can lead to various forms of behavior (i.e., conduct) that can lead to higher prices and profits (i.e., the economic performance) by the firms in it.

Consumer Franchise. The tacit agreement between the consumer and the firm to buy this firm's product over everyone else's provided the manufacturer provides a product at a reasonable price that is of consistently high quality and in sufficient quantity.

Consumer Sovereignty. The marketing principle that the needs of the consumer take precedence over all other needs in a business.

Contribution. Selling price per unit minus the direct cost of goods sold per unit.

Contribution Margin. The difference between selling price per unit and direct cost per unit. This difference is the contribution per unit to overhead and fixed costs.

Controlling. That one of the four functions of management which deals with measuring the progress of the firm toward the goals established in the planning function.

Cooperative. A business that is owned, operated, and patronized primarily by the owners and that does business at cost.

Corporation. A state-chartered legal entity that has a legal existence apart from its owners and that issues stock.

Cost, Average. Total cost divided by output in units.

Cost of Goods Sold. The direct costs of producing the goods sold during the current accounting period.

Critical Tasks. Those tasks that must be done well in a business in order to accomplish the corporate purpose, or that if done poorly will cause the firm to fail.

Cross-Price Elasticity. The percentage change in quantity demanded of a product in response to a known percentage change in price of that product's substitute or complement.

Demand. A series of price and quantity relationships showing how much consumers are willing and able to buy at various prices.

Demand, Law of. The observation that consumers typically buy less of a good as the price rises, and more as it falls..

Derived Demand. The demand for one item that is at least partly determined by the demand for another item.

Diminishing Marginal Utility. The situation where the consumption of additional units of a good or service adds less to total satisfaction (i.e., utility) than does consumption of the previous unit.

Diminishing Returns, Law of. The observation that, given at least one fixed resource, the application of increasing amounts of variable inputs will lead to output increasing first at an increasing rate, then increasing at a decreasing rate, then reaching a maximum, and finally declining.

Directing. That one of the four functions of management which deals with the implementation of the goals set in planning, using organization and controls.

Distribution. The physical movement of commodities or products from one part of the marketing system to another.

Distribution, Exclusive. The situation in which a firm selects just a few intermediaries to handle its products in specified territories.

Distribution, Intensive. The situation in which a firm sells its products through any outlet that is willing to take it.

Distribution, Selective. The situation in which a firm sells only through those intermediaries that it selects, but does not give middlemen an exclusive right to sell the product.

Diversification, Market. Selling new products in new markets.

Dog. A product for which the firm lacks market dominance and for which the market potential for growth is low.

Dominant Core. The largest firms in an industry with the largest market share.

Economic Efficiency. The point in the production function where profits are maximized. Technical efficiency is normally a prerequisite to economic efficiency.

Economics. The study of how scarce resources are allocated between competing needs.

Economy of Scale. The increase (decrease) in output when all inputs are increased (decreased) by the same proportion.

Economy of Size. The reduction in average cost per unit that normally occurs as plant size is increased. It typically arises from more efficient use of inputs.

Efficiency. The level of output divided by the level of input required to achieve it.

Efficiency, Pricing. How close the market price of a resource comes to its full value.

Elastic Demand. The condition where the percentage of change in quantity demanded is greater than the percentage of change in price, income, and so on.

Elasticity, Income. The percentage change in quantity demanded in response to a known percentage change in income.

Elasticity, Supply. The percentage change in the quantity supplied in response to a known percentage change in the price of the item, price of substitute goods, income, and so on.

Elasticity of Demand. The percentage change in the quantity demanded in response to a known percentage change in another variable such as the price of the item, price of substitute goods, income, and so on.

Exchange Function. The physical activity of buying and selling a good or service, with ownership and possession passing from buyer to seller.

Food Product. Normally a differentiated product that often carries a brand name whose ingredients began as agricultural commodities (wheat, milk, shell eggs, etc.) that were first processed into a different form (flour, pasteurized milk, frozen eggs) and then transformed again in manufacturing to make a product purchased by consumers (cakes, pies, cupcakes).

Forecasting. The process of developing an estimate of the future.

Forward Contracting. Selling all or part of a crop for an agreed upon price before it is harvested.

Financing. One of the nine required marketing functions that helps overcome the value separation barrier to greater consumer satisfaction. By financing production and marketing activities before products are sold it is possible to avoid possible cash flow difficulties and facilitate the operation of the marketing system.

Fixed Costs. Those costs that do not vary with the level of output.

Form Utility. The additional satisfaction that consumers gain from the transformation of a good from one physical form to another.

Four Functions of Management. Planning, organizing, controlling, and directing.

Futures Contract. A legal contract on a commodity traded on a commodity exchange that specifies the price, quality, and quantity to be delivered at some predetermined time in the future.

Goods, Consumer. Products used by the final consumer.

Goods, Convenience. Low-cost goods that are purchased frequently with little thought, effort, or comparison shopping.

Goods, Durable. Goods that are not immediately consumed in use.

Goods, Emergency. A subcategory of convenience goods that is purchased at the time of immediate need.

Goods, Impulse. A subcategory of convenience goods whose purchase is generally unplanned and is decided upon only when the goods are seen.

Goods, Industrial. Goods used to produce other goods.

Goods, Nondurable. Goods that are consumed in use.

Goods, Shopping. A subcategory of consumer goods that includes items that require some thought and comparison as to the selection of product quality, price, style and so forth.

Goods, Specialty. A subcategory of consumer goods that includes items that have a unique characteristic or brand name that causes the consumer to make a special effort to seek them for purchase.

Goods, Staple. A subcategory of convenience goods that includes items purchased with little planning.

Goods, Unsought. A subcategory of consumer goods that includes items that are either unknown to consumers or normally not sought by most consumers.

Grades and Standards. One of the nine required marketing functions that helps overcome the information separation that limits consumer satisfaction. The use of uniform grades and standards facilitates the buying and selling of products in the market.

Gross Margin. On the income statement, total dollar sales minus cost of goods sold.

Hedging. Simultaneously taking equal but opposite positions in the cash and futures markets so as to minimize price risk.

Inelastic Demand. The condition where the percentage change in quantity demanded is less than the percentage change in price, income, and so on.

Information Separation. One of the barriers to greater consumer satisfaction in the economic system overcome by marketing. Information separation is overcome by providing a large flow of accurate and timely information about anything that might affect the market to all potential market participants.

Input. Any resource used in production.

Integration, Horizontal. The situation in which a firm moves to do a larger share of the marketing activities at one level in the marketing system. For example, a food retailer tries to gain a larger market share of retail sales in a market.

Integration, Vertical. The situation in which a firm moves from where it has been in the marketing system either backward toward the beginning of the marketing channel or forward toward the ultimate consumer. Firms typically integrate vertically to gain greater control and higher profits. For example, a food manufacturer may forward integrate by opening restaurants that feature the foods it manufactures.

Inventory. The amount of unsold products or inputs to production on hand at some time.

Liabilities. A firm's debts.

Line Position. A job in an organization that has direct authority to make decisions.

Loss Leader. A highly advertised low price on an item that is designed to entice customers to come to buy. The intent is that customers will also buy other items once in the store so that the seller can earn a profit from all that is purchased and raise the store's total level of sales and profits.

Management. Accomplishing tasks through people.

Manager. The one responsible for seeing that tasks are done.

Marginal Cost. The change in cost associated with the production of an additional unit of output.

Marginal Revenue. The change in revenue associated with the production of an additional unit of output.

Market. A group of current or potential consumers with similar unmet needs and purchasing power.

Market Development. Developing the sales of existing products in new markets.

Market Information. One of the nine required marketing functions that must be done to overcome information separation for greater consumer satisfaction in the economic system. The ability of all potential market participants to have access to timely and accurate information that could affect the market facilitates the operation of the marketing system.

Marketing. All those business activities that help satisfy consumer needs by coordinating the flow of goods and services from producers to consumers or users.

Marketing, Direct. The situation in which producers sell their products directly to consumers without the use of middlemen.

Marketing, Indirect. The situation in which producers sell their products to consumers through the use of middlemen.

Marketing, Pull. An approach to marketing where consumers are given a strong promotional effort to buy a product.

Marketing, Push. An approach to marketing where channel intermediaries are given a strong promotional effort to sell a product.

Marketing Areas, Law of. The observation that when more than one supply point is available to serve an area, each plant will extend its marketing area until the sum of its production and transportation costs is just equal to that of another supply point. This will insure that the plant with the lowest total delivered cost will service each area.

Marketing Bill. The difference between the price that the processing-manufacturing sector pays for raw agricultural commodities from the production agriculture sector and the price its receives for food products from consumers after it has processed them into food products that are sold at the times, places, and forms that consumers desire.

Marketing Channel. The path a product follows from the farm gate to the consumer.

Marketing Concept. The concept that marketing is the determination of consumer needs and the purpose of the business organization should be the profitable fulfillment of these consumer needs.

Marketing Management The planning, organizing, controlling, and directing of all the firm's business activities that help satisfy consumer demands and help the firm accomplish its goal of maximizing its long run profits.

Marketing Margin. The difference between the price consumers pay for a product and the price received by producers for the raw product.

Marketing Mix. Four controllable variables that all begin with the letter "P"—product, price, place, and promotion—that when used together as part of the managers' tactical plan can help the firm to completely satisfy consumer needs in the target market. Based on a concept put forth by Jerome McCarthy.

Marketing Plan. A complete assessment of all the factor surrounding the consumer needs the firm is hoping to fill.

Market Niche. An identifiable segment of a larger market.

Market Penetration. Increasing the sales of current products in present market areas or capturing a large market share quickly with a new product.

Market Potential. Total level of sales possible in a target market for all firms.

Market Share. The percentage of total sales from the target market achieved by a single firm.

Markup. The amount of money or percentage added to the direct cost of goods to arrive at the selling price. The markup must be figured on the selling price *not* the cost. For example, 20 percent added to cost will *not* yield a 20 percent profit. To earn a 20 percent profit, 25 percent must be added to cost.

Mass Marketing. An approach to marketing that assumes that all consumers have the same set of needs and so the firm needs only to produce a single product and use a single marketing approach to meet the needs of all customers.

Merchandising. The way in which products are presented to consumers for sale.

Middlemen. Those members of the marketing system who are involved in the trade rather than the production of products.

Mix Pricing. The process of using loss leader pricing with regular prices in order to hit overall financial goals.

Net Cash Flow. The actual cash received minus actual cash paid out over a given period of time.

Net Worth. On a firm's balance sheet, what remains after liabilities are subtracted from assets.

Opportunity Cost. The cost of a resource as measured by its highest value in a forgone use.

Option. A contract that gives the right but not the obligation to buy or sell an agricultural futures contract at some specified time in the future for a price set at the time the option is purchased.

Organizing. That one of the four functions of management which deals with how the firm will be arranged to accomplish the goals set in the planning function.

Output. The result of the production process.

Ownership Separation. One of the barriers to greater consumer satisfaction in the economic system that is overcome by marketing. It accomplishes this through the transfer of ownership of a product from one individual to another.

Performance, Market. One of the elements in the evaluation of how markets operate as part of the structure-conduct-performance model. The structure of a market (i.e., the number of firms) can lead to various forms of behavior (i.e., conduct) that can lead to higher prices and profits (i.e., the economic performance) by the firms in it.

Place Utility. The satisfaction that consumers receive from having a product in the place where they want it.

Planning. One of the four functions of management which deals with all actions concerning the future of the business.

Possession Utility. The satisfaction that consumers receive from gaining possession of a product so that they can use it.

Price. The amount paid or asked for a product.

Price, F.O.B. The situation in which the selling price is set for a sale at the factory. The manufacturer will load it for free on board (f.o.b.) the transportation the buyer specifies. Once loaded, ownership of the good passes to the buyer, who pays for the cost of transportation and also assumes all risk for loss or damage from then on.

Price, Law of One. The observation that when markets are operating efficiently, there should be only one price for each product in a market after adjusting for the costs of adding time, place, and form utility.

Price, List. The published price for which the product is to sell.

Price, Seasonal Patterns of. Patterns of prices that recur within one year.

Price Cycles. Patterns of prices that recur in periods of longer than one year.

Price Determination. The process followed by economists to determine the factors influencing the prices of products. Normally done after the sale has been completed.

Price Discovery. The process used by buyers and sellers to arrive at the sale price during a transaction.

Pricing, Forward. The establishment of the exchange prices of a commodity or product before the physical transfer to the new owner.

Pricing, Market Penetration. A pricing policy where the initial price of a new good is set relatively low.

Pricing, Market Skimming. A pricing policy where the initial price of a new good is set very high, then moved down in stages as consumer demand is satisfied at each level of price.

Private Label. A brand used exclusively by a food retailer or wholesaler that is not normally widely advertised.

Processing. The conversion of products to different forms.

Processing-Manufacturing Sector. A major part of the three-part agribusiness system that meets consumers' demand for greater processing and convenience in the products they consume by processing and manufacturing food products from the raw agricultural commodities produced by production agriculture.

Product. Anything that gives consumers satisfaction.

Product, Generic. A product without a brand name.

Product Development. Offering users a new or improved product in existing market areas.

Production. The use of inputs to create an output that has economic value.

Production Agriculture. The centerpiece of the three-part agribusiness system that takes agricultural inputs and produces raw agricultural commodities.

Production Function. A depiction of the levels of output possible from various levels of and combinations of inputs.

Product Life Cycle. The distinctive stages that most products pass through from being a new product to being dropped from sale.

Product Line. The number and types of products the firm offers to sell.

Product Mix. The set of products included in a firm's product line.

Product Positioning. What the consumer thinks of when thinking of a firm's product (e.g., highest quality, lowest price. best service, and so on).

Product Benefit. What use of the product means to the buyer.

Profit. Total revenue minus total cost.

Publicity. Unpaid mass selling.

Put. The option contract for the right to sell a futures contract.

Quantity-Assortment Problem. The problem of product manufacturers being generally organized to turn out large quantities of a few products, while consumers seek to purchase small quantities of a relatively large assortment of products.

Question Mark. A product that does not occupy a dominant position in the market but is in a market with high growth potential.

Return on Assets (ROA). The ratio of net profits before tax to total assets.

Return on Investment (ROI). The ratio of net profit before tax to the level of invested capital.

Risk. The possibility of loss where the probabilities of various outcomes are known.

Risk, Business. The variation in net income that arises from normal fluctuations in business activity.

Risk, Casualty. Loss of life or loss of property due to unforeseen occurrences.

Risk, Financial. The risk that a firm will be unable to meet its financial obligations.

Risk, Market. The risk associated with changes in market supply and demand.

Risk, Personnel. The risk that arises from the illness, death, injury, or other loss of one of the principals in a business.

Risk, Physical. The risk that a product will deteriorate in quality due to physical changes arising from things such as insects, rodents, fires, poor handling and storage, and so on.

Risk, Price. The risk that a product will change in value due to changes in the market prices of inputs and outputs.

Risk, Production. The variation in product output due to factors beyond the control of the producer (e.g., weather, disease, pests, etc.).

Risk, Technological. The risk associated with (1) the adoption or nonadoption of new technology, or (2) obsolescence and ensuing equipment breakdowns.

Risk Taking. One of the nine required marketing functions that helps overcome the time separation barrier to greater consumer satisfaction in the economic system. By bearing some of the physical and price risk it facilitates the operation of the marketing system.

Robinson-Patman Act. A federal law that describes many of the practices that are considered unfair trade practices.

Sales Forecast. The level of sales a single firm can expect to receive from the target market.

Sales Promotion. All selling activities that complement personal and mass selling activities. This includes coupons, in-store signs, etc.

Selling. The performance of all those activities that help prospective customers fulfill their needs and wants with the firm's products.

Selling, Mass. Selling to a large number of potential consumers at one time. There are two forms of mass selling: advertising and publicity.

Selling Marketing Function. One of the nine required marketing functions that deals with how to sell products desired by others. The selling function overcomes the ownership separation to greater consumer satisfaction by making it possible for others to obtain what is for sale.

Selling, Personal. One-on-one selling by a salesperson.

Services. Nontangible products that cannot be held, stored, or touched. They can include benefits, activities or satisfactions that are offered for sale.

Sherman Antitrust Act. A federal law that forbids monopolies and prohibits combinations of firms that leads to restraint of interstate trade.

Shift in Demand. A change in quantity demanded at all prices that comes in response to changes other than in the product's own price.

Short Run. A time period short enough that at least one input is fixed.

Space Separation. One of the barriers to greater consumer satisfaction in the economic system that is overcome by marketing. It typically deals with having the product at the location desired by the consumer and is normally overcome by transporting the item to where it is desired.

Staff Position. A job that has no direct decision-making authority but does give advice to those that do.

Stages of Production. The three stages found on a production function. In stage I, total product is increasing at an increasing rate and production in this stage is inefficient. In stage II, total production is increasing at an decreasing rate with a positive marginal product and average product, and production in this stage is normally efficient. In stage III, total product is decreasing, marginal product is negative, and production in this stage is inefficient.

Star. A product that offers not only the potential for high market share but also has the potential for high market growth.

Storage. One of the nine required marketing functions that deals with overcoming the time separation barrier to greater consumer satisfaction.

Storing a product makes it possible for consumers to enjoy it some time in the future.

Strategic Planning. A plan for an ongoing firm that describes its overall approach to its business. The goal of strategic planning is to match profitable business opportunities with the firm's resource base.

Structure, Market. One of the elements in the evaluation of how markets operate as part of the structure-conduct-performance model. The structure of a market (i.e., the number of firms) can lead to various forms of behavior (i.e., conduct) that can lead to higher prices and profits (i.e., the economic performance) by the firms in it.

Supply. A series of price-quantity relationships showing how much producers are willing to supply at various prices.

Tactical Planning. Short-run, day-to-day plans made within the confines of the firm's overall long-range strategic plan to meet the requirements of the market.

Target Market. A relatively homogeneous group of consumers with unmet needs.

Target Marketing. An approach to marketing that realizes that consumer needs determine product characteristics and marketing programs. Under this approach firms adjust their production and marketing efforts to produce and sell goods that are designed to fill specific needs of targeted groups of consumers.

Technical Efficiency. The points on the production function where the level of output per unit of input is at a maximum for various levels of input, and could not be obtained with fewer inputs. A prerequisite to economic efficiency.

Time Separation. One of the barriers to greater consumer satisfaction in the economic system that is overcome by marketing. Through storage it is possible to insure that consumers will have a product they desire some time in the future.

Time Utility. The satisfaction that consumers gain from having a product available when they want it.

Total Cost. The sum of all fixed and variable costs of production.

Trademark. A symbol that need not be pronounceable but that customers can recognize and associate with a particular firm's products.

Transportation. One of the nine required marketing functions that helps overcome the space separation barrier to greater consumer satisfaction by transporting products to the locations that consumers most desire.

Uncertainty. The possibility of loss where the probabilities of various outcomes are not known.

Universal Product Code (UPC). A multiline code found on products that can be read by electronic scanners.

Unitary Demand. The condition where the percentage change in quantity demanded is exactly equal to the percentage change in price, income, and so on. It is also typically the point of highest total revenue.

USDA. United States Department of Agriculture.

Utility. The satisfaction one receives from ownership, control, or consumption of a product.

Value Separation. One of the barriers to greater consumer satisfaction overcome by marketing. Greater value typically in the form of convenience or form is given to the product through processing.

Variable Costs. Those costs that do vary with the level of output in the short run.

Workable Competition. The situation in which there is sufficient effective competition in a market to give both consumers and society most of the benefits that arise from perfect competition.

Index